april 18

COLUMBIA UNIVERSITY STUDIES IN ENGLISH AND COMPARATIVE LITERATURE

THE ELIZABETHAN FAIRIES

ROBIN GOODFELLOW

From *Robin Goodfellow, his mad prankes and merry jests,* 1628

THE ELIZABETHAN FAIRIES

THE FAIRIES OF FOLKLORE AND THE FAIRIES OF SHAKESPEARE

BY

MINOR WHITE LATHAM

1972

OCTAGON BOOKS

New York

Reprinted 1972

by special arrangement with Columbia University Press

OCTAGON BOOKS
A DIVISION OF FARRAR, STRAUS & GIROUX, INC.
19 Union Square West
New York, N. Y. 10003

Library of Congress Cataloging in Publication Data

Latham, Minor White, 1881-1968.
The Elizabethan fairies.
(Columbia University studies in English and comparative literature)
Reprint of the author's thesis, Columbia University, 1930.
Bibliography: p.
1. Fairies. 2. English literature—Early modern (to 1700)—History and criticism. 3. Shakespeare, William, 1564-1616—Characters—Fairies. I. Title. II. Series.

PR429.F3L3 1972 398.21'42 71-39032
ISBN 0-374-94811-9

Printed in U.S.A. by
NOBLE OFFSET PRINTERS, INC.
NEW YORK 3, N. Y.

TO

MY MOTHER

LOUISA WHITE LATHAM

PREFACE

Any investigation of the fairy mythology of the 16th century is immediately concerned with two problems: the problem of the native fairies of tradition, and the problem of the fairies of Shakespeare. In this essay an attempt has been made to study both conceptions of the fairy world; to present the traditional fairies of folklore, and the whole body of beliefs popularly held in the 16th and 17th centuries concerning them; and to trace the development of the fairies of Shakespeare, and their influence upon subsequent literature and folklore.

The completion of the work affords a most pleasant opportunity for the acknowledgment of invaluable aid and assistance. Mr. Frederic W. Erb and his assistants on the staff of the Library of Columbia University have my heartiest thanks for their continued aid and cooperation, as has Miss Helen Kline for the meticulous care and the efficiency with which the difficult work of preparing and proof reading the manuscript has been done. Professor E. M. Laney of Agnes Scott College has given me her most kind assistance in the work of verifying and compiling the bibliography. To Professors H. M. Ayres and W. W. Lawrence I am indebted for reading the manuscript and offering valuable suggestions. To Dean Virginia Crocheron Gildersleeve of Barnard College my debt of gratitude is great for her generous and unfailing assistance in furthering my endeavors.

Two persons have assisted me to whom I am unable to make any adequate acknowledgment. Dr. Gulielma Fell Alsop has by her untiring help and encouragement made this work possible. Professor Ashley H. Thorndike first suggested the subject to me, and from the beginning has generously given his time and scholarship. Whatever merit this volume possesses is due to his skillful and patient guidance and helpful criticism.

M. W. L.

Columbia University
December 30, 1929

CONTENTS

Introduction 1

I. The Origin and Nature of the Elizabethan Fairies 23

II. The Fairies: Their Appearance and Characteristics 65

III. The Fairies: Their Life on Earth 111

IV. The Changeling and the Witch 148

V. The Fairies of Shakespeare 176

VI. Robin Goodfellow 219

List of Texts and Authorities Consulted 263

Texts in Which References to the Fairies Occur . . . 296

Index 309

INTRODUCTION

Since the publication of the first textual criticism of Shakespeare's plays, the fairy mythology of Shakespeare and the popular fairy mythology of the 16th century and the difference and likeness between them have been subjects for scholarly research and discussion. The earlier as well as the later editors of Shakespeare in the 18th century made no distinction between the two conceptions of fairyland, but assumed that the fairies created by Shakespeare, the diminutive and benevolent fairies of *A Midsummer Night's Dream* being regarded as representative of all the fairies of Shakespeare, were the fairies of English tradition and rural belief. Several of the notes of Dr. Johnson [1] sum up the opinion which prevailed, especially his comment on the song of Ariel, as follows:

> The reason for which Ariel is introduced thus trifling is, that he and his companions are evidently of the fairy kind, an order of beings to which tradition has always ascribed a sort of diminutive agency, powerful but ludicrous, a humorous and frolick controlment of nature, well expressed by the songs of Ariel.[2]

Joseph Ritson, in the first modern critical investigation and discussion of the fairies of England,[3] found no differ-

[1] The definition of a fairy in the Dictionary of Dr. Johnson is significant: a fairy is a " Fabled being supposed to appear in a diminutive human form, and to dance in the meadows, and reward cleanliness in houses." London, 1866 ed.

[2] *The Plays of William Shakespeare* in Ten Volumes . . . to which are added Notes by Samuel Johnson and George Steevens, London, 1778, Vol. I: *The Tempest,* p. 34, footnote.

[3] *Fairy Tales, Now First Collected: to which are prefixed Two Dissertations: 1. On Pygmies. 2. On Fairies.* London, 1831.

ence between the fairies of Shakespeare and those of native tradition, but represented, as features characteristic of all English fairies, those particular features exemplified by the fairies of *A Midsummer Night's Dream:* namely, diminutiveness, amiability and charm. "The fairies," Ritson stated, "were exceedingly diminutive, but, it must be confessed, we shall not readily find their actual dimensions. They were small enough, however, if we may believe one of queen Titanias maids of honour, to conceal themselves in acorn shells." [4] Upon their amiability and charm, he was equally positive:

> . . . the idea of a fairy could never inspire any but pleasing sensations; these little people being always distinguished for their innocent mirth, and benevolent utility. It was far otherwise, indeed, with superstition and witchcraft, which, though equally false, were, nevertheless, as firmly believed; as they induced ignorance and bigotry to commit horrid crimes; but nothing of this kind is imputable to the fairies.[5]

In 1802–1803, Sir Walter Scott, in his essay "On the Fairies of Popular Superstition," [6] called attention to the influence of Shakespeare upon the fairies of native tradition. Among the causes which he assigned for the change in the characteristics of the English fairies from those of the traditional dwarfs or *berg-elfen* of the Gothic and Finnish tribes from whom he would have them derive,[7] he noted "the creative imagination of the sixteenth century": [8]

> Many poets of the sixteenth century, and above all, our immortal Shakespeare, deserting the hackneyed fictions of Greece and Rome,

[4] *Fairy Tales,* p. 35.
[5] *Ibid.,* p. 61, 1st footnote.
[6] *Minstrelsy of the Scottish Border,* 1803, Vol. II, pp. 174–241.
[7] *Ibid.,* p. 179.
[8] *Ibid.,* p. 180.

sought for machinery in the superstitions of their native country. "The fays, which nightly dance upon the wold," were an interesting subject; and the creative imagination of the bard, improving upon the vulgar belief, assigned to them many of those fanciful attributes and occupations, which posterity have since associated with the name of fairy. In such employments, as rearing the drooping flower, and arranging the disordered chamber, the fairies of South Britain gradually lost the harsher character of the dwarfs, or elves. Their choral dances were enlivened by the introduction of the merry goblin Puck, for whose freakish pranks they exchanged their original mischievous propensities. The fairies of Shakespeare, Drayton, and Mennis, therefore, at first exquisite fancy portraits, may be considered as having finally operated a change in the original which gave them birth.

While the fays of South Britain received such attractive and poetical embellishments, those of Scotland, who possessed no such advantage, retained more of their ancient, and appropriate character.[9]

The original folk fairies "of Britain, and more especially those of Scotland," Scott represented as "retaining the unamiable qualities, and diminutive size, of the Gothic elves."[10] The fairies of England he seems to have regarded as harmless.[11]

Scott's essay is an important document in the history of English fairy mythology, since it is one of the first[12] statements, if not the first, of Shakespeare's influence on the fairies of popular superstition and of Shakespeare's use of Robin Goodfellow, and one of the first statements

[9] *Ibid.,* Vol. II, pp. 222–224.

[10] *Ibid.,* p. 185.

[11] *Ibid.,* p. 178.

[12] J. O. Halliwell, in his *Memoranda on the Midsummer Night's Dream,* 1879, p. 13, states: "Charles Lamb, in a manuscript that I have seen, speaks of Shakespeare as having 'invented the fairies'; by which, I presume, he means that his refinement of the popular notion of them was sufficiently expansive to justify the strong epithet."

of the existence, in the 16th century, of two conceptions of fairyland, that of folk tradition and that created by Shakespeare.

The view advanced by Scott was elaborated by Nathan Drake in his " Dissertation on the Fairy Mythology, and on the Modifications which it received from the Genius of Shakespeare [13] published in 1817. He pointed out the existence in England of the fairies of popular tradition and the recurring characteristics of the " Fairy Mythology of England " from Gervase of Tilbury to William Warner.[14] He made a study of the fairy mythology of Shakespeare, basing his work upon four plays, *A Midsummer Night's Dream, Romeo and Juliet, Merry Wives of Windsor,* and *The Tempest,* and emphasized the originality of Shakespeare in the " delineation of this tribe of spirits." [15] He augmented the history of Robin Goodfellow with many new references, and called attention to the changes wrought upon him by Shakespeare.[16] He noted the influence of the fairy mythology of Shakespeare upon the subsequent poets of the 16th and 17th century.[17]

[13] *Shakespeare and His Times,* Paris, 1838, pp. 488–511.

[14] *Ibid.,* p. 502.

[15] *Ibid.,* pp. 502–508. Cf. p. 503:

" Of the originality of Shakespeare in the delineation of this tribe of spirits, or Fairies, nothing more is required in proof, than a combination or grouping of the principal features; a picture which, when contrasted with the Scandick system and that which had been built upon it in England and Scotland previous to his own time, will sufficiently show with what grace, amenity, and beauty, and with what an exuberant store of novel imagery, he has decorated these phantoms of the Gothic mythology."

[16] *Ibid.,* pp. 508–511.

[17] *Ibid.,* p. 511: " It is, in short, to his picture of the fairy world, that we are indebted for the ' Nymphidia ' of Drayton; the ' Robin Goodfellow ' of Jonson; the miniatures of Fletcher and Browne; the full-length portraits of Herrick; the sly allusions of Corbet, and the spirited and picturesque sketches of Milton."

His conclusions upon the subject of the fairy mythology of England and of Shakespeare can best be expressed in his own words:

> Upon the whole we may be allowed, from the preceding dissertation, to consider the following series of circumstances as entitled to the appellation of facts: namely, that the patria of our popular system of fairy mythology, was the Scandinavian Peninsula; that, on its admission into this country, it gradually underwent various modifications through the influence of Christianity, the introduction of classical associations, and the prevalence of feudal manners; but that ultimately two systems became established; one in Scotland, founded on the wild and more terrific parts of the Gothic mythology, and the other in England, built, indeed, on the same system, but from a selection of its milder features, and converted by the genius of Shakespeare into one of the most lovely creations of a sportive imagination. Such, in fact, has been the success of our bard in expanding and colouring the germs of Gothic fairyism; in assigning to its tiny agents new attributes and powers; and in clothing their ministration with the most light and exquisite imagery, that his portraits, in all their essential parts, have descended to us as indissolubly connected with, and indeed nearly, if not altogether, forming our ideas of the fairy tribe.[18]

To Drake, as may be noticed in the statement quoted above, the popular fairies of 16th century England were diminutive in stature. For the rest, they possessed "the same infernal origin, . . . the same mischievous and terrific character, and occasionally the same frolic and capricious wantonness," as the fairies of the "Scottish System" which "received and fostered that wilder and more gloomy portion of the creed which develops the agency and disposition of the Swart or Malignant tribe." [19]

Thomas Keightley in *The Fairy Mythology; illustra-*

[18] *Ibid.*, p. 511.

[19] Drake, *Shak. and His Times,* pp. 502 and 493.

tive of the Romance and Superstition of various Countries,[20] first published in 1828, supplemented in several important particulars the work of Drake. He collected and arranged in chronological order the "few scattered traditions" concerning the fairies of the people found in the writings of Gervase of Tilbury, Burton, Harsnet, etc., and in contemporary folk tales, and the "passages, treating of fairies and their exploits, from our principal poets" from Chaucer to George Darley.[21] He extended the study of the fairies of Shakespeare to all the plays of Shakespeare in which fairies are mentioned, with the exception of *Pericles, The Comedy of Errors, Richard II* and *Macbeth,* and pointed out specifically the contributions of Shakespeare and those of folklore to the conception of the fairies found in Shakespeare's plays and in English Poetry.[22]

His own idea of the fairies is particularly significant in any investigation of the differences between the two conceptions of fairyland, since, like his predecessors, he represented the fairies of England as diminutive beings more

[20] Though Keightley regarded Shakespeare as the "principal agent" in bringing about the change in the fairy mythology of England, he attributed to the appearance of the *Faerie Queene* more influence than had been granted by his predecessors.

"After the appearance of the *Faerie Queene,* all distinctions were confounded, the name and attributes of the real Fays or Fairies of romance were completely transferred to the little beings who, according to the popular belief, made 'the green sour ringlets whereof the ewe not bites.' The change thus operated by the poets established itself firmly among the people; a strong proof, if this idea be correct, of the power of the poetry of a nation in altering the phraseology of even the lowest classes of its society." *The Fairy Mythology,* 1833, London, Vol. I, p. 18.

[21] *Fairy Myth.,* Vol. II, pp. 104–118, 121–158.

[22] *Ibid.,* Vol. II, pp. 127–156.

mischievous than malignant, except for their "child-abstracting propensities." [23]

The commentators who followed Keightley —[24] Thoms,[25] Halliwell,[26] and Thiselton-Dyer —[27] added nothing of moment to the discussion,[28] and continued to stress the fact that Shakespeare created "the finest modern artistic realisation of the fairy kingdom," and to represent the fairies as "little people" of "diminutive stature," "tiny moralists," etc., never any bigger than little children in size.

In the more recent dissertations on the fairies of Shakespeare and of popular mythology — I refer particularly to Appendix A, "The Fairy World," which forms an important section of E. K. Chambers' edition of *A Midsummer Night's Dream,* 1893; to Alfred Nutt, *The Fairy Mythology of English Literature: its Origin and Nature,* 1897; [29] and to Frank Sidgwick, *The Sources and Analogues of "A Midsummer-Night's Dream,"* 1908 — the lines laid down by Drake and by Keightley have been followed, with several modifications, mainly concerned with the theory of the origin of the fairies and their derivation.

The older method of tracing the development of the

[23] *Ibid.,* Vol. II, p. 127; Vol. I, pp. 16, 18, and 20.

[24] See also Francis Douce, *Illustrations of Shakespeare and of Ancient Manners,* 1807; J. Hunter, *New Illustrations of the Life, Studies, and Writings of Shakespeare,* 1845; William Bell, *Shakespeare's Puck, and his Folkslore,* 1852–64; and Thomas Percy, *Reliques of Ancient English Poetry,* 1858.

[25] *Three Notelets on Shakespeare,* 1865.

[26] *Illustrations of the Fairy Mythology of A Midsummer Night's Dream,* Shak. Soc., London, 1845.

[27] *Folk Lore of Shakespeare,* 1883.

[28] The exceptions to this statement are the "Notelets" of Thoms on Puck and on Queen Mab.

[29] *Folk-Lore,* Vol. VIII, 1897, pp. 29–53 incl.

English fairies from some definite source, as the dwarfs and elves of Scandinavian or Teutonic origin or the Celtic fays, has been discarded in favor of the theory of a "fairy creed . . . common to all of the Aryan-speaking people of Europe, to the ancestors of Greek and Roman and Slavs, as well as to the ancestors of Celts and Teutons,"[30] or, to put it in other words, the belief in fairies is "clearly a relic of the pre-Christian religious ideas of our ancestors. These were much the same amongst Celts, Teutons and the primitive Graeco-Latin peoples."[31]

In other respects there is no marked difference between the conclusions of modern scholarship[32] and those of Drake and of Keightley. And in every instance the traditional fairies of the rural belief of the 16th century have been presented as small. Chambers states that

> The fairies . . . generally appear in the romances as of human stature. In the popular stories they are usually dwarfs or pigmies, about the size of small children. This is not an invariable rule.

[30] Nutt, *Fairy Myth. of Eng. Lit.*, p. 45.

[31] E. K. Chambers, "The Fairy World," App. A of Warwick ed. of *A Midsummer Night's Dream*, 1911 ed., p. 156. Cf. also Nutt, *Fairy Myth. of Eng. Lit.*, p. 45: "The attempt to discriminate modern national characteristics in the older stratum of European folklore is not only idle but mischievous, because based upon the unscientific assumption that existing differences, which are the outcome of comparatively recent historical conditions, have always existed."

[32] "The fairy of folk-lore in Shakespeare's day is nearly everything that the fairies of *A Midsummer-Night's Dream* are; we may possibly except their exiguity, their relations in love with mortals, and their hymeneal functions. His conception of their size as infinitesimal at least differs from that of the popular stories, where (as far as can be ascertained) they are shown to be about the size of mortal children." Sidgwick, *The Sources and Analogues of "A Midsummer-Night's Dream,"* 1908, p. 65. Cf. also Chambers, "Fairy World," pp. 157, 160, and 166; and Nutt, *Fairy Myth. of Eng. Lit.*, p. 36.

There is Tom Thumb, for example; . . . But Shakespeare has carried this idea further than any of his predecessors. His fairies, in *A Midsummer-Night's Dream* and in *Romeo and Juliet* though perhaps not in *The Merry Wives of Windsor,* where children are dressed up to imitate fairies, are at least spoken of as infinitesimally small.[33]

Sidgwick holds they were " about the size of mortal children." Nutt[34] comments upon the diminutive size of the fairy race in the following words:

I will only say that, possibly, the diminutive size of the fairy race belongs more especially to Teutonic tradition as developed within the last 2,000 years, and that in so far the popular element in Shakespeare's fairy world is, possibly, Teutonic rather than Celtic.[35]

Two examples of the present conception of the traditional fairies of Elizabethan England are to be found in P. H. Ditchfield's *The England of Shakespeare,* 1917, and in *Shakespeare's England,* chapter XVI, written by Professor H. Littledale, 1917.[36] According to the

[33] E. K. Chambers, " Fairy World," pp. 166–167.

[34] " . . . . so far as the outward guise and figure of his fairies is concerned, Shakespeare is borne out by a series of testimonies reaching back to the twelfth century Gervase of Tilbury and Gerald the Welshman, who give us glimpses of a world of diminutive and tricky sprites." *Fairy Myth. of Eng. Lit.,* p. 36.

[35] Nutt, *Fairy Myth. of Eng. Lit.,* p. 45. Cf. also p. 36.

[36] The following account of the fairies of England shows the possibilities of which the subject is capable:

" But the superstition which swayed king and peasant alike could also take attractive forms. The simple minds which recoiled before devil-lore and black magic could people their meadows and forests with fairies and elves, or indulge their fancies in that folklore which bound, and still binds, the past with the present. Every country-side would have its poetic myths, fancy-born and harmless, with which to enliven their many meetings and to invest with significance the common things of life. . . . But the innate poetry, as well as the majesty and

former, the fairies are "these gentle creatures" and "these pretty little elves."[37] According to the latter:

Fairies are essentially the little people. With their whims and caprices and tempers, they are shadows of humanity in miniature, and act as tiny but potent guardians, blessing the homes, rewarding the minor virtues, and punishing the minor trespasses of "human mortals." . . . Childlike themselves, they love children, and even steal them from their cradles, . . . the true fairies are nocturnal, and rank lower in the hierarchy of the supernatural. Prospero's spirits belong mainly to occult science; Oberon's fairies are a part of folklore.[38]

The chief conclusions of modern scholarship, therefore, concerning the fairies of popular mythology and those of Shakespeare's conception of fairyland, may be summed up as follows:

1. In England, in the 16th century, there were two conceptions of fairyland: "that of Shakespeare, who paints the Fairies, in *A Midsummer-Night's Dream* and elsewhere, as minute ethereal beings, . . . who hide themselves in the hollow of a nut, or the petals of a flower";[39] and that of popular tradition.

---

youthfulness of the Elizabethan mind, is nowhere more gloriously revealed than in its conception of that moonlit music-haunted world where fairies move; . . . It was an age in which a ray of moonshine was held to be a path along which delicate and unsubstantial creatures were tripping their aërial rounds. Just as a lurid glare was spread over moor and glen by Celtic imagination, lighting up witches and their magic, so over softer meadows shone that faint afterglow of medieval Fairyland, which daily fed the thoughts of peasants and the pens of poets." J. A. DeRothschild, *Shakespeare and His Day,* 1906, pp. 232–236. Cf. also Floris Delattre, *English Fairy Poetry,* 1912.

[37] *The England of Shakespeare,* 1917, p. 288.

[38] *Shakespeare's England,* 1917, Vol. I, pp. 536, 537 and 539. Cf. also A. A. Jack, *A Commentary on the Poetry of Chaucer and Spenser,* 1920, pp. 334–335.

[39] E. K. Chambers, "Fairy World," p. 149.

2. Shakespeare's conception of the fairies was adopted by many of the poets of his time and has, " through them . . . become traditional in English poetry and English art." [40]

3. Thanks to Shakespeare, " the modern English conception of the fairies is different from the conception prevalent in other countries, and infinitely more picturesque and pleasant." [41]

4. However Shakespeare modified the characteristics of the fairies of popular mythology, the traditional fairies of 16th century England were, in their original state, diminutive in size or small and distinguished by a certain amiability.[42]

This present study of the Elizabethan fairies has for its purpose the further examination of popular fairy my-

[40] *Ibid.*, p. 149. Cf. also Nutt, *Fairy Myth. of Eng. Lit.*, p. 31: " Scarce any one of Shakespeare's plays has had a literary influence so immediate, so widespread, and so enduring. As pictured by Shakespeare, the fairy realm became, almost at once, a convention of literature in which numberless poets sought inspiration and material. I need only mention Drayton, Ben Jonson, Herrick, Randolph, and Milton himself. Apart from any question of its relation to popular belief, of any grounding in popular fancy, Shakespeare's vision stood by itself, and was accepted as the ideal presentment of fairydom, which, for two centuries at least, has signified to the average Englishman of culture the world depicted in the *Midsummer Night's Dream.*"

[41] Sidgwick, *Sources and Analogues*, p. 35.

[42] John Masefield in his lecture, *Shakespeare and Spiritual Life*, of 1924, has called attention to the fact that the fairies of English tradition were large enough to pinch Falstaff and attend the fairy court in the woods near Athens. He has also noted the difference between the dispositions of the fairies of *A Midsummer Night's Dream* and those of popular English tradition. The former were not wild enough, nor unearthly, nor malicious enough to be folk fairies. Mr. Masefield seems to have arrived at his conclusions by poetic intuition and familiarity with modern folk belief, since he adduces no proof for his statements.

thology of the 16th century, and the fairy mythology of Shakespeare.

With the exception of the essay of Robert Kirk in 1691, *Secret Commonwealth, or, a Treatise displayeing the Chiefe Curiosities as they are in Use among diverse of the People of Scotland to this Day; An Essay of The Nature and Actions of the Subterranean (and, for the most Part,) Invisible People, heretofioir going under the name of ELVES, FAUNES, and FAIRIES, or the lyke, among the Low-Country Scots,* there exists no complete and detailed contemporary picture of the traditional fairy commonwealth of the 16th century, and no full account of the whole body of beliefs popularly held concerning the fairies and their intercourse with mortals during the period. To remedy this deficiency, I have ventured upon an endeavor to show, in the words of the Elizabethans themselves, and of their immediate successors of the 17th century, to what race of beings or spirits the fairies were believed to belong, and what the origins attributed to them; to reproduce the picture of their appearance and of the fairyland in which they were supposed to dwell; to give the intimate details of their natural history and of their earthly activities; and to trace the history and career of Robin Goodfellow.

Against this background of native fairy lore, I have attempted to present Shakespeare's fairies as exemplified in *A Midsummer Night's Dream, Romeo and Juliet,* and *The Tempest,* and to study their reputed origin and connections, especially with reference to their size. I have endeavored further to trace the development of the fairy mythology of Shakespeare and the influence which it exerted upon English literature and upon popular superstition.

The strong temptation to draw comparisons between

the fairies of the 16th century and those of the preceding centuries, to trace the relationship between them, and to discuss the probable derivation of the 16th century fairies, has been sternly resisted.

The method of using original sources as the chief material for this discussion has the disadvantage of necessitating a certain amount of repetition. Since most of the references to the fairies of the time were never intentional histories or conscious and scientific tabulations, but were casual and current comments, sometimes on one characteristic of the fairies and sometimes on several, to contemporaries to whom the fairies were well known, it is impossible to make use of new authorities and new quotations, in every case.

It has seemed necessary, in order to reproduce the everyday belief of the Elizabethans concerning the fairies, to treat the fairies not as mythical personages or as fanciful creations of the literary imagination or of popular superstition, but to regard them, as did their human contemporaries of the 16th century, as credible entities and as actual and existing beings. For this reason, where this essay is especially concerned with their domestic history and their intercourse with mortals, they have been represented according to the psychology of the folk who believed in them and saw them, and in the style in which they were discussed and referred to during the 16th century.

It might be well to add also that this particular study of the Elizabethan fairies by no means claims to be an exhaustive record of the occurrences of the belief in the fairies and of the representations of them in the 16th and 17th centuries. It is based upon an examination of the outstanding literature of the period and of whatever letters, chapbooks, popular ballads, diaries, commentaries and treatises on the subject are available. Though the number of elves and fairies found here has been great, it is most probable that a large number of these beings have escaped the notice of the present investigator. It has seemed safe, however, judging from the trend which the research has shown, to draw the conclusions summarized in the subsequent chapters.

For convenience of the reader, s is printed for ſ in the quotations. The old use of u and v, i and j, is preserved. VV and vv are replaced by W. and w.

The history of the material [43] in which the fairy lore of the period is to be found is as interesting and significant as are the references to the fairies themselves. As Alfred Nutt has noted, the time of the greatest flourishing of the fairies in literature extended approximately from the years 1570 to 1625. During this time, they were most "familiar," [44] and after the appearance of Spenser's *Faerie Queene* and of *A Midsummer Night's Dream,* "most fashionable."

In the beginning of the 16th century, there were few references to the fairies, and during the first half of the century the race of spirits, either as elves or fairies, made no great impression upon the records of 16th century life or literature. Though the fairies were surely a part of English civilization, as references in the dictionaries of the time indicate, they were too much the creatures of popular superstition and of folk belief to be referred to by learned scholars, or to be given a place in the poems of serious poets. The exceptions to this rule are the

[43] No references have been made to the English and Scottish ballads, in which a great deal of material on fairies and fairy lore is to be found, since it is impossible to determine the original dates of these ballads.

[44] See *The Plays of Shakespeare,* 1778, Vol. III, p. 127, notes by Johnson and Steevens.

translations by Lord Berners of Froissart's *Chronicle* and of *Huon of Burdeux*. With these exceptions and the recognition accorded the fairies in the early dictionaries and the homely similes of Tyndale, which kept alive in print the name and fame of Robin Goodfellow, the fairies, as they came into prominence later, had no place in the literature of the period.

As far as can be ascertained, neither Hawes nor Skelton nor Barclay makes any mention of them. There is no record of them in the *Utopia* of Sir Thomas More, in *The Governour* of Sir Thomas Elyot, or in most of the works of Roger Ascham. A careful reading of the plays of John Bale, with one exception, and of the interludes of John Heywood, and of other interludes of the period, reveals neither elves nor fairies.

Though a reference to "mad peevish elves" occurs in *Ralph Roister Doister,* the race is not mentioned in *Tottel's Miscellany,* in the earliest edition of the *Mirror for Magistrates,* or in *Gorboduc.*

In the Scottish literature of the same period, the fairies are continually referred to and made use of. The *Exposition in Matthew* by John Major contains one of the earliest descriptions of the brownie. In Gawin Douglas's translation of the *Aeneid* is to be found one of the earliest definitions of the fairies. They are mentioned at least once by Dunbar and many times by Sir David Lyndesay.

After the publication of Douglas's translation of the *Aeneid* in 1553 in England, the fairies begin to appear in English translations of Virgil and of Ovid, brought into literary prominence as the English equivalent of the nymphs and hamadryads of the Latin originals. The translation of the *Aeneid* by Thomas Phaër makes mention of the fairies; the translation of Ovid's *Metamorphoses* by Golding gives space and poetic embellishment repeatedly to the fairies and elves; and the translation of the four books of the *Aeneid* by Stanyhurst makes a number of references to hobgoblins. In the translation of *La Spiritata* from the Italian, there are interpolated among the spirits mentioned in the Italian original, the native red and white fairy, Robin Goodfellow, Hobgoblin, pucks, and puckerels.

At the same time in the plays and interludes, elves and fairies begin to be referred to, as in *Gammer Gurtons Nedle, Misogonus, Jacob and Esau, King Darius, Common Conditions,* and *John Bon and Mast Parson.*

Outside of the translations and plays, they occupy very little attention in English literature. Googe, with the exception of his translation of Naogeorgus, Turberville and Gascoigne make no mention of them. The agricultural poems of Thomas Tusser, with two exceptions, and the earlier works of Churchyard claim no acquaintance with them, nor does the *Paradise of Dainty Devices,* or *England's Helicon.*

In Scotland, however, their presence and their traits were not forgotten. On the contrary, belief in their power and in their reality was so great that, in 1576, Edinburgh witnessed the burning at the stake of a Scotch woman for "repairing" with the fairies and the Queen of Elfame, a spectacle which was to be repeated until 1640 and later.

In 1575, "the Queen of the Fayry" played no small part in the entertainment presented before Elizabeth at Woodstock,[45] and, in 1578, at the entertainment accorded her at Norwich, the fairies were represented in some detail in an entertainment devised by Churchyard. At the

[45] "The fairy lore of royal progress and of court masque and play was probably launched at Woodstock on its successful career." C. R. Baskervill, "The Genesis of Spenser's Queen of Faerie," *Modern Philology,* Vol. 18, May, 1920, p. 53.

same time, in the second edition of a *Mirror for Magistrates,* they were given a certain prominence in connection with the history of Dame Elianor Cobham.

From this time until the death of King James, they were, as Dr. Johnson stated, much in fashion. Literary England, as well as ordinary England, court and citizen, witnessed them in pageants and royal progresses, saw them represented on the stage, played the rôle of the fairies in masques and in practical jokes, read of them in poems and pamphlets, and sang of their beauty and power, not forgetting to make use of a charm against their wickedness on going to bed.

Among the writers who were most conversant with the fairy lore of the period and in many instances most given to making use of it, are Scot, Camden, Warner, Puttenham, Lyly, Spenser, Nashe, Greene, Drayton, Sir John Harington, Thomas Middleton, Churchyard, James VI of Scotland, Dekker, Fairfax, Fulke Greville, Beaumont and Fletcher, Heywood, Rowlands, Hall, Burton, Shakespeare and Jonson.[46]

Among those to whom the fairies made little or no appeal, are Kyd; Sir Philip Sidney; Stubbes, whose *Anatomie of Abuses,* contrary to expectation, fails to refer to the fairies or to the superstitious practices in regard to them; Marlowe, in whose *Dido* (attributed in part to Nashe) alone, is a reference to a changeling; Daniel; Marston; James Howell; John Taylor; Ford; Peele, who, in spite of his knowledge of folklore as shown in *The Old Wives' Tale,* makes but one reference to fairies; and many of the writers of the sonnets.

At the death of James I, approximately, the concern

[46] In the works of Shakespeare and of Jonson is to be found the most complete knowledge of the folk fairies. Jonson, in particular, showed himself most conversant with the fairy lore of his period and represented it most accurately.

with fairy lore underwent a change. The fairies of *A Midsummer Night's Dream,* as will be seen later, became the fashion and gradually usurped the place of the fairies of folklore in the works of most of the outstanding poets of the time with the exception of Cowley, who referred to the folk fairy, and of Milton, who celebrated the traditional fairies of the folk save in the matter of their size. Only in the philosophical and religious treatises, and in discourses proving the existence or nonexistence of witches, as the works of Henry More, Glanvil, John Webster, Edward Fairfax, Harsnet, Hobbes, and Robert Kirk are the fairies of folklore to be found.

The most striking absence of interest in fairy lore is to be noted in the works of Sir Thomas Browne, especially his dissertation on *Vulgar and Common Errors,* where the fairies and the belief in the fairies are not mentioned except for a reference to fairy or elf stones. This is not the case, however, with Butler's *Hudibras,* where the superstitions of the folk with regard to witches and fairies and Robin Goodfellow are recorded.[47]

[47] For the convenience of the reader, the texts containing references to the fairies and Robin Goodfellow, have been arranged in a separate bibliography and are to be found at the end of Chap. VI.

There are a number of questions which occur to one's mind in regard to the prominence of the fairies during the 16th century in England. Did their vogue spring from a growing familiarity with the poems of Chaucer and Gower, and with the medieval romances? Did an almost universal knowledge of classical mythology and a familiarity with the wood gods and spirits of Rome and Greece turn the literary man's thoughts to his own folklore? Was it the growing number of poets from the lower classes, fresh from the country and from the smaller villages and towns (where belief in the fairies was a matter of course), bound by no slavish adherence to authority nor limited by the dignity of scholarship, who put the fairies into poems and plays as naturally as had the classical poets, the nymphs and satyrs? The answers to these questions will always be conjectural.

In connection with the sources which contain the fairy lore of the 16th and 17th centuries, it is well to call attention to the fact, as did Robert Burton in the footnotes appended to his statements concerning the fairies in *The Anatomy of Melancholy,* that in the 16th century the terms *fairies* and *elves,* and later *fairy elves,* were used to denote the same beings.[48]

It is well to note also that, in specific instances, there was an implied or expressed distinction made in the use of the two terms.[49] The word *elves* in particular, had a number of meanings. In some cases, elves seem to have been regarded as beings more wicked than fairies. This distinction is most apparent in those localities where oral tradition and folk tales concerning elves and fairies, instead of romances and scholars' treatises about them, prevailed, as, in Scotland, where the terms the *Queen of Elfame* and the *Elf Queen, elf folk* and *elf boys* were used almost exclusively by the common folk in the evidence given in witchcraft trials. This is true also in the early literature of the 16th century, where the term *elf* was used to denote a wicked person or being, as for instance, in the *Historie of Jacob and Esau,*[50] *Godly Queen Hester,*[51] *The Palice of Honour* by Gawin Douglas,[52] *Three Laws,*[53] Stanyhurst's translation of the *Aeneid* of

[48] Shilleto ed., 1896, Vol. I, pp. 219 and 220.

[49] The following note from Dr. Johnson's definition of *elf* in his Dictionary, is as pertinent now as in 1755: "Still, an exact definition, stating how an elf differed from a fairy on the one side, and from a goblin on the other, not to mention dwarfs and fiends, is impracticable."

[50] Farmer, *Early English Dramatists,* 2d ser., 1906, II, 2 & 4; V, 10.

[51] Farmer, *Early English Dramatists,* 2d ser., 1906, p. 262.

[52] Pinkerton, *Scotish Poems,* 1792, Vol. I, p. 60.

[53] John Bale, Farmer ed., 1907, p. 23.

Virgil,[54] *The Flyting of Montgomerie and Polwart,*[55] *The Marriage of Wit and Science,*[56] Joseph Hall's *Carmen Funebre Caroli Horni,*[57] and later in William Browne's *Fido.*[58]

In other instances the term *elf* was used both as a term of affection and to denote a silly or foolish person — as in *Misogonus,*[59] *Diana* of Henry Constable,[60] *The Buggbears,*[61] *Common Conditions,*[62] *The Muses Elizium,*[63] *Gallathea,*[64] and the *Historie of Promos and Cassandra.*[65]

The word *elf* was used also to denote a misshapen man in the *Medulla Grāmatice,*[66] and in Palsgrave's *Lesclarcissement de La Langue Francayse,* in addition to *fée,* is rendered *nain.*

There would seem also to have existed a feeling that elves were in some way subservient to the queen of fairies or to the fairies themselves, if the use of the two terms in *A Midsummer Night's Dream,* and in *Merry Wives of Windsor,* in both of which plays the queen of fairies speaks of her subjects as elves; in the *Alchemist,* where the arrival of the fairy court following the fairy queen is announced by the line:

[54] *The Fovrth Booke of Virgil His Aeneis,* Arber ed., 1880.

[55] *Poems of Alexander Montgomerie,* Stevenson ed., 1910, ll. 482–495.

[56] Farmer, *Early English Dramatists,* 4th ser., 1908, IV, 1.

[57] Grosart ed., 1879, Verse 5.

[58] Hazlitt ed., 1869, ll. 47–50.

[59] *Early Plays from the Italian,* Bond ed., 1911, I, 1.

[60] Lee ed., 1904, Sonnet 32.

[61] *Early Plays from the Italian,* Bond ed., 1911, I, 3.

[62] Farmer, *Early English Dramatists,* 4th ser., 1908, pp. 192 and 223.

[63] Drayton, Spenser Soc. ed., 1892, *The Third Nimphal.*

[64] John Lyly, Bond ed., 1902, V, 3.

[65] Geo. Whetstone, Students' Facsimile ed., 1910, I, 3.

[66] See *Catholicon Anglicum,* E. E. T. S. ed., 1881, note, p. 113.

Look, the elves are come;[67]

and in Hobbes' *Leviathan,* in which it is stated,

When the Fairies are displeased with any body, they are said to send their Elves, to pinch them,[68]

can be taken as an indication of a distinction between elves and fairies, rather than as an example of the usual loose use of the terms.

A notable example of the distinction made in the 16th century between the two terms, is to be found in "The Eight Booke" of Golding's translation of Ovid's *Metamorphoses:*

The Woodnymphes with the losses of the woods and theyrs right sore
Amazed, gathered on a knot, and all in mourning weede
Went sad too Ceres, praying her too wreake that wicked deede
Of Erisicthons. Ceres was content it should bee so
And with the mooving of her head in nodding too and fro,
She shooke the feeldes which laden were with frutefull Harvest tho.
And therewithall a punishment most piteous shee proceedes
Too put in practyse: were it not that his most heynous deedes,
No pitie did deserve to have at any bodies hand.
With helplesse hungar him to pyne, in purpose shee did stand.
And forasmuch as shee herself and famin myght not meete,
(For fate forbiddeth famin too abyde within the leete
Where plentie is) she thus bespake a *fayrie of the hill.*
There lyeth in the utmost bounds of Tartarie the chill
A Dreerie place, a wretched soyle, a barreine plot: no grayne,
No frute, no tree, is growing there: but there dooth ay remayne
Unweeldsome cold, with trembling feare, and palenesse white as clowt,

[67] Jonson, Gifford ed., 1846, III, 2.

[68] Rpt. of 1651 ed., Oxford, 1909, p. 545. Cf. also C. Middleton, *The Famous Historie of Chinon of England,* E. E. T. S. ed., 1925, p. 30.

And foodlesse famin. Will thou her immediatly withowt
Delay too shed hirself intoo the stomacke of the wretch,
And let no plentie staunch her force, but let her working stretch
Above the powre of mee. And least the longnesse of the way
May make thee wearie, take thou heere my charyot: take I say
My draggons for to beare thee through the aire. In saying so
She gave hir them. The *Nymph* mounts up: and flying thence as tho
Alyghts in Scythy land, and up the cragged top of hye
Mount Caucasus did cause hir Snakes with much a doo too stye,
Where seeking long for famin, shee the gaptoothd *elfe* did spye
Amid a barreine stony feeld a ramping up the grasse
With ougly nayles, and chanking it. Her face pale colourd was.
Hir heare was harsh and shirle, her eyes were sunken in her head.
Her lyppes were hore with filth, her teeth were furd and rusty read;
Her skinne was starched, and so sheere a man myght well espye
The verie bowels in her bulk how every one did lye.
And eke above her coorbed loynes her withered hippes were seene.
In stead of belly was a space where belly should have beene.
Her breast did hang so sagging downe as that a man would weene
That scarcely to her ridgebone had hir ribbes beene fastened well;
Her leannesse made her joynts bolne big, and kneepannes for too swell,
And with exceeding mighty knubs her heeles behynd boynd out.
Now when the *Nymph* behild this *elfe* a farre (she was in dout
Too come too neere her:) shee declarde her Ladies message. And
In that same little whyle although the *Nymph* aloof did stand,
And though shee were but newly come, yit seemed shee too feele
The force of famin.[69]

[69] Rouse ed., 1904, ll. 966–1009.

CHAPTER I

THE ORIGIN AND NATURE OF THE ELIZABETHAN FAIRIES[1]

Although the 16th century witnessed the most astounding use and glorification of the fairies in literature, and the creation of a literary conception of fairyland, it was understood by poet and scholar that the fairies, with certain notable exceptions,[2] were not figures of

[1] The term "Elizabethan" in this essay is not confined to the reign of Elizabeth, but is used to cover the years from 1558 to 1603 and those of the first quarter of the 17th century which should more properly be termed Jacobean. The 16th century believed in the fairies and wrote about them. The 17th century continued to believe in the fairies of the 16th century and discussed them. There is no sharp line of demarcation between the two periods in regard to fairy lore and fairy mythology.

[2] *A Midsummer Night's Dream, Romeo and Juliet,* and the *Faerie Queene.* In these works also the fairies represented possessed a number of traits of the folk fairies. The inconsistency of both Shakespeare and Spenser in the treatment of the literary race of fairies which each created, is very marked. In the case of the former, note the description of Mab, of infinitesimal dimensions and poetic and fanciful occupation, yet

> " . . . . that very Mab
> That plats the manes of horses in the night;
> And bakes the elf-locks in foul sluttish hairs,
> Which, once untangled, much misfortune bodes."

In the case of the latter, as both Scott and Keightley note, the stealing of changelings in Book I, Canto X and Book III, Canto III of the *Faerie Queene,* and the designation of the progeny of the fairies as "base Elfin brood" were injudicious and incongruous inconsistencies, utterly at variance with the conception of the fairies presented in the *Faerie Queene,* and with the personality, character and

literary invention or of a literary inheritance, but were the traditional fairies of rural belief, a race of English and Elizabethan spirits, indigenous to the country and the century,[3] who made their way into scholarly recognition and into literary records, neither from the established categories of demons or devils, nor from the romances of preceding centuries, but from the fields and forests of England and from the living traditions and contemporary belief of the English folk.

In pageants, plays, poems and tracts, the fairies appeared inevitably as creatures of common tradition and popular report. Even in the works of those poets in the 17th century,[4] who, for one purpose or another, consciously imitated the pattern of the literary fairies of *A Midsummer Night's Dream* or of those who presented the fays of romance in masque or pageant, attention was called to the fact of the differences between the beings thus represented and the native fairies, as may be seen, for example, in the *Nimphidia* of Drayton,[5] and in the masque, *Oberon, the Fairy Prince,* of Ben Jonson.[6]

reputation of Belphoebe, born of a "Fairie." See also Book VI, Canto X, where Sir Calidore, himself a fairy, is unable to distinguish between "nymphes, or faeries, or enchaunted show"; and the June Eclogue of the *Shepheardes Calender,* where "elvish ghosts" are contrasted with "frendly Faeries," the Glosse by E. K. on "Frendly faeries" utterly belying any friendliness.

[3] "The fairies or elves of the British isles are peculiar to this part of the world, and are not, so far as literary information or oral tradition enables us to judge, to be found in any other country." Joseph Ritson, "Dissertation on Fairies," *Fairy Tales,* 1831, p. 26.

[4] See Chap. V.

[5] *Minor Poems,* Brett ed., 1907, Stanzas 8, 9 and 10.

[6] *Masques and Entertainments by Ben Jonson,* Morley ed., 1890, p. 154. Cf. also Wm. Browne, *Britannia's Pastorals,* Hazlitt ed., 1869, Vols. I and II, Books 1 and 3; the fairy poems of Herrick;

The fact that the fairies of the 16th century were the fairies of the folk and of native tradition was generally recognized by scholars. One has only to turn to the initial statements with which a discussion or definition of the fairies is prefaced to discover that this is true. Here, again and again, in essay or in treatise, they are referred to as "our Fairies," or identified as figures of popular belief in such phrases as "those little Puppet-Spirits, which they call Elves or Fairies";[7] "They be also those, whiche be called ladies of the fayry";[8] "Some put our Fairies into this rank";[9] "Apparition of these kind of Creatures, which the common people call Fayries";[10] "That fourth kinde of Spirits, . . . amongst vs was called the Phairie . . . or our good neighbours";[11] "Robin good-fellowes some, some call them Fairies."[12]

The most notable example of the conception of the fairies as English spirits and as traditional beings, by a scholar of the period, is to be seen in Burton's *A Digression on the Nature of Spirits, bad Angels, or Deviles,* among whom he included the fairies. After attempting to classify them in the recognized categories of spirits, especially in the sixth rank of sublunary devils, and after

and Spenser, *The Faerie Queene,* Cambridge ed., 1908, Book I, Canto X, Stanza LXV; in which both the traditional fairies and the literary fairies are represented.

[7] Henry More, *An Antidote against Atheism,* 4th ed., 1712, p. 121.

[8] *Bibliotheca Eliotae,* L ante A, 3d ed., London, 1559.

[9] Robert Burton, *The Anatomy of Melancholy,* Shilleto ed., 1896, Vol. I, p. 219.

[10] John Webster, *The Displaying of Supposed Witchcraft,* 1676 ed., p. 41.

[11] James VI of Scotland, *Daemonologie,* 1616, p. 132.

[12] Thomas Heywood, *The Hierarchie of the blessed Angells,* 1635, p. 574.

classifying them, both as watery and as terrestrial spirits, he identifies the fairies of his time as follows:

Terrestrial devils are those Lares, Genii, Fauns, Satyrs, Wood-nymphs, Foliots, Fairies, Robin Goodfellows, Trolli, &c. which as they are most conversant with men, so they do them most harm. Some think it was they alone that kept the heathen people in awe of old, and had so many idols and temples erected to them. . . . Some put our Fairies into this rank, which have been in former times adored with much superstition, with sweeping their houses, and setting of a pail of clean water, good victuals, and the like, and then they should not be pinched, but find money in their shoes, and be fortunate in their enterprizes. These are they that dance on heaths and greens, as Lavater thinks with Trithemius, &, as Olaus Magnus adds, leave that green circle, which we commonly find in plain fields, which others hold to proceed from a meteor falling, or some accidental rankness of the ground; so Nature sports herself. They are sometimes seen by old women and children.[13]

The particular characteristics which Burton chose as marks by which to identify the fairies: the awe which they inspired; the type of worship they demanded; their domestic interests; their methods of punishment and reward; and the visible evidences of their earthly activities, were the peculiar characteristics of the Elizabethan fairies which made them a separate and distinct race of fairies — the coarse and country fairies, as Ben Jonson called them, and which differentiated them as a race from the fairies of preceding centuries.[14]

---

[13] *Anat. of Mel.,* Vol. I, pp. 219–220.

[14] There is no doubt that the 16th century fairies possessed some of the racial characteristics with which the fays of romance were also endowed. Whether these were derived from the fays of the romances or whether they were traits possessed in common by all fairies is a matter for speculation.

The fairy lore found in Chaucer makes mention of none of the characteristic features of the fairy lore described by Burton, except

Certainly, the fairies represented in *The Anatomy of Melancholy* as "our Fairies" were not the fays of romance. These were mysterious ladies, "primarily enchantresses," and "often regarded as mortal"[15] with "no limitations of beauty, age or resources."[16] They dwelt in some inaccessible country concealed from human eyes by glamour, or in some mysterious islands of the ocean, or in the far-off island paradise of Avalon, usually unapproachable save through their guidance or that of one of their messengers.[17] They came into the world of mortals to gain a knight's love. In seeking this love,

> . . . the fée . . . is . . . a queenly princess. She does not humbly accept a marriage forced upon her, but comes from a distant land solely to carry back the hero whom she loves, — not in the future to be a wife patiently enduring all sorts of indignities, but a proud supernatural mistress whose commands when not followed to the letter bring sorrow to him whose life even is in her hands.[18]

They concerned themselves with pleasure and the joys of love, and used their power to shift their shapes, to build enchanted dwellings, to fashion magic objects, to take dire revenge on mortals who offended them,[19] and to insure for their mortal lovers, youth and never-ending bliss

---

the dancing of the fairies, their bewitchment of mortals and the fact that they are "conversant with men," all of which traits are common to all fairies.

[15] E. K. Chambers, "The Fairy World," Appendix A of Warwick edition of *A Midsummer Night's Dream,* 1893 ed., p. 151.

[16] W. H. Schofield, *The Lays of Graelent and Lanval,* rpt. from Mod. Lang. Assn. Publns., Vol. XV, No. 2, Baltimore, 1900.

[17] See H. C. Coote, "Neo-Latin Fay," *The Folk-Lore Record,* Vol. II, 1879, p. 5; Alfred Nutt, "The Fairy Mythology of English Literature, *Folk-Lore,* Vol. 8, 1897, p. 37.

[18] W. H. Schofield, "The Lay of Guingamor," *Harvard Studies and Notes in Philology and Literature,* Vol. 5, 1896, p. 236.

[19] L. A. Paton, *Studies in the Fairy Mythology of Arthurian Romance,* 1903, p. 147.

as long as they remained in fairyland. As may be seen, they were not the fairies of sixpences and shoes.[20]

If it was understood in the 16th century that the fairies were the contemporary fairies of tradition and of the English folk, it was a matter of common belief that they were real and actual beings. Not only were they believed to exist but they were known to appear in visible and material form,[21] or, as Robert Kirk stated in 1691, they were

[20] See L. F. A. Maury, *Les Fées Du Moyen Age,* 1843, pp. 23–24: "Femmes mystérieuses tenant à la fois du caractère de l'homme et de Dieu, magiciennes auxquelles l'avenir dévoilait parfois ses secrets, enchanteresses aux mains desquelles était livrée la destinée des humains; sur leur tête, en un mot, vinrent se confondre et se concentrer les attributs de toutes les déesses gauloises et des druidesses qui les servaient. Ces femmes, le peuple leur donna le nom de magiciennes, de fees, de sorcières; mais il les désigna spécialement par le nom de fata, sous lequel ses ancêtres avaient honoré les parques identifiees aux déessesmères, par celuis de fata, qui ne renfermait rien de plus, au reste, à ses yeux, que l'idee d'enchantement. De fata, on avait fait fae, fee, fieerie, comme de pratum, prata, on avait fait prae, pre, prairie; et ce mot de fae voulut dire simplement 'enchante'; en ce sens, il etait adjectif.

Lancelot du Lac, 1553 ed., p. v, rptd. in E. K. Chambers, "Fairy World," p. 151: "En cellui temps estoient appellées fées toutes celles qui s'entermettoient d'enchantements et de charmes, et moult en estoit pour lors principallement en la Grand Bretagne, et scavoient la force et la vertue de parolles, des pierres et des herbes, parquoy elles estoient tenue en jeunesse, et en beaulte et en grandes richesses comment elles divisoient. Et ce fut estably au temps de Merlin le prophete."

Cf. also A. C. L. Brown, "Iwain," *Harvard Studies and Notes in Philology and Literature,* Vol. 8; and Alfred Nutt, "Studies on the Legend of the Holy Grail," *Folk Lore,* London, 1888, p. 232.

[21] E. K. Chambers in "The Fairy World," p. 156, makes the statement that "The fairies were supposed to exist, but no longer to appear," citing, as illustrations of his contention, Chaucer's remark in "The Tale of the Wyf of Bathe" that they were driven away by the

. . . no Nonentities or Phantasms, Creatures proceiding from ane affrighted Apprehensione, confused or crazed Sense, but Realities, appearing to a stable Man in his awaking Sense, and enduring a rationall Tryall of their Being.[22]

There is ample evidence of the belief in the reality and actual being of the fairies in the recognized existence in Elizabethan life of the changeling, a visible and material being and a member of the fairy race, and in the recognition by English law, and more especially by Scottish law of mortals made witches by fairies who appeared to them and invested them with their powers.[23]

The severall notorious and lewd Cousonages of John West and Alice West, falsely called the King and Queene of Fayries, practised verie lately both in this citie and many places neere adjoyning: to the impoverishing of many simple people, as well men as women, and the arraignment and conviction, on the 14th of January, 1613, of the two impostors whose crime consisted in impersonating the king and queen of fairies, furnishes a significant illustration of the belief in visible and actual fairies at the beginning of the 17th century.[24]

piety of the limatours, and Bishop Corbet's lament in *The Faerye's Farewell* that the Reformation had caused their disappearance. I am forced to dissent from Mr. Chambers' statement that they were not supposed to appear.

[22] *Secret Commonwealth,* Lang ed., London, 1893, pp. 27–28.

[23] See authorities quoted in Chap. IV, in which the subject of changelings and witches has been treated separately.

[24] A tract rpt. in Hazlitt, *Fairy Tales, . . . illustrating Shakespeare,* London, 1875, pp. 222–238. Cf. also J. P. Collier, *Bibliographical Account of Early English Literature,* 1866, Vol. II, p. 205: ". . . the real value of the tract consists in the manner in which it shows, that just about the time that Shakespeare ceased to write, the belief in the existence of fairies was so prevalent among the lower orders. West and his wife were not themselves 'King and Queen of the Fairies,' but persons who asserted that they had irresistible influence

That they were believed to exist and to appear is patent also in any examination made of the spells used against their power and of the ceremonies and observances relative to their presence, practised automatically by the contemporaries of Spenser, of Shakespeare and of Fletcher. The universal knowledge of their appearance, their characteristics and their antipathies, bears witness, also, to a belief in a visible and a material race (if the term "material" may be applied to supernatural beings), as does the immediate recognition of them and identification of them by these features.

More conclusive, still, of the common faith in the existence of the fairies is the use made of them on the stage, where they appear as beings whose materialization is not an infrequent or an improbable happening. Falstaff, for example, in *Merry Wives of Windsor,* suffers under no illusion that the fairies who dance around him in Windsor Forest are mythical beings or creatures invented in old wives' tales. To him, if his fear or his actions are at all indicative, the fairies are real and fearful spirits who appear to mortals and who must not be spoken to under pain of death.[25] The lawyer's clerk of *The Alchemist* does not consider an interview with the queen of the fairies an impossible feat, or her appearance to him,

with their mysterious majesties. On the strength of their miraculous foreknowledge, people of all classes resorted to them for their information regarding life, death, or loss of property.

"At last they were detected and arraigned, as the title-page informs us, on the 14th January, 1613, but what punishment was inflicted upon them does not appear; and at the end of the tract 'a second arraignment' is spoken of, as if they were soon again to be tried for other offences of the like kind."

[25] V, 5. The quotations from Shakespeare are taken from *The Plays and Poems of William Shakespeare,* edited by Edmond Malone, London, 1821, 21 vols.

after due ceremonies, an extraordinary occurrence.[26] To Morion and his man, Ratsbane, in *The Valiant Welshman,* the sight of the fairy queen in her usual haunts is nothing to be wondered at.[27] Maria, in *Lusts Dominion,* does not regard the appearance of the fairies to her as an improbable happening, but follows the usual ritual practised on such occasions.[28] And the materialization of the fairies in *Endimion* is treated neither as an exceptional nor an unusual event, and the devastation wrought upon their victim is repaired by herbs known and used as the remedy for such injuries.[29]

The belief in fairies as visible and actual spirits is, also, a matter of record among the scholars of the period. E. K., in the June Glosse of *The Shepheardes Calender,* of 1579, calls attention to the fact that "The opinion of faeries and elfes is very old, and yet sticketh very religiously in the myndes of some." [30] "Well, thanks be to God," comments Reginald Scot, speaking in 1584 of the terrors of the night, among whom he included the fairies and changelings, "this wretched and cowardly infidelity, since the preaching of the gospel, is in part forgotten: and doubtlesse, the rest of those illusions will in short time (by Gods grace) be detected and vanish away." [31] Edward Fairfax stated in 1621:

> Yet in this flourishing time of the Gospel, and in this clear day of knowledge, it cannot but offend the conscience of every zealous Christian to see the people of God still buried in the night of superstition, and lie dead in the grave of paganism; so many are the strange follies, rooted in the opinion of the vulgar, concerning the

26 Ben Jonson, Gifford ed., I, 1 and III, 2.

27 Students' Facsimile ed., 1913, II, 5.

28 Dodsley ed., 1874, Vol. XIV, III, 2.

29 John Lyly, Bond ed., 1902, Vol. III, IV, 3.

30 *The Complete Works of Spenser,* Cambridge ed., p. 31.

31 *The Discovery of Witchcraft,* 1651 ed., printed by R. C., p. 113.

walking of souls in this or that house, the dancing of Fairies on this rock or that mountain, the changing of infants in their cradles, and the like.[32]

"The times are not past the ken of our memory," according to Bishop Hall, "since the frequent, and in some part true, reports of those familiar devils, fairies, and goblins, wherewith many places were commonly haunted:[33] the rarity whereof, in these latter times, is sufficient to descry the difference betwixt the state of ignorant superstition and the clear light of the gospel. I doubt not but there were many frauds intermixed both in the acting and relating divers of these occurrences; but he that shall detract from the truth of all, may as well deny there were men living in those ages before us."[34]

". . . and there are many that do believe and affirm that there are such people," John Webster writes in 1673,[35]

And we our selves having practised the art of medicine in all its parts in the North of England, where Ignorance, Popery, and

[32] "A Discourse of Witchcraft. As it was acted in the Family of Mr. Edward Fairfax of Fuystone in the County of York, in the year 1621." *Miscellanies* of the Philobiblon Society, 1858–59, Vol. V, p. 17.

[33] See in this connection Pierre leLoyer, *Discovrs, et Histoires des Spectres, Visions et Apparitions des Esprits, Anges, Demons, et Ames, se Monstrans visibles aux hommes.* Paris, MDCV, p. 201: "Et au reste les Escossois Albins au Aubeins, ou Allibavvns, comme encore on les appelle en quelques lieux d'Escosse, ont esté diffamez iulques à present d'auoir eu des Nymphes ou Fees visibles, appellees Belles gens, Elfes ou Fairs, foles qui aiment les homes, & cerchent de conuerser auec eux comme Demons Succubes, & depuis qu'vne fois elles les ont amadouez & iouy d'eux, c'est chose fort perilleuse de se pouuoir departir de leur conuersation."

[34] *The Invisible World,* Wynter ed., 1862, Vol. 8, p. 202.

[35] *Disp. of Sup. Witch.,* p. 302. Cf. also *Ibid.,* p. 283. On the "reality" of the fairies, compare the discussions as to the reality of Shakespeare's ghosts, in E. E. Stoll, *Shakespeare Studies,* 1927.

superstition doth much abound, and where for the most part the common people, if they chance to have any sort of the Epilepsie, Palsie, Convulsions or the like, do presently perswade themselves that they are bewitched, forespoken, blasted, fairy-taken, or haunted with some evil spirit, and the like; and if you should by plain reasons shew them, that they are deceived, and that there is no such matter, but that it is a natural disease, say what you can they shall not believe you, but account you a Physician of small or no value, and whatsoever you do to them, it shall hardly do them any good at all, because of the fixedness of their depraved and prepossessed imagination.[36]

So late as 1725, according to Henry Bourne in *Antiquitates Vulgares,*

Another Part of this Conversation generally turns upon Fairies. These, they tell you, have frequently been heard and seen, nay that there are some still living who were stollen away by them and confined seven Years.[37]

As to the particular nature and race of the fairies and their origin, 16th century opinion was divided. In one point only was there complete agreement. Whoever or whatever they were, they belonged to the category of wicked spirits.

[36] *Disp. of Sup. Witch.,* pp. 323–324.

[37] 1725 ed., p. 82. Cf. also Warton, *History of English Poetry,* 1775–81, Vol. 3, p. 496; John Beaumont, *An Historical, Physiological and Theological Treatise of Spirits, Apparitions, Witchcrafts and other Magical Practices,* London, 1705, pp. 104–105; William Camden, *Britannia,* Holland trans., 1610, pp. 146–147; and Addison, *The Spectator,* No. 419, as follows: ". . . our forefathers loved to astonish themselves with the apprehensions of witchcraft, prodigies, charms, and inchantments. There was not a village in England that had not a ghost in it; the churchyards were all haunted; every large common had a circle of fairies belonging to it, and there was scarce a shepherd to be met with who had not seen a spirit." Cf. also *The Spectator,* Nos. 12, 110 and 117.

This is apparent in the definitions and classifications given them by scholars of the period; [38] in the connection with witches and witchcraft ascribed to them; [39] in the recognition by English and Scottish law of fairies as spirits of the devil, and in the execution of mortals for dealing with them; [40] in the practices, such as stealing changelings and carrying away mortals, bewitching human beings with disease or blindness, blasting crops and cattle, attributed to them; [41] in the residence in Hell assigned them; [42] and in the spells and charms known and used against their power by mortals.[43]

In all the pages of their record, with the exception of the fairies of Shakespeare's mythology, and the fairies of Spenser,[44] the fairies as a race are never referred to as

[38] See Chap. I, pp. 41–48 and 52–61.

[39] See Chap. IV, pp. 163–175.

[40] See Chap. IV, pp. 168–175.

[41] See Chap. III, pp. 123–129, 137; Chap. IV, pp. 151–154.

[42] See Chap. II, pp. 109–110.

[43] See Chap. IV, p. 162; Chap. III, 127–129; Chap. I, 37–39. Cf. also Kirk, *Sec. Comm.*, pp. 7–8: "They remove to other Lodgings at the Beginning of each Quarter of the Year, . . . and thereby have made it a Custome to this Day among the Scottish-Irish to keep Church duely evry first Sunday of the Quarter to sene or hallow themselves, their Corns and Cattell, from the Shots and Stealth of these wandring Tribes; and many of these superstitious People will not be seen in Church againe till the nixt Quarter begin, as if no Duty were to be learned or done by them, but all the Use of Worship and Sermons were to save them from these Arrows that fly in the Dark." Cf. also *Ibid.*, pp. 15–16: "They are said to have . . . no discernible Religion, Love, or Devotion towards God, the blessed Maker of all: they disappear whenever they hear his Name invocked, or the Name of JESUS, (at which all do bow willinglie, or by constraint, that dwell above or beneath within the Earth, Philip. 2. 10;) nor can they act ought at that Time after hearing of that sacred Name."

[44] The friendly fairies of the June Eclogue of *The Shepheardes*

good spirits, except when this adjective is applied to them as a matter of propitiation or of fear,[45] or to single out some particular member of the race who is pleased, for some reason or other, to show a favor to mortals.

This conception of the fairies seems almost incredible when it is remembered that the *Faerie Queene* was written in honor of Elizabeth, and that she was repeatedly complimented by masques and entertainments in which the fairies or the fairy queen appeared; and that the fairy masques of Jonson were presented in honor of Anne of Denmark and James I of England.

The difficulty of the fairies' wickedness in the case of Elizabeth, however, was, in most instances, overcome either by creating a new race of fairies, as in the *Faerie Queene,* or by representing the fairies stripped of their wicked and base nature, as in the *Entertainment at Elvetham,*[46] *The Queenes Majesties Entertainment at Woodstocke,*[47] or in the *Queens Entertainment at Suffolk and Norfolk.*[48]

Calender are an exception to this rule. The inconsistency between the adjective used here in regard to them and the Glosse which explains " Frendly faeries " has already been noted. Spenser may have had in mind an especial race of fairies, as in the *Faerie Queene,* or the fairies here designated may have been friendly for the occasion.

45 " These Siths, or FAIRIES, they call Sleagh Maith, or the Good People, it would seem, to prevent the Dint of their ill Attempts, (for the Irish use to bless all they fear Harme of;) " Kirk, *Sec. Comm.,* p. 5.

46 John Nichols, *The Progresses and Public Processions of Queen Elizabeth,* 1823, Vol. III, pp. 118–119.

47 Publns. of Mod. Lang. Assn. of America, Vol. 26, 1911, p. 98;

" This loue hath caused me transforme my face,
and in your hue to come before your eyne,
now white, then blacke, your frende the fayery Queene."

48 Nichols, *Prog. of Eliz.,* Vol. II, p. 186:

" And therewithall, the blacke infernall spreetes
Ranne out of hell, the earth so trembling than,

The fairies who appeared before James I who, in Scotland, had given his royal consent and assistance to burning witches for haunting and repairing with the fairies, and had authoritatively pronounced them delusions and creatures of the devil, were portrayed as the train of Oberon, and Oberon himself, who was, both in *Huon of Burdeux* and in the masque itself, a Christian and pious fairy. The fairies of the entertainment at Apthorp, before Anne of Denmark, are not so easily accounted for unless it was understood that all fairies appearing before royalty were denatured, or that they, as the song here seems to indicate, were rendered blessed and good by the presence of royal blood. The entire use of fairies as complimentary fairies in royal masques and entertainments is one of the contradictions of the fairy lore of the period, though in most cases it is to be noted that they appeared in these cases in their capacity of giving gifts and bestowing good fortune.

The degree of the fairies' wickedness and the extent of their infernal connections were never definitely settled, but varied with the circumstances, as witchcraft, with which they were connected or with the belief and superstition of the scholar who wrote concerning them. In spite of the fact that they were known to belong to the rank of evil spirits and devils, both in folk tales and in

---

And like young laddes they hopt about the streetes.
The satyres wilde, in forme and shape of man
Crept through the wooddes, and thickets full of breeres,
The water nymphes, and feyries streight appears
In uncouth formes, and fashion strange to view:
The hagges of hell, that hatefull are of kind,
To please the time, had learnd a nature new,
And all those things that man can call to mind
Were gladde to come, and do their dutie throwe."

treatises of scholars, a curious uncertainty is evidenced in regard to the exact nature of the fairies' wickedness, and, in some cases, a perceptible reluctance to condemn them utterly or to brand them irretrievably with the stigma of infernal spirits, possibly, because of their notorious generosity and their habits of bestowing good fortune and rich gifts on their favorites.

An idea of the personality of the fairies and of the varying degrees of their wickedness is to be found in the charms and spells with which, like the Carpenter in " The Milleres Tale " of Chaucer, the ordinary subjects of Elizabeth would protect themselves and others " from elves and fro wightes." [49]

> Till after long time myrke, when blest
> Were windowes, dares, and lights,
> And pails were fild, and hathes were swept,
> 'Gainst fairie-elues and sprits,[50]

or, as the Reverend George Giffard puts it in 1593:

> Herein also lyeth a more foule abhomination, and that is the abusing and horrible prophaning of the most blessed name of God, and the Holy Scriptures unto witcheries, charmes, and conjurations, and unto all divellish arts. Such an one is haunted with a fayrie, or a spirit: he must learne a charme compounded of some strange speeches, and the names of God intermingled, or weare some part of S. Johns Gospell or such like.[51]

> From fairies, and the tempters of the night,
> Guard me, beseech ye!,[52]

[49] Skeat ed., 1894, ll. 292–300.

[50] Wm. Warner, *Albion's England,* Booke V, Chalmers ed., Vol. 4, p. 564.

[51] *A Dialogue Concerning Witches and Witchcrafts,* Percy Soc. Publns., Vol. 8, 1843, pp. 53–54.

[52] *Cymb.,* II, 2. Cf. also Camden, *Britannia,* Holland trans., p. 147; and *C. of E.,* II, 2.

ran one charm for protection, unless a mortal thought himself in immediate danger, when he was grateful for a more potent spell, as:

From elves, hobs, and fairies,
That trouble our dairies,
From fire-drakes and fiends,
And such as the devil sends,
Defend us, good Heaven! [53]

or

Saint Francis, and Saint Benedight,
Blesse this house from wicked wight;
From the night-mare, and the goblin,
That is hight Good-fellow Robin;
Keep it from all evil spirits,
Fairies, weezels, rats, and ferrets:
From Curfew-time
To the next prime.[54]

For other purposes, there were the following charms:

Peace and charity within,
Neuer touch't with deadly sin:
I cast my holy water poore,
On this wall and on this doore,
That from euill shall defend,
And keepe you from the vgly fiend:
Euill spirit by night nor day,
Shall approach or come this way;
Elfe nor Fary by this grace,
Day nor night shall haunt this place.[55]

or

First I conjure the be Sanct Marie,
Be Alrisch king and Queene of Farie,

[53] Fletcher, Darley ed., 1851, *Monsieur Thomas,* IV, 6.

[54] Cartwright, *The Ordinary,* III, 1, Dodsley, 1780, Vol. X.

[55] *The Merry Devill of Edmonton,* 1608, Students' Facsimile ed., 1911, p. following D2.

And be the Trinitie to tarie,
 Quhill thow the treuth haue taull:
Be Christ and his Apostilles twell,
Be Sanctis of Heuin and hewis of Hell,
Be auld Sanct Tastian him sell,
 Be Peter and be Paull.

Be Mathew, Mark, be Luik and Johne,
Be Lethe, Stix and Acherone,
Be hellische furies euerie one,
 Quhair Pluto is the Prince:
That thow depart and do na wonder,
Be lichtning, quhirle wind, hayle nor thunder,
That beast nor bodie get na blunder,
 Nor harme quhen thow gais hence.

Throw power I charge the of the Paip,
Thow neyther girne, gowl, glowme, nor gaip,
Lyke Anker saidell, like unsell Aip,
 Lyke Owle nor Alrische Elfe:
Lyke fyrie Dragon full of feir,
Lyke Warwolf, Lyon, Bull nor Beir,
Bot pas ȝow hence as thow come heir,
 In lykenes of thy selfe.[56]

Nowhere is the common acceptance of the fairies, either as infernal spirits or as lesser wicked beings, more apparent, also, than in the fact of their inclusion among the bugbears or in the lists of evil beings by whom the folk were kept in continual fear, as in *The Discovery of Witchcraft,* where elves, fairies and changelings are given a place with the Devil and the familiar and fearful beings of England:

But in our childhood our mothers maids have so terrified us with an ugly devil having hornes on his head, fire in his mouth, and a

[56] *Philotus,* rpt. from Charteris ed., Bannatyne Club, 1835, Act II, Stanzas 122–124.

taile in his breech, eyes like a bason, fanges like a dog, clawes like a bear, a skinne like a Niger, and a voice roring like a Lion, whereby we start and are afraid when we hear one cry Bough: and they have so fraied us with bull-beggers, spirits, witches, urchens, elves, hags, fairies, satyrs, pans, faunes, sylens, kit with the cansticke, tritons, centaures, dwarfes, giants, imps, calcars, conjurors, nymphes, changelings, Incubus, Robin good fellow, the spoorn, the mare, the man in the oke, the hellwaine, the firedrake, the puckle, Tom thombe, hob-gobblin, Tom tumbler boneles, and such other bugs, that we are afraid of our own shadowes.[57]

Among the spirits enumerated in *The Buggbears*,[58] "the whyte & red fearye" and "Garret" are to be found, added by the English adapter and translator of *Le Spiritata* of Grazzini to the roll of spirits, both amiable and "yll," of the Italian original. They appear, too, in the list of wicked spirits in *A Mirror for Magistrates*, edition 1578;[59] in *The Battle of Alcazar;*[60] in *A Declaration of egregious Popish Impostures;*[61] in *Comus;*[62] in *The Faithful Shepherdess;*[63] and in Joseph Hall's poems.[64]

[57] Scot, 1651 ed., p. 113.

[58] *Early Plays from the Italian,* Bond ed., 1911, III, 3, p. 117.

[59] Haslewood ed., 1815, Vol. II, p. 121.

[60] Geo. Peele, Malone Soc. Rpt., 1907, IV, 2, l. 1231.

[61] Samuel Harsnet, 1603 ed., p. 134.

[62] Milton, Cambridge ed., 1899, ll. 432–437.

[63] Fletcher, Darley ed., 1851, I, 1

In the plays of Beaumont and Fletcher, with the possible exception of *The Faithful Shepherdess,* where the good qualities of the fairies are depicted in most instances, the fairies are always referred to as beings of the deepest dyed villainy and wickedness.

[64] *Carmen Funebre Caroli Horni,* 1596, Grosart ed., 1879, p. 217, verse 5:

"Now shall the wanton Deuils daunce in rings
In euerie mede, and euerie heath hore:
The Eluish Faeries and the Gobelins:

In regard to the origin of the fairies, there were, in general, three beliefs or theories. These have been summed up by the anonymous author of *A Discourse concerning Devils and Spirits,* as follows:

Many have insisted upon the Natures of these Astral Spirits: some alledging, That they are part of the faln Angels, and consequently subject to the torments of Hell at the last Judgment: Others, That they are the departed souls of men and women, confined to these outward Elements until the Consummation: Lastly, others, as Del rio, Nagar the Indian Magician, and the Platonists affirm, That their nature is middle between Heaven and Hell; and that they reign in a third Kingdom from both, having no other judgment or doom to expect for ever.[65]

The identification of the fairies as fallen angels had been one of the earliest origins assigned to them. According to *The Early South-English Legendary* of the 13th century,[66] in the account of the fall of Lucifer:

for al-so sone as ore louerd I-maud: heouene and eorþe and helle,
he makede him furst and is felawes: ase ich ov mai here telle.
And he ase-sone ase he was imaud: he bi-gan to smite in pruyte:
Al-so heiȝ ase ore louerd he wolde beo: he bi-ȝat þare-with wel
luyte.
Manie heolden faste with him: and nouȝt alle of one lore:
And manie likeden wel is dedene: some lasse and some more,
Some ferden ase huy ne rouȝten: noþer of on .ne of oþur.
þare ne bi-lefte in heouene non of heom: ne heore maister noþer.
Seint Miȝhel was maister to driuen heom: out of heuene a-doun:
þat was þe batayle þat he made: with þe luþere dragoun.

The hoofed Satyres silent heretofore:
Religion, vertue, Muses, holie mirth
Haue now forsworne the late forsaken earth."

[65] Rpt. in Appendix II of Reginald Scot, *The Discoverie of Witchcraft,* Nicholson rpt., 1886, p. 495.

[66] See Introduction, E. E. T. S. ed., 1887, pp. viii and x.

þe maister-dragoun lucifer: and is riȝte felawes ech-on
þat faste heolden with is pruyte: he drof heom to helle anon.
Ake huy þat heolden sumdel with him: and nouȝt fulliche so faste,
Out of heouene he drof heom: and In-to þe lofte heom caste,
Al here bi-neþe toward þe eorþe: þare mest tempeste is:
And þare heo schullen in tempest and in pine beo: to þe daye of dome, i-wis;
And ase hore gult þe more was: heore pine was al-so,
þe worse stude heom [was] i-take: heore penaunce for-to do.
Ake to helle huy ne schullen nouȝt: are domes-day i-wende;
Ak þare huy schullen after-ward: bi-leue with-outen ende.
Oþure þare weren þat for heom: sumdel in mis-þouȝte weren,
Ake natheles huy heolden betere with god: and vnneþe fur-bere:
þulke wenden out of heouene al-so: and a-boue þe oþure beoth,
An heiȝ onder þe firmament: and godes wille i-seoth,
And so schullen sumdel in pine beo: a-non to þe worldes ende,
Ake huy schullen at domes-day: a-ȝein to heouene wende.
In eorthþeliche parays: some beoth ȝeot al-so,
And in oþur studes on eorþe: heore penaunce for-to do. —
For heore defaute in heouene: þoruȝ ore louerdes grace
Man was formest on eorþe i-wrouȝt: to fulfulle þulke place.

. . . .

And ofte in fourme of wommane: In many derne weye
grete compaygnie men i-seoth of heom: boþe hoppie and pleiȝe,
þat Eluene beoth i-cleopede: and ofte heo comiez to toune,
And bi daye muche in wodes heo beoth: and bi niȝte ope heiȝe dounes.
þat beoth þe wrechche gostes: þat out of heuene weren i-nome,
And manie of heom a-domesday: ȝeot schullen to reste come.[67]

In the 17th century this theory of their origin was frequently advanced, and in one instance in the 16th century, in *The Famous Historie of Chinon of England,* by Christopher Middleton, the fairies are defined as

[67] E. E. T. S. ed., p. 305, ll. 181–210; p. 307, ll. 253–258.

such creatures as we call Fairies, whome some imagine to be those spirites that fell downe vpon the earth, and since that time inhabit the seuerall corners thereof.[68]

There is a reason, however, for the infrequent designation of the fairies as fallen angels, for they were traditionally regarded as outraged and dangerous whenever they were called evil spirits. Especially is this characteristic apparent in the encounter of Anne Jefferies with

[68] E. E. T. S. ed., 1925, p. 39. This is the only instance I have been able to find in the 16th century where the fairies are definitely stated to be fallen angels. In this connection see also Nashe, *Pierce Penilesse His Svpplication to the Diuell,* McKerrow ed., 1904–1910, Vol. I, p. 229, where a likeness between these angels and fairies appears; Burton, *Anat. of Mel.,* Vol. I, p. 206; J. M. Synge, *The Aran Islands,* 1911, p. 33; and W. P. Ker, in "The Craven Angels," *Modern Language Review,* Vol. 6, 1911, pp. 86–87, states:

"It may be due in part to the Platonic demonology, as stated by St Augustine, de Civ. Dei, VIII, mainly after Apuleius de Deo Socratis, ultimately from the description of daemons in the Symposium. The passages were well known; they may be found in the common-place book printed in the Rolls edition of R. de Diceto, Vol. I, p. 46. Geoffrey of Monmouth quotes Apuleius, in a chapter on the birth of Merlin. It was from Apuleius that Chaucer got the 'eyrish bestes' of the House of Fame; these are the 'aeria animalia' of Apuleius and St Augustine — the daemons of the air —

many a citezeyn
Of which that speketh dan Plato.

. . . .

The Fairy Genesis can be understood as a half learned transference of this argument and belief from the aerial daemons (described by philosophers and theologians) to the race of elves as known in folklore — 'far from heaven, and safe from hell.' The elves, with their half human nature, need explaining as well as the Platonic daemons; and the theory that explains the 'eyrish bestes' will do also for the people of the fairy-knolls."

them, in 1645,[69] where they were reported to repudiate the term, "Evil Spirits," and to refer the magistrates and ministers who used such terms, to the First Epistle of St. John, Chapter IV, Verse 1:

> Dearly Beloved, believe not every Spirit, but try the Spirits, whether they are of God, &c.

The belief that the fairies were souls of men departed, on the other hand, seems to have been a common and established article of faith. In the dictionaries and in plays, they are frequently confused with ghosts. The *Historia de Gentibus Septentrionalibus* of Olaus Magnus designates the fairies as among those

> of which they hold this opinion, that the Souls of those men, that give themselves to Corporal Pleasures, and make themselves as it were slaves unto them, and obey the force of their Lusts, violating the Laws of God and men, when they are out of their bodies, and wander about the Earth. In the number whereof they think those men to be, who even in these our days, are wont to come to help men, to labour in the Night, and to dress Horses and Cattel.[70]

[69] J. Morgan, *Phoenix Britannicus,* London, 1732, p. 550: Letter from Moses Pitt to Dr. Edward Fowler, May 1, 1696. Cf. also *Huon of Burdeux, Berners trans.,* E. E. T. S. ed., 1882–84, Vol. I, pt. 1, p. 69.

[70] *A Compendious History of the Goths, Swedes & Vandals,* 1658 trans., Book III, Chap. X, Of the Night Dances of the Fairies, and Ghosts, p. 43. Olai Magni, *Gentivm Septentrionaliv̄ Historiae Breviarivm,* 1652, Lib. III, Chap. X, De Elvarum, id est, spectrorum nocturna chorea, p. 108: "Hunc nocturnum monstrorum ludum vocant incolae Choream Elvarum: de quibus eam habent opinionem, quod animi eorum hominum, qui se corporeis voluptatibus dedunt, earumq; quasi ministros se praebent, impulsuique libidinum obediunt, ac divina & humana jura violant, corporibus elapsi circum terram ipsam volutantur. E quorum numero credunt eos esse, qui se adhuc nostro seculo in effigie humana accommodare solent ministeriis hominum, nocturnis horis laborando, equosque & jumenta curando, ut infra de ministerio daemonum hoc eodem libro ostendetur." Cf. also John Beaumont, *Treatise of Spirits,* p. 104.

Robert Kirk cites this idea of the fairies' origin as one of several, held by the lowland Scotch:

> But other Men of the Second Sight, being illiterate, and unwary in their Observations, learn from those; one averring those subterranean People to be departed Souls, attending awhile in this inferior State, and clothed with Bodies procured throwgh their Almsdeeds in this Lyfe; fluid, active, aetheriall Vehicles to hold them, that they may not scatter, or wander, and be lost in the Totum, or their first Nothing; [71]

and Hobbes, in his *Leviathan*, makes fairies and ghosts [72] the same order of beings:

> The Ecclesiastiques are Spirituall men, and Ghostly Fathers. The Fairies are Spirits and Ghosts. Fairies and Ghosts inhabite Darknesse, Solitudes, and Graves. The Ecclesiastiques walke in Obscurity of Doctrine, in Monasteries, Churches, and Church-yards.[73]

[71] *Sec. Comm.*, p. 18.

[72] It must have been this conception of the fairies to which Shakespeare was referring when Puck reminded Oberon in *M. N. D.*, III, 2:

> "My fairy lord, this must be done with haste;
> For night's swift dragons cut the clouds full fast,
> And yonder shines Aurora's harbinger;
> At whose approach, ghosts, wandering here and there,
> Troop home to church-yards: damned spirits all,
> That in cross-ways and floods have burial,
> Already to their wormy beds are gone;
> For fear lest day should look their shames upon,
> They wilfully themselves exile from light,
> And must for aye consort with black-brow'd night."

[73] Rpt. of 1651 ed., Oxford, 1909, p. 545. Cf. also trans. of *Aeneid* by Stanyhurst, Arber ed., 1880, pp. 68, 108, 111; and Burton, *Anat. of Mel.*, Vol. I, p. 206, as follows: "There is a foolish opinion, which some hold, that they are the souls of men departed, good and more noble were deified, the baser grovelled on the ground, or in the lower parts, and were devils."

The connection between the fairies and the souls of departed men is to be seen, also, in the confessions of a number of witches who recognized among the "gude wichtis" their friends and neighbors long dead,[74] and in the "relations" of mortals "conversant amongst Faeries" who "have seen several of their Neighbours or Familiar acquaintance in the habit they were wont to weare, notwithstanding they were known to have been dead some years before."[75]

The third belief: namely, that the fairies were of a nature "middle between Heaven and Hell" and reigned in a third kingdom from both, was frequently held.

This is one of the conceptions of the fairies found among the Scotch:

> These Siths, or FAIRIES, they call Sleagh Maith, or the Good People, it would seem, to prevent the Dint of their ill Attempts, (for the Irish use to bless all they fear Harme of;) and are said to be of a midle Nature betuixt Man and Angel, as were Daemons thought to be of old; of intelligent studious Spirits, and light changable Bodies, (lyke those called Astral,) somewhat of the Nature of a condensed Cloud, and best seen in Twilight. Thes Bodies be so plyable thorough the Subtilty of the Spirits that agitate them, that they can make them appear or disappear att Pleasure.[76]

And it would seem, from the following statements, that the author of *A Discourse concerning Devils and Spirits* inclines to the belief that the fairies were of a middle nature between heaven and hell:

> But to speak more nearly unto their natures, they are of the source of the Stars, and have their degrees of continuance, where of some live hundreds, some thousands of years: Their food is the Gas of the Water, and the Blas of the Air: And in their Aspects,

[74] See Chap. IV, pp. 170–173.
[75] *Dis. conc. D. & S.*, p. 505.
[76] Kirk, *Sec. Comm.*, p. 5.

or countenances, they differ as to vigour and cheerfulness: They occupy various places of this world; as Woods, Mountains, Waters, Air, fiery Flames, Clouds, Starrs, Mines, and hid Treasures: as also antient Buildings, and places of the slain. Some again are familiar in Houses, and do frequently converse with, and appear unto mortals.

They are capable of hunger, grief, passion, and vexation: they have not any thing in them that should bring them unto God: being meerly composed of the most spiritual part of the Elemeuts: And when they are worn out, they return into their proper essence or primary quality again; as Ice when it is resolved into water.[77]

John Webster, in *The Displaying of Supposed Witchcraft,* explains:

. . . if the thing were truly related (a most convincing Relation, to prove the Existence of Spirits, called, The Devil of Mascon) . . . as to the matter of fact, that it must needs be some Creature of a middle Nature, and no evil Spirit, both because it was such a sportful and mannerly Creature, that it would leave them, and not disturb them at their devotions; as also . . . because it denied that it was a Devil, and professed that it hoped to be saved by Christ.[78]

[77] Page 495.

[78] Page 41. Webster is here speaking of the fairies. Cf. also Peter Heylyn, *Cosmographie in foure Books contayning the Chorographie and Historie of the Whole World and all the Principal Kingdomes Provinces Seas and Isles thereof,* London, 1677, Appendix, p. 161.

It is interesting to note that this theory of the fairies is to be found in Robert of Gloucester's *Chronicle,* Hearne ed., Oxford, 1724, Vol. I, p. 130:

"Þe clerkes seide, þat yt is in philosophie y fonde,
Þat þer beþ in þe eir an hey, fer fro þe gronde,
As a maner gostes, wyȝtes as it be,
And me may hem ofte on erþe in wylde studes y se,
And ofte in monne's fourme wymmen heo comeþ to,
And ofte in wymmen forme þei comeþ to men al so,
Þat men clepuþ eluene, . . ."

In addition to the three theories usually held regarding the origin of the fairies, there was a further theory — that the names " elfes and goblins " as well as the beings so designated, came from the Guelfes and Gibelins, after the fashion described by E. K. in the June Glosse of *The Shepheardes Calender,*

. . . the truth is, that there be no such thinges, nor yet the shadowes of the things, . . . the sooth is, that when all Italy was distraicte into the factions of the Guelfes and the Gibelins, being two famous houses in Florence, the name began, through their great mischiefes and many outrages, to be so odious, or rather dreadfull, in the peoples eares, that if theyr children at any time were frowarde and wanton, they would say to them that the Guelfe or the Gibeline came. Which words nowe from them (as many thinge els) be come into our usage, and, for Guelfes and Gibelines, we say elfes and goblins.[79]

In the *Cosmographie* of Heylyn, the same origin is assigned the fairies,[80] as is the case, also, in *Etymologicon Linguae Anglicanae* of Stephen Skinner, 1671, where, among other theories of the origin of the word, the following account is given:

Goblins, à Fr. G. Gobelins, Lemures, Spectra, Terriculamenta, . . . Manduci: Elves and Goblins, q.d. Guelfs and Ghibelins, quibus olim terribilissimis nominibus infantes territare solebant nutrices. Sic Praeceptor meus, sed est mera conjectura.

In the matter of the exact identification of the fairies, or of the particular category of spirits and supernatural beings to which they belonged, there were a number of beliefs and of opinions.

By translators of the classics and by men of literary training and attainments, fairies and elves were believed

[79] Page 31.
[80] Lib. I, p. 113.

to be, or at least were made, the native British equivalent of classical nymphs and fauns.[81] This identification occurs very early in the translation of the *Aeneid* by Gawin Douglas, in the following passage:

Thir woddis and thir schawis all, quod he,
Sum tyme inhabyt war and occupyit
With Nymphis and Fawnys apon euery syde,
Quhilk fairfolkis, or than elvys, clepyng we,
That war engendryt in this sam cuntre,
That with ane kynd of men yborn, but leys,
Furth of ald stokkis and hard runtis of treis;
Quhilkis nowder maneris had nor polecy,
Ne couth thai eir the ground, nor occupy
The plewis, nor the oxin ȝok infeir,
Nor ȝit had craft to conquys nor wyn geir,
Nor kepe thar moblis quhen it gadderit was;
Bot, as thir bestis, or the doillit as,
Thar fude of treis dyd in woddis fet,
Or of the wild veneson scharp to get.[81a]

Phaër in his translation of the same passage,

Haec nemora indigenae Fauni Nymphaeque tenebant,
Gensque virum truncis et duro robore nata . . .

makes use of somewhat the same idea:

[81] E. K. Chambers in "The Fairy World," p. 154, has called attention to the identification of the fairies with the nymphs, fauns, etc.

[81a] *The Aeneid of Virgil* translated into Scottish verse by Gawin Douglas, Bannatyne Club, Edinburgh, 1839. *The Aucht Buke of Eneados,* p. 478. Cf. also Eden's *Decades, The fyrst Decade, First printed in 1511,* Arber ed., 1885, p. 101: "These Zemes, they beleue to send plentie and frutefulnes of those rootes, as the antiquitie beleued suche fayries or spirites as they cauled Dryades, Hamadryades, Satyros, Panes, and Nereides, to haue the cure and prouidence of the sea, wooddes, and sprynges and fountaynes, assigninge to euery thynge, theyr peculier goddes."

These woods (cþ he) sometime both Fauns, Nimphs, and Gods of
groũde,
And fairy Queenes did kepe, and vnder them a nacion rough;
A people saluage strong, and borne in tronks of timber tough:
Who neither nurture knew, nor trade of life, nor bullocks taught,
Nor goods vpstoare they could, nor wisely spare those things thei
caught.
But bowes of trees them fed, and hunting hard them kept from
cold,
Furst from Olympus mount (right neare the skies) good Saturn
old,
Whan he from Ioue did flee, and from his kingdoms outlawd stood,
He first that wayward kittish kynde disperst in hilles, and wood,
Did bring to thrift, and gaue them lawes, and all the land this
waye
Did Latium cal, . . . [82]

Golding in 1565–1567 [83] seems to have taken the similitude between the fairies and elves and nymphs and

[82] *The eygth booke of Aeneidos,* ll. 335–345. *The whole .xii. Bookes of the Aeneidos of Virgill.* Whereof the first .ix. and part of the tenth, were conuerted into English Meeter by Thomas Phaër Esquier, and the residue supplied, and the whole worke together newly set forth by Thomas Twyne Gentleman. London, 1573.

[83] *The xv. Bookes of P. Ouidius Naso, entytuled Metamorphosis,* translated oute of Latin into English meeter, by Arthur Golding Gentleman. A Worke very pleasaunt and delectable. Imprynted at London, by William Seres, 1567. Rouse ed., London, 1904.

It is interesting to observe that the translation of the same passages by George Sandys, published 1626, makes no mention of fairies or elves, as for instance, Book XIV, ll. 584–586:

"In which hee saw a darksome denne forgrowne with busshes hye,
And watred with a little spring. The halfegoate Pan that howre
Possessed it: but heertoofore it was the fayryes bowre,"

is translated by Sandys as

"A Cave, inviron'd with a sylvan shade,
Distilling streames. By halfe-goate Pan possest;
Which erst the Wood-nymphs with their beauties blest."

hamadryads as a matter of course, to judge from the number of instances in which the wood spirits of the Latin original are translated *fairies:* as, in Book IX, line 408, where *Nymphis latura* becomes *fayries of the Lake;* Book XI, line 171, where *nymphis* is rendered *fayrye elves;* Book XIV, line 586, where *nymphae* becomes *fayryes;* Book I, line 859, *hamadryadas, Fairie;* and Book IV, line 370, *naiadum, Waterfaries.* And in the earliest rhyming dictionary of the time, the *Manipvlvs Vocabvlorvm* by P. Leuins, 1570, *faunus* is given as the equivalent for *Faýrye* and *Satyrus, faunus* as the equivalent of *elfe.*[84]

To Thomas Churchyard in 1578, and, it must be surmised, to the Queen and courtiers to whom he presented his entertainments, the likeness between nymphs and fairies is so close that they not only appear together, the fairies being introduced by the nymphs as follows:

The Phayries are another kinde of elfes that daunce in darke,
Yet can light candles in the night, and vanish like a sparke;
And make a noyse and rumbling great among the dishes oft,
And wake the sleepie sluggish maydes that lyes in kitchen loft.
And when in field they treade the grasse, from water we repayre,
And hoppe and skippe with them sometime as weather waxeth fayre;[85]

but the difference between the two is so indistinguishable that the costumes which were to have adorned the nymphs of the water are used later as the costumes of the fairies:

Yea, out of hedge we crept indeede, where close in caves we lay,
And knowing by the brute of fame a Queene must passe this way,
To make hir laugh, we clapt on coates of segges and bulrush both,

[84] E. E. T. S. ed., 1867. Cf. also *Medulla Grāmatice,* 1468, Note, p. 113, *Catholicon Anglicum,* E. E. T. S., 1881: "Satirus. An elfe or a mysshapyn man."

[85] *The Queen's Entertainment in Suffolk and Norfolk,* 1578: Nichols, *Prog. of Eliz.,* Vol. II, p. 210.

That she should know, and world should say, Lo there thy Phayries
goth,
Like Furies madde, and Satyres wild: . . .[86]

The conception of "The Robbin-good-fellowes, Elfes, Fairies, Hobgoblins of our latter age" as the same beings "which idolatrous former daies and the fantasticall world of Greece ycleaped Fawnes, Satyres, Dryades, & Hamadryades"[87] set forth by Nashe in 1593, is repeatedly found in the works of most of the earlier and later Elizabethans. Even James VI of Scotland, committed though he is to the belief that the fairies are illusions of the devil, or the devil himself, does not fail to designate them also as

That fourth kinde of Spirits, which by the Gentiles was called Diana, and her wandering court, and amongst vs was called the Phairie (as I told you) or our good neighbours.[88]

In the dictionaries of the period, with few exceptions, the elves and fairies are also defined in terms of classical mythology but, in this case, they are most frequently given as the English equivalent of *lamiae* and *strygia,* both of whom are wicked and evil beings, than of nymphs and of satyrs.[89] The *Promptorium Parvulorum,*[90] com-

[86] *Ibid.,* pp. 212–213.

[87] *The Terrors of the Night,* McKerrow ed., 1904–10, Vol. I, p. 347. Cf. also *The Maydes Metamorphosis,* III, 1, in Bullen, *A Coll. of Old Eng. Plays,* 1882, Vol. I: "No Fayrie Nymph"; Froissart's *Chronicles,* trans. Berners, 1812, Vol. II, p. 700, Concerning the island of Chyfolignie, "the fayry and the nympes be moche conuersaunt there." This conception had appeared in Eden's *Decades,* printed 1555, in *The Firste Booke of the Decades of the Ocean* of Peter Martyr, printed in Latin, 1511.

[88] *Daemon.,* p. 132.

[89] See Huloet's *Dictionarie* . . . corrected by John Higgins, 1572: fayres or Elves — Lamiae, Empusae, Laruae, Lemures, Les fees.

[90] E. E. T. S. ed., 1908.

piled 1440, defines *elf* as "spyryt, lamia, -e; fem"; the *Catholicon Anglicum* of 1483,[91] "an Elfe; lamia, eumenis, dicta Ab eu, quod est bonum, & mene, defectus"; (the word *fairy* is not given in either book); the *Vulgaria*[92] of Horman, 1519, renders "The fayre hath chaunged my chylde," "Strix, vel lamia pro meo suum paruulum, supposuit."

Although the *Bibliotheca Eliotae* of 1532 makes *elfes* or *fayries* the English equivalent of *nymphae, naides, dryades* and *hamadryades* (all feminine gender), the terms *an elfe, the fairie,* and *ladies of the fayry* are to be found among the definitions of Larva, Strix and Lamiae:

> Larua, ae, f.g. and Laruae, arum, plur. a spirite, whyche appereth in the nyght tyme. some call it a hegge. some a goblyn. some a goste or an elfe. also a masker, or he that weareth a visour. also the visour it selfe.
>
> Strix, strigis, fae. ge. a shricheoule, a witche that chaungeth the fauour of children, the hegge or fairie.
>
> Lamiae, be women, whyche beholdying chyldren, or geuynge to them gyftes, doo alter the forme of theym: whyche children be afterwarde called elfes, or taken with the fayrie, and some suche women will sucke the bloud from chyldren. They be also those, whiche be called ladies of the fayry, whyche dooe allure yong men to company carnally with theym: and after that they bee consumed in the acte of lecherye, they coucte to deuoure theym.[93]

In *A Worlde of Wordes*[94] by John Florio, 1598, in

[91] E. E. T. S. ed., 1881.

[92] *Catholicon Anglicum,* E. E. T. S., 1881, note p. 113. It is significant that in nearly every case in which the fairies are used in the dictionaries, they are identified by wicked and cruel characteristics.

[93] *Bibl. Eliotae,* L ante A, and S ante T.

[94] Pages 197 and 401–402. Larva according to Florio is defined as "a vizard, or a maske, a vision, a night-ghost, a hag, a spirit, a hobgoblin, a walking or appearing spirit." — p. 198. "Fata, a fairie, a witch, an enchantres, an elfe." — p. 127.

the latter part of the century, the fairy is again defined as *Lamia*[95] and as *Strega,* and *lamia,* in addition to other meanings, is rendered as:

Also a witch, a sorceresse or a hag. Also women that were thought to haue such eies as they could put out and put in at their pleasure, or rather certaine diuels in a counterfeit shape, which with flatterings allured faire yoong springals and boies, and taking vpon them the likenes and fashion of women were thought to deuoure them and bring them to destruction. Some thought them to be ladies of the fairies or such as make children afraide, or such witches as sucke childrens blood to kill them.

Strega, a witch, a sorceresse, a charmer, a hag or fairie such as our elders thought to change the fauour of children.

These are the definitions of the fairy also that appear in Minsheu's *The Guide into the tongues,* of 1617:

Fairie à Belg: Váerlick siue Vréselik, i. timendus, horibilis, terribilis, à vresen, i. timere: propter terrorem quem inopinato suo aduentu incutere solent. B. Toouerinne, à tooueren, i. incantare: traduntur enim juuenes ac potissimum speciosos incantationibus in sui amorem pellicere, ac pellectos deuorare. T. Nácht mummel, à nacht, i. nox & mummel, i. larua: q. noctis larua. Quo nomine Lamias quoque appellatas fuisse testatur. Philostrat: in Apollon, & Cael: Rhodig: lib: 29 cap: 5. L. Lámia, ae & Lámiae, arum. . . . l. insatiabili gulae auiditate deglutio, propter rationem suprà allatam. Ab antiquis, mulieres esse putabantur, siue veriùs daemonum quaedam phantasmata, quae formosarum mulierum specie assumpta, pueros pariter & juuenes blanditijs allectos vorare credebantur. Hae quum foris essent egregiae oculata, domi

[95] See Bourne, *Antiq. Vulgares,* 1725, p. 83: "Now in all this there is really nothing, but an old fabulous Story, which has been handed down even to our Days from the Times of Heathenism, of a certain Sort of Beings called Lamiae, which were esteem'd so mischievous and cruel, as to take away young Children and slay them. These, together with the Fauns, the Gods of the Woods, seem to have form'd the Notion of Fairies."

prorsus cacutiebant. Chrysostomus Dion in intima Africa feras quasdam esse scribit muliebri facie, quae & ipsae Lamiae dicuntur, vberibus autem totoque corpore adeò specioso vt nullo pictoris ingenio similes affingi queant, quibus retectis homines in fraudem alliciant, captosque deuorent. Isidor: á laniando vult, quidam à . . . helol, qua voce noctua, vel nycticorax aut denique Lamia significari solet, vel dicitur Lamia á rubore & sortibus oculorum, . . . Nam ex oculis de affectione animi aut moribus, facilè capitur iudicium, & vero incantatricum quod rubeant & sordescant, quis non audijt, Maro alludit, oculus fascinat agnos.[96]

The identification of the fairies with beings of classical mythology or with wicked monsters of antiquity was by no means the only idea of them that prevailed. By a number of authorities, they were held to be the devil himself or beings of his substance and nature. The reference to the fairies in the works of Sir David Lyndesay would indicate a close resemblance between the "Feind and the Farie-folk" and the association of the one with the other as the following passages from *Ane Satyre of the thrie Estaits* show:

DISSAIT.

Now am I buskit, and quha can spy —
The Deuill stik me! — gif this be I?
If this be I, or not, I can not weill say.
Or hes the Feind or Farie-folk borne me away? [97]

SPRITVALITIE.

Pas on, Madame, — we knaw ȝow nocht; —
Or, be him that the warld wrocht!
Ȝour cumming sall be richt deir coft,
Gif ȝe mak langer tarie.

[96] 1617 ed., p. 187.
[97] E. E. T. S., 1865–71, Vol. 35–37–47, pp. 401–402.

ABBOT.

But doubt, wee will baith leif and die
With our luif, Sensualitie.
Wee will haif na mair deall with the
Then with the Queene of Farie.[98]

FLATTRIE.

I na mair will remaine besyd ȝow,
Bot counsell ȝow, rycht weill to gyde ȝow,
Byd nocht on Correctioun.
Fair-weil! I will na langer tarie.
I pray the alrich Queene of Farie
To be ȝour protectioun.[99]

SENSVALITIE.

. . . .
Adeu, Sir King! I may na langer tary.
I cair nocht that: als gude luife cums as gais.
I recommend ȝow to the Queene of Farie.
I se ȝe will be gydit with my fais.[100]

FALSET.

. . . .
Adew! I may na langer tarie,
I man pas to the King of Farie,
Or ellis the rycht to hell.[101]

In Lord Berners' translation of *Huon of Burdeux*, 1534, Huon has no hesitation in calling Oberon "ye deuyll," [102] or of expressing his wonder "how he can speke of god almyghty/ for I thinke he be a deuyll of hell/." [103]

[98] *Ibid.*, pp. 422–423.
[99] *Ibid.*, p. 433.
[100] *Ibid.*, p. 440.
[101] *Ibid.*, p. 532.
[102] E. E. T. S. ed., Vol. I, pt. I, p. 69.
[103] *Ibid.*, p. 71.

James VI of Scotland identifies the fairies with the devil himself:

Epi: That kind of the diuels coursing in the earth, may be diuided in foure different kindes, whereby he affraieth and troubleth the bodies of men: For of the abusing of the soule, I haue spoken alreadie. The first is, where spirits trouble some houses or solitarie places: The second, where Spirits follow vpon certaine persons, and at diuers houres trouble them: The third, when they enter within them and possesse them: The fourth is these kinde of Spirits that are called vulgarly the Fairie: Of the three former kinds, ye heard already, how they may artificially be made by Witchcraft to trouble folke: . . . But generally I must forewarne you of one thing before I enter in this purpose: that is, that although in my discoursing of them, I deuide them in diuers kinds, ye must notwithstanding thereof note my phrase of speaking in that: For doubtleslie they are in effect, but all one kinde of Spirits, who for abusing the more of mankinde, take on these sundrie shapes, and vse diuers formes of outward actions, as if some were of nature better then other.[104]

Thomas Heywood regards them as wicked spirits

> . . . . such as we call
> Hob-goblins, Fairies, Satyrs, and those all
> Sathan by strange illusions doth employ,
> How Mankinde to insidiate and destroy.[105]

Nashe associates them with the Devil.[106] Hobbes makes Beelzebub, prince of demons, their king;[107] and Burton regards them as devils under the dominion of the Devil;[108] while the *Mirror for Magistrates* enumerates them among "all infernall powers."[109]

104 *Daemon.*, p. 123.

105 *Hierarchie*, p. 568.

106 *Terr. of the Night*, Vol. I, p. 347.

107 *Leviathan*, p. 544.

108 *Anat. of Mel.*, Vol. I, p. 216.

109 Page 121.

The laws of Scotland pronounced the fairies "spretis of the devill" [110] and the records of the trials of witches in England, and literature and dissertations on witchcraft identified them with the devil, either as inhabitants of Hell [111] or as familiar spirits of the devil.[112]

In spite of the nature assigned the fairies by law, a large body of scholarly opinion tended to minimize their identification with the devil himself, and seems to have regarded them as spirits having no connection with heaven and yet not absolutely wicked nor wholly in the power of Satan or of his race, but, as their origins — especially as fallen angels — would make them, spirits connected with the devil and in his power because of their former sins and "confined until the day of judgment to this sublunary world." [113] According to this conception of them, they were specifically classified as sublunary devils, and put in the ranks of watery spirits, terrestrial spirits, or domestic devils.

It was as terrestrial spirits that they were more generally accepted. In this category, they are put by Nashe,[114] by Thomas Heywood,[115] and by Robert Kirk.[116] Here, too, they are classified by Burton,[117] and by Lavater,[118] and by the author of *A Discourse concerning Devils and Spirits* whose statement can be taken as representative of this conception of the fairies:

[110] Pitcairn, *Crim. Trials,* 1833, Vol. I, pt. 2, pp. 51 and 162.

[111] See Chap. II, pp. 72–73.

[112] See Chap. IV, pp. 121–122.

[113] Burton, *Anat. of Mel.,* Vol. I, p. 216.

[114] *Pierce Penilesse,* Vol. I, p. 238.

[115] *Hierarchie,* pp. 503–504, 510.

[116] *Sec. Comm.,* p. 11.

[117] *Anat. of Mel.,* Vol. I, p. 217.

[118] *Of Ghostes and Spirites walking by nyght,* Eng. trans. 1572, p. 49.

Subordinate unto these of the Air are the Terrestrial Spirits, which are of several degrees according to the places which they occupy, as Woods, Moun/tains, Caves, Fens, Mines, Ruins, Desolate places, and Antient Buildings, calld by the Antient Heathens after various names, as Nymphs, Satyrs, Lamii, Dryades, Sylvanes, Cobali, &c. And more particularly the Faeries, who do principally inhabit the Mountains, and Caverns of the Earth.[119]

As water devils they are classified by Thomas Heywood,[120] by Elyot,[121] and by Florio,[122] and tentatively ranked by Burton as follows:

Water-devils are those Naiades or Water-nymphs, which have been heretofore conversant about waters and rivers. The water (as Paracelsus thinks) is their Chaos, wherein they live; some call them Fairies and say that Habundia is their Queen; these cause inundations, many times shipwrecks, and deceive men divers ways, as Succubae, or otherwise, appearing most part, (saith Trithemius), in women's shapes.[123]

With water nymphs, as has already been seen, they are made synonymous by Golding,[124] and by Churchyard.[125] And as fairies of the sea, they appear in Eden's *Decades:*

But if they be wrought with the cunninge hande of Phidias or Praxiteles, and shaped to the similitude of the fayre nimphes or fayeres of the sea (cauled Nereiades) or the fayres of the wods, (cauled Hamadriades) they shal neuer lacke byers.[126]

[119] Page 510.
[120] *Hierarchie,* p. 506.
[121] *Bibl. Eliotae.*
[122] *A Worlde of Wordes,* p. 236.
[123] *Anat. of Mel.,* Vol. I, p. 219.
[124] *Op. cit.,* Chap. I, pp. 50–51.
[125] Nichols, *Prog. of Eliz.,* Vol. II, p. 210. Cf. also Chap. II, pp. 100–101.
[126] Page 12 of "The Firste Booke of the Decades of the Ocean," written by Peter Martyr. First printed in 1511: in *The first Three*

They were also, as sublunary devils, regarded as familiar or domestic devils. This is the definition given them by Reginald Scot, who puts them in the same category with "bugs, Incubus, Robin good fellow, and other familiar or domestical spirits and divels."[127] Samuel Rowlands considers the fairies domestic spirits:

In old wiues dayes, that in old time did liue

. . . .

Great store of Goblins, Faries, Bugs, Night-mares,
Vrchins, and Elues, to many a house repaires,[128]

as does Harsnet in *A Declaration of egregious Popish Impostures,*[129] Kirk in *Secret Commonwealth,*[130] Ben Jonson in the *Masque of Oberon,*[131] and Edward Fairfax

English books on America. 1555 A.D. Being chiefly Translations, Compilations, &c., by Richard Eden, . . . Arber ed., 1885, p. 74.

These are but a few examples of the connection of the fairies with water either as watery devils or as the same race as water nymphs. The association of the fairies with water, as is well known, was one of the features of their history during the centuries preceding the 16th century, and a love of water and springs was a characteristic of the elves of early English literature as well as of the fairies of romance and of Chaucer. Cf. also Francis Douce, *Illustrations of Shakspeare, and of Ancient Manners,* 1807, Vol. I, p. 389: "Fairies were also, from their supposed place of residence, denominated waternymphs, in the Teutonic languages wasserfrauwen, wassernixen, nocka, necker and nicker; terms, excepting the first, manifestly connected with the Scotish nicneven, and most probably with our old nick." Cf. also Huloet, *Abecedarium,* printed 1552, corrected by John Higgins, 1572 (known as Huloet's *Dictionarie*):

"Fayries or Elves of the hylls Oreades
Fayes or Nymphes of the Sea, the daughters of Nereus and
Doric having the forme of women."

[127] *Dis. of Witch.,* 1651 ed., p. 364.

[128] *More Knaues Yet? Of Ghoasts and Goblins.* Hunterian Club ed., 1880, Vol. 2, p. 41.

[129] Page 133.

[130] Page 6.

[131] Morley ed., p. 154.

in *A Discourse of Witchcraft,* from which the following account is taken:

The heathen Romans brought into this land, besides the multiplicity of their greater gods, certain domestic deities, peculiar to every place, house, and heath, these were their Paenates in general, and with them they coupled Genius, Daemon, Lari, &c. which the Saxons, heathens also, did not abolish at their entrance, though names more barbarous were given to these Deities and Semideities, as Thor, Woden, Easter, for the greater; and for the domestic, Hobthuss, Robin Goodfellow, Hobgoblin; and for the nymphs and sylvans they had Elves and Fairies.[132]

Whether the fairies were regarded as domestic spirits or water devils, or were made the English equivalents of lamiae, strygia, larvae, nymphs or satyrs, or whether they had their beginning as fallen angels, as the ghosts of men departed, as beings of a middle nature outside the pale of salvation, or as a verbal corruption of Guelfs and Gibelines, their classifications and origins leave little reason to doubt that their reputation was an evil one and that their race was considered wicked. The one exception to this statement might seem to be their identification with nymphs and hamadryads. To the Elizabethans, however, as Christian writers and Christian poets, nymphs and dryads were pagan and heathen spirits of idolatrous former days, and to the common people they were evil and fearful beings, if the long lists of wicked spirits, among whom the nymphs were included, are representative of popular bugbears.[133]

[132] Preface to Reader, p. 18.

[133] It would seem certain that, in the earlier part of the century, nymphs, to the common people, were real and visible beings in their own right. Cf. the enumeration of the beings used to terrify children in Scot's *Dis. of Witch.,* 1651 ed., p. 113; and in *The Buggbears,* p. 117, where nymphs are mentioned along with Rawhead, bloudibone

In connection with the general feeling that the nature of the fairies was more or less wicked, it is significant that their existence and belief in their existence was ascribed by Protestant scholars to the teachings and influence of the Catholic Church.[134] The statement by Bishop Harsnet in 1603,

> What a world of hel-worke, deuil-worke, and Elue worke had we walking amongst vs heere in England, what time that popish mist had befogged the eyes of our poore people.[135]

had already been anticipated by Chapman,[136] by Reginald

---

and witches. Cf. also Lyly, *Endimion,* IV, 3; *Shakspere's Holinshed,* Boswell-Stone ed., 1896, p. 24. Especially interesting is a woodcut of nymphs, appearing in Caxton's translation of *Six Books of Metamorphoseos,* Pepys Ms., Shakspeare Press, London, 1819: The facon of Dyane.

[134] In one instance at least the fairies' connection with the Church of Rome was known and voiced by a country woman of Scotland who represented them, or, at least, their agent, as being dissatisfied with the Protestant faith and prophesying that the true religion would soon return: "(16.) INTERROGAT, Quhat sche thocht of the new law? Ansuerit, That sche had spokin with Thom about that mater; bot Thom ansuerit, That this new law was nocht gude; and that the auld ffayth suld cum hame agane, but nocht sic as it was befoir." Pitcairn, *Crim. Trials,* Vol. I, pt. 2, p. 56. Cf. also William Browne, *An Elegie on the Countesse Dowager of Pembrooke,* Hazlitt ed., 1869, Vol. II, p. 308:

> "For should the world but know that thou wert gone,
> Our Age too prone to Irreligion,
> Knoweing soe much divinitie in thee,
> Might thence conclude noe immortalitye.
> And I belieue the Puritans themselues
> Would be seduc'd to thinke, that Ghostes & Elves
> Doe haunt vs yet, in hope that thou would'st deigne
> To visitt vs, as when thou liv'd'st againe."

[135] *Declaration,* p. 133.

[136] *An Humerous dayes Myrth,* Pearson rpt. of 1599 ed., Vol. I, p. 57.

Scot,[137] by E. K.,[138] by James VI of Scotland,[139] and by many others. Nor did writers of the 17th century fail to stress the fairies' connection with the Church of Rome, as any examination of Fairfax's *Discourse of Witchcraft*,[140] the *Leviathan* of Hobbes,[141] or the poems of Bishop Corbet [142] will show.

The only difference between the beliefs of scholars concerning the nature of fairies and the idea of the fairies held by the folk (as can be seen from a comparison of the charms and spells against them, the popular practices of the folk in regard to them and the statements of James VI of Scotland, Scot, Burton and Fairfax quoted above) was that of definition and of credulity. The former endeavored to classify them in one of the learned categories of spirits or mythological beings, to trace their derivation and origin, and, in many instances, to disap-

137 *Dis. of Witch.*, 1651 ed., "To the Readers."

138 Spenser, *Shep. Cal.*, June Glosse.

139 *Daemon.*, p. 132.

140 Preface to Reader, p. 17.

141 Page 545.

142 *The Faerye's Farewell*, Vol. 5, Chalmers ed., 1810, p. 582:

> "By which we note the Faries
> Were of the old profession;
> Theyre songs were Ave Maryes;
> Theyre daunces were procession:
> But now, alas! they all are dead,
> Or gone beyond the seas;
> Or farther for religion fled,
> Or elce they take theyre ease."

See also Bourne, *Antiq. Vulgares*, p. 84: "This Opinion, in the benighted Ages of Popery, when Hobgoblins and Sprights were in every City and Town and Village, by every Water and in every Wood, was very common. But when that Cloud was dispell'd, and the Day sprung up, those Spirits which wander'd in the Night of Ignorance and Error, did really vanish at the Dawn of Truth and the Light of Knowledge." Cf. also Warton, *Hist. of Eng. Poetry*, Vol. III, p. 496.

prove their existence; the latter accepted them as fearful beings as much a part of life as they themselves.

To both scholar and old wife and to the inhabitants of England — if the evidence furnished by the references to the fairies from literature and folklore, found on the preceding pages, can be accepted as sufficiently indicative of the nature and race of the fairies of the 16th century — the fairies of Shakespeare's time were the traditional fairies of the country, distinct in nationality from other spirits of the time, as "the deuill and his dam," ghosts, or Rawhead and Bloudibone. They existed as real and actual supernatural beings and appeared under certain circumstances in visible form. In the main, they were fallen angels, or departed souls with a more or less evil past, or creatures of a middle nature between heaven and hell. As such beings, they were not numbered among the good spirits but were placed in the category of wicked spirits, or in the class, to quote Olaus Magnus, of "monstrous things, and innumerable Delusions . . . by which men were extreamly terrified, or torn to pieces and slain." [143]

[143] *A Compendious History of the Goths, Swedes and Vandals,* Bk. III, p. 43.

Chapter II

THE FAIRIES: THEIR APPEARANCE AND CHARACTERISTICS [1]

When Dr. Johnson observed that common tradition had made the fairies of Shakespeare's time familiar,[2] he spoke more truly than he was probably aware. For one of the most striking features of their Elizabethan existence is the general recognition of them by their mortal contemporaries, and the intimate and universal knowledge of their appearance and their characteristics. And this, in spite of the fact that — unlike the modern fairies of today — the fairies of the 16th century had few of the very striking and distinctive features, as the gauzy wings and diminutive stature of the modern fairies, which would establish them at first sight as fairies!

Perhaps no better method of presenting the fairies, as the Elizabethans saw them, can be followed than to contrast them with the picture of the fairies of today, found in actual photographs, made or believed to have been

[1] In most of the references to the fairies in the 16th century, they are treated as real and existing entities. For this reason it is almost impossible, when quoting or citing these references, to refer to the fairies as a supposititious race or to treat them as mythical beings. In this chapter, therefore, and in several of the subsequent chapters, they are represented, according to the psychology of the folk who believed in them and saw them and in the style in which they were discussed and referred to in the 16th century, as living beings.

[2] *The Plays of William Shakspeare,* 1778, notes by Johnson and Steevens, M. N. D., V, 2, in Vol. III, p. 127: "Fairies in his time were much in fashion; common tradition had made them familiar, and Spenser's poem had made them great."

made of them in 1917.[3] Here they appear as diminutive beings, mostly female, clad in diaphanous trailing draperies, with butterfly wings and flowing hair, poised on stalks of grass or on the knee of a child.

Had these photographs been shown to an inhabitant of 16th century England, he would have had to inquire who the very diminutive beings with wings were, and he would have repudiated with scorn, the contention that these pictures were pictures of the fairies.

The picture of fairies as he saw them, is to be found in Bovet's *Pandaemonium:*

> Those that have had occasion to travel that way, have frequently seen them there, appearing like men and women of a stature generally near the smaller size of men; their habits used to be of red, blew, or green, according to the old way of country garb, with high-crown'd hats. One time about fifty years since, a person . . . was riding towards his home that way, and saw just before him, on the side of the hill, a great company of people, that seemed to him like country folks, assembled, as at a fair.[4]

If one is to judge by this record and other records of the fairies' materializations and appearances, real or theatrical, the description of the fairies as "near the smaller size of men" would seem to represent the idea of their figures and of their measurements held, with few exceptions, during the 16th century. With these propor-

[3] See photographs facing pp. 65, 80 and 81 of *The Coming of the Fairies,* by Sir Arthur Conan Doyle, 1922. The book was written to prove the present existence of the fairies, and the photographs of them, taken by a medium, were offered as evidence of their reality. The photographic plates were subsequently acknowledged as spurious, but the pictures of the fairies produced upon them represent the popular conception of the fairies' appearance and proportions.

[4] Richard Bovet, "*Pandaemonium, or the Devil's Cloyster, being a further blow to modern Sadduceism, proving the existence of witches and spirits,*" London, 1684; rpt. in Hazlitt, *Fairy Tales,* 1875, p. 335.

tions they were not only recognized when they appeared in person, but in many cases human beings were mistaken for them.

Before taking up a detailed examination of the material in which the evidence in regard to the size and figure of the fairies is to be found, it is well to call attention to the fact, to quote Mr. Sidgwick, "that even today it is not easy to shake off the inherited impression that the fairies are only what Shakespeare shows them to be."[5] Especially is this true in regard to the stature of the fairies who, like those made familiar by Shakespeare, are regarded as diminutive or very small.

So deep-rooted is this conception of the diminutiveness of the fairies that, in many instances, an investigation of their size and figure either proceeds upon the assumption of their diminutiveness, as in the case of Ritson,[6] and of Keightley,[7] or is subjected to the demand that the evidence adduced refutes the fact that they were diminutive —a conception of them of which the 16th century did not seem to have been aware, and which it was not, therefore, at any pains to refute by a differentiation of largeness in contradistinction to smallness.

It must be remembered that the proportions of the fairies of the 16th century were as familiar to the Elizabethans as are the proportions of the fairies of Shakespeare and of their descendants to any lettered person of today. In the latter case, the smallness of the fairies is so much a matter of course that no one in writing about them or referring to them, finds himself under the neces-

[5] Frank Sidgwick, *The Sources and Analogues of "A Midsummer-Night's Dream,"* 1908, p. 35.

[6] *Fairy Tales,* pp. 28 and 35.

[7] Thomas Keightley, *Fairy Mythology,* 1833, Vol. II, pp. 121, 126 and 127.

sity to designate them by the term *little*. To him and to his reader, the adjective and the word *fairy* are almost synonymous. A somewhat similar state of mind in regard to the proportions of fairies prevailed in the 16th century. So much were their measurements, as "near the smaller size of men," a matter of course that the Elizabethan, in referring to the fairies or writing about them, found himself under no compulsion to describe their proportions or to designate their stature by the term *large*.

The idea of the size and proportions of the native fairy of the 16th century, therefore, cannot be derived from any definite description of their stature or from any explicit statement of their measurements except in a few instances, like that of *Pandaemonium*, mostly confined to the late 17th century when belief in the existence of the fairies was dying out. On the other hand, it seems both logical and reasonable to take as evidence of their size and figure the fact that they are described repeatedly as men and women,[8] and to assume that the proportions and measurements of those persons with whom they were compared and of those for whom they were mistaken, were the proportions and measurements, with little variation, of the fairies. Their size and stature also can be reckoned from the evidence afforded by the representations made of them on the stage or in masque and pageant.

In those instances in which the stature or the figure of the fairies is described, they are represented as possessing

[8] It might be urged that the description of the fairies as men and women furnishes no evidence of their size, and may well mean small or diminutive men and women. The terms men and women usually connote full-grown adults of normal size. In the medieval romances, where the fays are described as women, no suspicion of smallness is attached to the term.

figures of adult human size; in general, as Bovet states, "near the smaller size of men," or as taking upon themselves the usual mortal stature when they materialized. The fairy whom a witch, Joan Tyrrye, met in 1555 was a man "having a white rod in his hand, and she came to him, thinking to make an acquaintance of him."[9] When Bessie Dunlop in 1576 first saw the fairies, she went up to the "kill-end" and there, she confessed, "sche saw twelf persounes, aucht wemene and four men." When she was asked if she "sperit at Thom quhat persounes thai war? Ansuerit, That thai war the gude wychtis that wynnit in the Court of Elfame."[10] Alesoun Peirsoun, executed in 1588 for witchcraft, stated that when the fairies appeared, there "apperit to hir . . . ane lustie mane, with mony mene and wemen with him."[11] The fairy who became the familiar spirit of Joan Willimott in 1618 appeared "in the shape and forme of a Woman."[12]

According to the description of the fairies found in *Robin Goodfellow; his mad prankes, and merry Jests*, 1628, they were "goodly proper personages";[13] according to that given by Anne Jefferies in 1645, they appeared as "six Persons of a small Stature";[14] according to that

[9] See Holworthy, *Discoveries in the Diocesan Registry, Wells*, p. 6, quoted in G. L. Kittredge, *Witchcraft in Old and New England*, 1929, p. 254.

[10] Pitcairn, *Crim. Trials*, Vol. I, pt. 2, pp. 52 and 53.

[11] *Ibid.*, Vol. I, pt. 2, p. 163.

[12] "The Examination of Ioan Willimott, taken the second day of March, 1618. A Collection of Rare and Curious Tracts, relating to Witchcraft in the counties of Kent, Essex, Suffolk, Norfolk, and Lincoln, between the years 1618 and 1664," London, 1838; p. 17 of *The Wonderfvl Discoverie of the Witchcrafts of Margaret and Phillip Flower*, . . .

[13] Rpt. Hazlitt, *Fairy Tales*, 1875, p. 179.

[14] J. Morgan, *Phoenix Brit.*, p. 547.

of Durant Hotham, a fairy was "a fair Woman in fine cloaths." [15] Robert Kirk represented them as "a Multitude of Wight's, like furious hardie Men"; [16] while the anonymous author of *A Discourse concerning Devils and Spirits* described them as "being like Men, and Women, Souldiers, Kings, and Ladyes Children, and Horsemen." [17]

Heywood, referring to "Sylvans, Fauns, Satyrs, Folletti, Paredry, &c. all included within the number of such as wee call Familiar Spirits," stated ". . . they can assume the shapes and figures of men, and eat, drinke, sit at table, talke and discourse after the manner of our fellowes; so that they may be easily tooke for some friend or acquaintance." [18]

As has already been seen, the likeness of fairies to nymphs and fauns, to satyrs and hamadryads was repeatedly noted, and the identification of the fairies as the English equivalent of the latter repeatedly made. So identical were their measurements that when both were represented in pageant or progress, the same actors who took the part of nymphs were used to represent the fairies, as in the Entertainment at Norwich by Churchyard.[19] The stature of the nymphs and dryads according to common knowledge was that of human maidens and women. And if the figure of the fairies is to be reckoned from their identification as nymphs, the same proportions should hold good in their case.

In the dictionaries of Elyot, Florio and Minsheu of the early and late 16th century and the early 17th century, it will be remembered that *the fairies* or *ladies of*

[15] Webster, *Disp. of Sup. Witch.*, p. 301.

[16] *Sec. Comm.*, p. 27.

[17] Page 510.

[18] *Hierarchie*, pp. 599–600.

[19] Nichols, *Prog. of Eliz.*, Vol. II, p. 199.

the fairies were likened to lamiae and strygia, who were represented as beings in the form of full-grown women. Hence it is to be inferred that the *ladies of the fayry* possessed the same stature, especially as there is no indication of any variation.[20] In other dictionaries, as the *Medulla Grāmatice* and the *Manipvlvs Vocabvlorvm, elf* is defined as *satirus* or *faunus*.[21] Neither of these beings was smaller than a full grown woman or a small man.

Not only were the proportions of the fairies and the nymphs identical so that one was mistaken for the other, as is shown definitely in *Endimion:*

Enter Fayries.

But what are these so fayre fiendes that cause my hayres to stand vpright, and spirits to fall downe? Hags — out alas! Nymphes! — I craue pardon.[22]

but their measurements were also regarded as similar to those of goddesses with whom they were confused in many a chance encounter.

In Holinshed's *Chronicle of Scotland,* it is recorded that the "thrée women in strange and wild apparell," who met Banquo and Macbeth "suddenlie in the middest of a laund," were, according to "the common opinion" "the weird sisters, that is (as ye would say) the goddesses of destinie, or else some nymphs or feiries." [23] The similarity between fairies and the goddesses of destiny here is especially significant, since in the original source of Holinshed, Hector Boece's *Scotorvm Historiae a Prima Gentis Origine,* and in the immediate source of

[20] See Chap. I, pp. 52–55.

[21] See Chap. I, p. 51.

[22] Lyly, IV, 3.

[23] Holinshed, *Chronicles of England, Scotland, and Ireland,* 1807–1808, Vol. 5, pp. 268–269.

Holinshed's *Chronicle of Scotland, The History and Chronicles of Scotland* by Hector Boece, translated by John Bellenden, from which this account is taken, the term, " three women," is the only designation given the three beings who appeared. The explanation of these women as fairies was added by Holinshed. Had the diminutiveness or perceptible smallness of the fairies been as pronounced a characteristic of the race in 1577 as today, it would have been almost impossible to have confused them with goddesses whose figures were never represented as undersize.

The statement of Burton that the water devils or water nymphs were called fairies, is followed by the explanation that such a one was " Egeria, with whom Numa was so familiar, Diana, Ceres, &c."[24] William Browne in *Britannia's Pastorals* notes the fairies' likeness to a human maiden, or to one of the nine Muses, or to Venus or Proserpina:

> Maiden, arise, repli'd the new-borne Maid:
> " Pure Innocence the senslesse stones will aide.
> Nor of the Fairie troope, nor Muses nine;
> Nor am I Venus, nor of Proserpine:
> But daughter to a lusty aged Swaine."[25]

The following quotation from *Euphues* seems most indicative not only of the beauty of the fairies, but also of their size and figure:

> As the Ladies in this blessed Islande are deuout and braue, so are they chast and beautifull, insomuch that when I first behelde them, I could not tell whether some mist had bleared myne eyes, or some strang enchauntment altered my mynde, for it may bee, thought I, that in this Islãd, either some Artemidorus or Lisi-

[24] *Anat. of Mel.*, p. 219.

[25] Vol. I, Song 4, Book I, p. 110. Cf. also Scot, *Dis. of Witch.*, 1651 ed., p. 52.

mandro, or some old Nigromancer did inhabit, who would shewe me Fayries, or the bodie of Helen, or the new shape of Venus.[26]

The ladies he referred to are the ladies of England, who are further described in the same paragraph as

of pure complexion . . . their eyes percing like the Sun beames, . . . their speach pleasant & sweete, . . . their gate comly, their bodies straight, their hands white, al things that man could wish, or women woulde haue, . . . And to these beautifull mouldes, chast minds: to these comely bodies tẽperance.

Had there been as great and as striking a difference between the proportions of the fairies and those of mortal ladies as is the case today, it would scarcely have occurred to the mind of any person, in spite of the fairies' reputation for beauty, to confuse them with the body of Helen or of Venus, or to compare ordinary ladies to them without noting, as could easily have been the case here, the discrepancy between their measurements.

That there was little difference between the fairies' figure and that of mortal ladies can be seen also in the plays of the period. In *The Pilgrim,* Alinda and Juletta are taken for fairies.[27] Marina in *Pericles* is identified by her father at first sight as a fairy:

But are you flesh and blood?
Have you a working pulse? and are no fairy?
No motion? [28]

In *Monsieur Thomas,* Thomas, dressed in his sister's clothes and described as "a strange thing like a gentlewoman," is regarded and treated like a fairy or evil spirit.[29] The men appearing as morris dancers in *The*

[26] John Lyly, Bond ed., 1902, Vol. II, p. 200.
[27] Fletcher, Darley ed., 1851, V, 4.
[28] V, 1.
[29] Fletcher, V, 8.

Gypsies Metamorphosed are described as "a sort of overgrown fairies." [30]

The size of the fairies can almost be reckoned from Imogen, mistaken for a fairy in *Cymbeline,* so carefully has Shakespeare measured her:

> PIS. Well then, here's the point:
> You must forget to be a woman; change
> Command into obedience; fear, and niceness,
> (The handmaids of all women, or, more truly,
> Woman its pretty self,) into a waggish courage;
> Ready in gibes, quick-answer'd, saucy, and
> As quarrellous as the weasel: nay, you must
> Forget that rarest treasure of your cheek,
> Exposing it (but, O, the harder heart!
> Alack no remedy!) to the greedy touch
> Of common-kissing Titan; and forget
> Your laboursome and dainty trims, wherein
> You made great Juno angry.
> IMO. Nay, be brief:
> I see into thy end, and am almost
> A man already.
> PIS. First, make yourself but like one.
> Fore-thinking this, I have already fit,
> ('Tis in my cloak-bag,) doublet, hat, hose, all
> That answer to them: Would you, in their serving,
> And with what imitation you can borrow
> From youth of such a season, 'for noble Lucius
> Present yourself, . . . [31]

In this garb and with this carriage, Imogen is mistaken for a fairy, and her figure and theirs are designated by the phrases:

[30] Ben Jonson, *Masques and Entertainments,* Morley ed., 1890, p. 272.

[31] III, 4. Cf. also Fletcher, Darley ed., 1851, *The Night-Walker,* I, 2; Fletcher, Darley ed., 1851, *The Pilgrim,* III, 4; and the anonymous *Historie of Jacob and Esau,* Farmer ed., 1906, II, 2.

> By Jupiter, an angel!

and

> Behold divineness
> No elder than a boy![32]

The measurements of the fairies do not have to rest solely upon the authority of literary evidence or of theatrical representations. The accounts of the presentation of the fairies in entertainments and devices show the popular idea of their figure.

"I drewe my boyes unto me, that were the Nymphes on the water, . . . with such garments and stuffe necessarie as fitted my purpose," is the statement of Thomas Churchyard in his description of "the Queenes Majestie's Entertainment" at Norwich, 1578, "to play by a device and degrees the Phayries."[33] These were the boys of whom Churchyard had already stated that "divers of those that knew them before (albeit they were barefaced) coulde scarce knowe them in their garments; and sundrie tooke them to be yong girles and wenches, prepared for the nonce."[34]

> Nan Page my daughter, and my little son,
> And three or four more of their growth, we'll dress
> Like urchins, ouphes, and fairies,[35]

were the casting directions for the representation of the fairy kingdom in *Merry Wives of Windsor.* The use of the adjective *little* applied to *son* in the folio[36] and to *fairy* in the quarto[37] as well as the subsequent statement by Ford that

[32] III, 6.

[33] Nichols, *Prog. of Eliz.,* Vol. II, p. 211.

[34] *Ibid.,* Vol. II, p. 199.

[35] IV, 4.

[36] IV, 4.

[37] Scene xv, *litle* boyes; *litle* Fayrie; Griggs facsimile, 1881

The children must
Be practised well to this, or they'll ne'er do't [38]

would seem to indicate that the fairies, here represented and mistaken for authentic inhabitants of fairyland, by Falstaff, were noticeably small, but the adjective, on closer examination, would seem to be one more of affection than of measurement.

It is true that neither the exact age nor the size of Anne Page or of her little brother is known. Anne Page, however, was old enough and grown enough to be of marriageable age, and two, at least, of the children of her growth and of that of the "little son" were of such size as to be described as a "great lubberly boy" [39] or

[38] IV, 4.

[39] V, 5.

"SLEN. I came yonder at Eton to marry mistress Anne Page, and she's a great lubberly boy: If it had not been i' the church, I would have swinged him, or he should have swinged me. If I did not think it had been Anne Page, would I might never stir, and 'tis a post-master's boy.

PAGE. Upon my life then you took the wrong.

SLEN. What need you tell me that? I think so, when I took a boy for a girl: If I had been married to him, for all he was in woman's apparel, I would not have had him.

PAGE. Why, this is your own folly. Did not I tell you, how you should know my daughter by her garments?

SLEN. I went to her in white, and cry'd, mum, and she cryed budget, as Anne and I had appointed; and yet it was not Anne, but a post-master's boy.

. . . .

CAIUS. Vere is mistress Page? By gar, I am cozened; I ha' married un garçon, a boy; un paisan, by gar, a boy; it is not Anne Page: by gar, I am cozened.

MRS. PAGE. Why, did you take her in green?

CAIUS. Ay, be gar, and 'tis a boy: . . ."

Had there been any noticeable discrepancy between the figures of Anne Page and of her company, there would have been no need for so much instruction to her various suitors about her disguise.

"un garçon, a boy; un paisan," and to be mistaken for her and almost married out of hand by Slender and by the doctor. Also among the fairies in the quarto are Dame Quickly and Sir Hugh, the latter of whom, in spite of the adjective little applied to the fairies, stated, "I was Also a Fairie."

In *The Masque of Oberon,* presented before King James, in 1610–1611, the part of the Fairy Prince was taken by Prince Henry, age seventeen, well proportioned and of good height, and the Prince of Wales was "accompanyed with [modernized spelling] twelue others, viz. two Earles, three Barons, fiue Knights, and two esquiers." [40]

The description and treatment of Mab and her fairies who danced around Queen Anne at Apthorp,[41] and that of the "Queen of the Fayry drawen with 6. children . . . the Boies brauely attired," [42] who appeared to Queen Elizabeth at Woodstock, furnish no indication of any variation in size from that of ordinary mortals. As far as any evidence to the contrary can be found, the parts of the fairy queen and her maidens who came into the garden at Elvetham were taken by maidens of the ordinary size of maidens.[43]

[40] *The Annales, or Generall Chronicle of England, begun first by maister Iohn Stow, and after him continued and augmented with matters forreyne, and domestique, auncient and moderne, vnto the ende of this present yeere, 1614.* By Edmond Howes, gentleman. London, 1615; p. 910.

[41] Ben Jonson, *Masques and Entertainments,* Morley ed., 1890, The Satyr.

[42] *The Queenes Majesties Entertainment at Woodstocke,* p. 98.

[43] Nichols, *Prog. of Eliz.,* Vol. III, p. 118. In the first day's entertainment at Elvetham, six virgins took part, three of whom represented the three Graces and three, the Hours. As the number of fairy maidens is six also, it would seem that the six virgins of the first day's entertainment took the part of the six fairy maidens on the fourth day.

The fairy rulers, as far as can be ascertained, were always represented as full-grown women. ". . . ane stout woman com in to hir, . . . That was the Quene of Elfame," [44] was the testimony of Bessie Dunlop, given in 1576. "The king of Fearrie is a braw man, weill favoured, and broad faced, &c." the witch, Issobell Gowdie, confessed in 1667.[45]

In England, also, only adult men and women seem to have taken the part of fairy rulers. Dol Common, full-grown, played the Fairy Queen of the *Alchemist,*[46] as did a man, the Fairy Queen in the *Valiant Welshman.*[47] An adult actor boasted to Greene that he was "as famous for Delphrigus, and the king of Fairies, as euer was any of my time," [48] and Dame Quickly in the quarto,[49] and Anne Page in the folio,[50] represented the Fairy Queen in *Merry Wives of Windsor.* It is especially noticeable, also, that Titania in *A Midsummer Night's Dream,* surrounded by an infinitesimal court in the diminutive rendition of fairyland, was represented as large enough to wind the figure of Bottom in her arms.[51]

The one diminutive ruler of the fairy kingdom was Queen Mab of *Romeo and Juliet,* whose rulership is apparent only in her title. Every other fairy ruler (Oberon was notoriously enchanted out of his growth) till the second quarter of the 17th century, as far as can be seen, was represented as of adult size.

[44] Pitcairn, *Crim. Trials,* Vol. I, pt. 2, p. 57.

[45] *Ibid.,* Gen. App., p. 604.

[46] Jonson, Gifford ed., III, 2.

[47] II, 1.

[48] Greene, *Groats-worth of Wit,* Grosart ed., 1881–1886, Vol. 12, p. 131.

[49] Scene xviii.

[50] V, 5.

[51] IV, 1.

Finally the fact may be regarded as evidence indicative of the fairies' dimensions that, before *A Midsummer Night's Dream,* except in the few instances given below (as far as I have been able to ascertain), the fairies were never designated as little. And in the works of most of the writers of the period, especially those of the 16th and the early 17th centuries, and of those who were not consciously imitating the fairies of *A Midsummer Night's Dream,* the fairies were never represented as very small beings, nor were their activities or occupations those of a diminutive race. This is true of the fairies represented by Lyly, Fletcher, Dekker, Nashe, Burton, Shakespeare (except in three plays), Reginald Scot, James VI of Scotland, Thomas Heywood, Jonson (except in *The Sad Shepherd*), Spenser, and of those found in the works of the early translators of the classics — Golding, Phaër, Stanyhurst, Douglas — in the records of witchcraft trials, and in all cases in Scotland.

One of the earliest instances in which there is any indication of the very small size of the fairies is that of the definition of elf as *nain* found in *Lesclarcissement de La Langue Francayse* of Palsgrave.[52] Whether this use of *nain* has reference to a misshapen person, as is the case in the *Medulla Grāmatice,* or to a diminutive person, cannot be said. The second instance of this kind is to be found in Act II, Scene 4 of the *Historie of Jacob and Esau,* in which Mido speaks of running " like a little elf." Mido is a small boy who leads the blind Isaac. He refers to himself as little, and is designated repeatedly by the other characters as little.[53] The simile, " like a little elf " here, therefore, may be made in reference to Mido's own figure rather than to the figure of a fairy.

[52] 1852 ed.

[53] I, 4 and III, 1.

In *Huon of Burdeux,* Oberon is described as three feet high. His smallness is noticed and explained as the result of enchantment. The other fairies in the romance are represented as of the size of men.[54]

With the exception of these instances, the fairies in the 16th century before 1594 do not seem to have been represented as diminutive or very small. To judge by the evidence submitted above, they were, as Anne Jefferies described them, " a small Sort of Airy People " [55] who appeared " like Men, and Women, Souldiers, Kings, Ladyes Children, and Horse-men cloathed in green." [56]

Although there seems to have been nothing striking about the figure of the fairies, their beauty, as may have been seen, was extraordinary. With few exceptions, they possessed such perfection of lineament and of feature that the terror which their materialization caused could not overcome the impression of beauty which their appearance produced. " To hell I shall not goe," was the conclusion of Raffe in *Gallathea,*[57] so fascinated by the sight of the fairies that he could not resist following them, " for so faire faces neuer can haue such hard fortunes."

The beauty of the boys who represented the fairies at Norwich was made a matter of special comment by Churchyard:

> And touching the beautie of the Nimphes, they seemed to be the chosen children of a world, and became theyr attire so wel, that their beauty might have abused a right good judgement.[58]

Upon the loveliness of Imogen and of Marina, both of whom were taken for fairies, Shakespeare and the cast of

[54] E. E. T. S. ed., Vol. I, pt. 1, pp. 72–73; and Vol. I, pt. 2, p. 540.

[55] J. Morgan, *Phoenix Brit.,* p. 545.

[56] *Dis. conc. D. & S.,* p. 510.

[57] John Lyly, II, 3.

[58] Nichols, *Prog. of Eliz.,* Vol. II, p. 199.

Cymbeline and of *Pericles* brought all the powers of the adjective to bear, Marina, particularly, being of

> That excellent complexion, which did steal
> The eyes of young and old.[59]

Oberon in *Huon of Burdeux* had an " aungelyke vysage, so that there is no mortall man that seethe hym but that taketh grete pleasure to beholde his fase." [60]

The fairies in the poems of Bishop Corbet, as in the *Endimion* of Lyly, were regarded as " prettie ladies." [61] According to the statement of William Lilly, they were " Those glorious creatures " and " these angelical creatures " of whom it is not " given to very many persons to endure their glorious aspects." [62] And even in the witchcraft trials, the fairies were " verrie semelie lyke to se." [63]

The transcendent quality of the beauty usually attributed to them is shown also in the lines of the *New Year's Gift, Addressed to the Queen, 1600,* " A Ryddle of the Princesse Paragon ":

> I saw marche in a meadowe greene,
> A fayrer wight then feirye queene

with " face, and corsage paragon "

> Suche as these blessed sprightes of paradise
> Are woonte to assume, or such as lovers weene
> They see sometimes in sleepe and dainty dreame,

[59] IV, 1.

[60] E. E. T. S. ed., Vol. I, pt. I, p. 63.

[61] Corbet, *The Faerye's Farewell,* Stanza 3, p. 582; and *Endimion,* IV, 3.

[62] *William Lilly's History of His Life and Times from the Year 1602 to 1681,* Hunt & Clarke ed., 1826, p. 98.

[63] Pitcairn, *Crim. Trials,* Vol. I, pt. 2, p. 53. Cf. also Thomas Middleton, Bullen ed., 1885, Vol. 6, *The Spanish Gypsy,* I, 5, ll. 106–118.

In femall forme a Goddesse, and noe Queene,
Fitter to rule a Worlde then a Realme.[64]

If it is remembered that this was only one of the many occasions when the beauty of Elizabeth was compared to that of the fairies, and that she, as here, was selected as the one person in England beautiful enough to surpass them in loveliness, little doubt of their beauty can be entertained.

With such general evidence of the beauty imputed to the fairies, it is significant to find that masks and vizards were required for the actors who represented them. In the disguise of spirits in *The Buggbears,* the actors who played the rôle of spirits had on " visars like develes," [65] and possibly a number of other kinds of visors, since it is noted that they went " a sprityng . . . with thys face & that face and you goodman good face " or " lyke buggbeares wth vysardes to make old sootes dyssardes." [66] The use of the customary masks is stressed in *Merry Wives of Windsor* where the troupe of fairies " must all be mask'd and vizarded." [67] And the omission of masks in the representation of the fairies at Norwich is so unusual that it requires a statement from the devisor.[68]

Such visors, for use both in devices of fairies and in other disguisings, like those of the 14th and 15th centuries, were " well and handsomely made," being " peyntid visers, diffourmyd or colourid visages in eny

[64] Nichols, *Prog. of Eliz.,* Vol. III, Parthe VII, p. 474 and Parthe VIII, p. 476.

[65] IV, 1.

[66] II, 4.

[67] IV, 6.

[68] Nichols, *Prog. of Eliz.,* Vol. II, p. 199.

wyse." [69] And handsome and ugly visors must have been kept in stock and were readily obtained, to judge from the ease with which Master Ford bought them for his fairies, and from the custom recorded by Lavater:

> It is a common custome in many places, that at a certaine time of the yeare, one with a nette or visarde on his face maketh Children afrayde, to the ende that ever after they should laboure and be obediente to their Parentes: afterward they tel them that those which they saw, were Bugs, Witches, and Hagges, which thing they verily believe, and are commonly miserablie afrayde.[70]

The necessity for a mask or vizard is explicable, when it is taken into account that the fairies of the 16th century were of different complexions — black, gray, green, white, red and sometimes bluc.

In the play of *The Buggbears,* assigned to the years 1564–1565, the "whyte & red fearye" was included among the spirits of the time.[71] The examination of John Walsh, tried for witchcraft in 1566, contained the statement that "ther be .iii. kindes of Feries, white,

[69] E. K. Chambers, *Medieval Stage,* 1903, Vol. I, p. 394. Cf. also Peter Cunningham, *Extracts from the Accounts of the Revels at Court in the Reigns of Queen Elizabeth and King James I,* Shak. Soc. ed., 1842.

[70] *De Spectris,* Eng. trans., 1572, p. 21. Cf. also Nathan Drake, *Shakspeare and his Times,* 1838, p. 154; Joseph Strutt, *Horda Angel Cynnan,* 1775–1776, Vol. II, p. 94 and Vol. III, p. 144; Thomas Dekker, *The Comedie of Olde Fortunatus,* Pearson rpt., 1873, Vol. I, p. 104; Stow's *Annales,* p. 918; and Francis Douce, *Illus. of Shak.,* Vol. I, p. 78.

The word *Larva* was used in the *Bibl. Eliotae* of 1532 to mean either "hegge," "goblyn," "a goste or an elfe. also a masker, or he that weareth a visour. also the visour it selfe"; and in 1598 in Florio's *Worlde of Wordes* to mean "a vizard, or a maske," "a hag, a spirit, a hobgoblin."

[71] Page 117.

greene, and black." [72] According to *The Discovery of Witchcraft,* there were " white spirits and blacke spirits, gray spirits and red spirits," [73] and in *Macbeth,* beings with the same varied complexions were invoked.[74]

When any man hath caught a fall upon the ground [William Camden related in the *Britannia*], forthwith hee starteth uppe againe on his feete, and turneth himselfe round three times toward his right hand, with his sworde, skein, or knife hee diggeth into the earth, and fetcheth up a turfe, for that, they say, the earth doth yeelde a spirite: and if within some two or three daies he fell sicke, there is sent a woman skilfull in that kinde unto the said place, and there she saith on this wise. I call thee P. from the East and West, South, and North, from the forests, woods, rivers, meeres, the wilde wood-fayries, white, redde, blacke, &c.[75]

Be thou ghost that cannot rest,
Or a shadow of the bless'd,
Be thou black, or white, or green,
Be thou heard, or to be seen —

was the prayer used to exorcise the spirit or fairy in *Monsieur Thomas.*[76]

In 1618 the fairies were referred to as blue. " . . . tell me how thou are us'd amongst ye faries, those little ringleaders, those white and blew faries " — Bob, the Buttrie Spirit, asked of Robin Goodfellow in *A Masque at Cole-Orton.*[77]

[72] *Examination of John Walsh,* rpt. in M. A. Murray, *The Witch-Cult in Western Europe,* Oxford, 1921, p. 240.

[73] Scot, 1651 ed., p. 388.

[74] IV, 1.

[75] Ireland, Holland trans., pp. 146–147.

[76] Fletcher, V, 8.

[77] *Die Maske von Cole-Orton,* in R. Brotanek, " Die Englischen Maskenspiele," in *Wiener Beiträge zur Englischen Philologie,* Vol. XV, Wien and Leipzig, 1902, p. 330.

Of all the colors and complexions affected by the fairies, black seems to have been the most prominent. The Queen of the Fayry, who appeared to Elizabeth at Woodstock, expressly states that her original complexion was black:

> This loue hath caused me transforme my face,
> and in your hue to come before your eyne,
> now white, then blacke, your frende the fayery Queene.[78]

As may have been noticed also, it was the black fairy who was always numbered among the fairy company and always mentioned by color whenever the fairies were exorcised or summoned. This may have been due both to the fact that these fairies, the "swart faery of the mine"[79] of Milton, were distinguished from the rest of the fairies, being

> . . . ye dancing spiritts of the Pittes: such as look to Toms Aegiptians here, & helpe them hole & drive sharp theire Picks & their moindrils, keepe away the dampe & keepe in theire Candles, draine the Sough & hold them out of ye hollows;[80]

and that they were, as John Walsh stated, "the woorst."[81]

Perhaps one of the best authorities for the colors of the fairies' complexions is *Merry Wives of Windsor*. Here, after great verbal and material pains have been taken to dress the fairies in white and green costumes, they are summoned by the fairy crier:

> Fairies, black, grey, green, and white,
> You moon-shine revellers, and shades of night.[82]

[78] *The Queenes Majesties Entertainment at Woodstocke,* p. 98.
[79] *Comus,* l. 436.
[80] *Cole-Orton,* p. 330.
[81] *Exam. of John Walsh,* p. 240.
[82] V, 5.

This apostrophe made to the company of boys and Mistress Anne Page and Sir Hugh, must have taken into account the color of the visors which had been bought for them which were well illuminated by the round of waxen tapers on the heads of the wearers. There is little possibility that the terms, black and grey, could have been applied to the actors' costumes. These, if words could make them so, were green and white, and it was in these two colors and these only, that Anne Page could be dressed and in these two colors that the boys were mistaken for Anne Page:

Nan Page my daughter, and my little son,
And three or four more of their growth, we'll dress
Like urchins, ouphes, and fairies, green and white.[83]

Now, thus it rests:
Her father means she shall be all in white,
. . . . her mother hath intended,
The better to denote her to the doctor,
(For they must all be mask'd and vizarded,)
That, quaint in green, she shall be loose enrob'd,
With ribbands pendant, flaring, 'bout her head.[84]

The green and white of the Windsor fairies were the colors of the costumes usually affected by all Elizabethan fairies. White they used many times, so many times that they and their relatives were called "White Nymphs." [85] But green was their favorite color and silk their only wearing, if the ballad maker or the citizen had his way,

[83] IV, 4.

[84] IV, 6. It might be contended that the black or grey could refer to the costumes worn by Sir Hugh or Pistol. The jackanapes, whom Sir Hugh represented, was usually dressed in green, and the costume of Pistol could not have been referred to, since Pistol acted as the fairy crier.

[85] Heywood, *Hierarchie,* p. 507.

which is not to be wondered at, considering the romantic glamour which haunts both color and fabric to this present day. "There were with King Obreon a many fayries, all attyred in greene silke," the author of *Robin Goodfellow; his mad prankes, and merry Jests,* insisted.[86] ". . . like Men, and Women, Souldiers, Kings, and Ladyes Children, and Horse-men cloathed in green," [87] was the comment on the fairy costumes in 1665. They rode into sight "on ahallow even," in Scotland, "all graithid into greine," [88] and were dressed in the same color in the *Psalmes, Sonets, & Songs of Sadness and Pietie* [89] of William Byrd. So much given to green were they that in 1696, when Anne Jefferies saw them, they appeared as "six small People, all in Green Clothes," [90] and as late as 1726 Waldron recounts their materialization in the Isle of Man "all drest in green, and gallantly mounted." [91]

Despite their preference for the color, there was no one particular shade of green which they most affected. Their costumes took on all the tones which the earth, from which the fairies must have taken their color, decked itself, and varied from yellow to green to brown. It was as "yellow-skirted" fairies that they were referred to in *The English Parnassus,*[92] and as the "finest

[86] Rpt. in J. O. Halliwell, *Illus. of the Fairy Myth. of M. N. D.,* Shak. Soc., 1845, p. 142.

[87] *Dis. conc. D. & S.,* p. 510.

[88] Montgomerie, p. 151.

[89] *Lyrics from the Song-books of the Elizabethan Age,* A. H. Bullen ed., London, 1891, p. 34. Cf. also William Dunbar, *Golden Targe,* Scottish Text Soc. ed., 1893, Vol. II, l. 125.

[90] Morgan, *Phoenix Brit.,* p. 548.

[91] Waldron, *A Description of the Isle of Man,* 1726, p. 33. Cf. also Bourne, *Antiq. Vulgares,* p. 83: "They are always clad in Green."

[92] Josua Poole, 1677 ed., p. 332.

olive-coloured spirits," in *The Gipsies Metamorphosed* of Ben Jonson.[93] The familiar spirits or fairies known to Issobell Gowdie in 1667, presented themselves in several shades of green, "Som of thaim apeirit in sadd-dun, som in grasse-grein, som in sea-grein, and som in yallow." [94] And the fairies of *A Midsummer Night's Dream* wore coats of the rear-mice or the cast skin of a snake.[95]

It is impossible to state, with absolute certainty, the cut and style of the clothes of the fairies. Except on the rarest occasions, no detailed description is given of their dress. In the accounts of the revels or in the inventories of the theatrical companies, this omission is most apparent. The one mention of fairy costumes, in *The booke of the Inventary of the goods of my Lord Admeralles Men,* specifies: "Item, iij payer of red strasers, and iij fares gowne of buckrome." [96] The ex-

[93] Morley ed., p. 272.

[94] Pitcairn, *Crim. Trials,* Gen. App., p. 615.

[95] II, 3 and II, 2.

[96] *Henslowe Papers,* Greg ed., 1907, App., p. 114.

There are no fairy costumes specified in the *Documents Relating to the Office of the Revels in the time of Queen Elizabeth.* In this connection (Feuillerat ed., 1908, p. 43) it is interesting to note the great detail with which repeatedly the costumes of the nymphs are described here:

"Womens Maskes

Dyana and vj Nymphes Huntresses withe her.

one vpper garmente and one nether garmente of purple Clothe of sylver tyssued the blacke side tinsell the vpper garment frenged with narrowe frenge of cullen golde and the nether garment frenged with frenge of vennys golde withe gylte bells.

. . . .

vj kirtells of purple Clothe of golde frenge withe Cullen sylver. vij partelettes of white taffita and vij payre of sleves of gloves on the same."

pense account for the costumes of the masque of Oberon, played January 1610–1611, furnishes evidence of the magnificence of the clothing of Oberon and his train,[97] as does the description of the Queen of the Fayry in *The Queenes Majesties Entertainment at Woodstocke,*[98] but beyond the use of silver embroidery, and the phrase, " very costly apparrelled," there is no indication in either reference of the cut or fashion of the clothes of the fairy court.

There is no doubt, however, that the fairies had a traditional or national costume of their own, and that the Elizabethans were most familiar with it, judging from their references to such disguisings as:

. . . they shewed him two attired like the king and queene of fayries, and by them elves and goblings,[99]

God's will then, queen of Fairy,
On with your tire,[100]

The water nymphes, and feyries streight appears
In uncouth formes, and fashion strange to view.[101]

In *Merry Wives of Windsor,* much trouble and great pains were taken to make Anne Page and her troupe of boys instantly recognizable as fairies. To this end, they finally appeared " mask'd and vizarded " and " loose enrob'd " in " white and green " with " ribbands pendant, flaring, 'bout " their heads upon which were " rounds of waxen tapers." [102] The nymphs, whose costumes later

[97] Cunningham, *Extr. from Accts. of Revels in Reigns of Eliz. and James I,* Introd., pp. viii–ix.

[98] Page 98.

[99] *Cozenages of the Wests,* Hazlitt rpt., p. 227.

[100] Jonson, Gifford ed., *Alchemist,* III, 2.

[101] Nichols, *Prog. of Eliz.,* Vol. II, p. 186.

[102] IV, 4 and 6.

served as fairy costumes in Queen Elizabeth's Progress at Norwich, had,

eyther upon white silke or fine linnen, greene segges, stiched cunningly on a long garment, so well wrought, and set on, as scarce any whit might be perceived. And every Nimph had in hir hand a great bundell of bulrushes, and had on hir head a garland of ivie, under the whiche ivie was a coyfe of mosse, and under the mosse was here long goodly heare like golden tresses, that covered hir shoulders, and in a manner raughte downe unto hir middle.[103]

An idea of the fairies' dress can be gained also, from the apparel of the characters who were mistaken for fairies in the plays of the period. Imogen in *Cymbeline* was in page's clothes when she was likened to a fairy,[104] as was Alathe in *The Night-Walker*.[105] Marina in *Pericles* was dressed in the usual costume of a gentlewoman when she was identified with the fairy race,[106] and Thomas in *Monsieur Thomas* was masquerading in his sister's clothes when he was given the rôle of a fairy or spirit.[107] From these instances, it would seem that the fairies at times wore the usual male and female attire of the country. This conclusion is corroborated by Bovet, who, describing the fairies in 1684, states that " their habits used to be of red, blew, or green, according to the old way of country garb, with high-crown'd hats." [108]

[103] Nichols, *Prog. of Eliz.*, Vol. II, p. 199.

[104] III, 6.

[105] Fletcher, I, 1.

[106] V, 1.

[107] Fletcher, IV, 6.

[108] *Pandaemonium,* Hazlitt rpt., p. 335.

In the woodcut found in *Robin Goodfellow; his mad prankes, and merry Jests,* 1628, picturing Robin Goodfellow, presumably, in the midst of the fairy dance, the fairies are represented as men and women in high-crowned hats.

In Scotland, with the exception of the "nymphes or feiries" who met Banquo and Macbeth, clad "in strange and wild apparell, resembling creatures of elder world," [109] the fairies seem to have worn the costumes of the country. Always when they appeared in 1576 to Bessie Dunlop, "The men wer cled in gentilmennis clething, and the wemene had all plaiddis round about thame." [110] Andro Man, burnt as a wizard for repairing with the fairies, insisted that the "elphis hes schapes and claythis lyk men." [111]

This preference for mortal clothes was also recorded by Robert Kirk:

> Their Apparell . . . is like that of the People and Countrey under which they live: so are they seen to wear Plaids and variegated Garments in the Highlands of Scotland, and Suanochs therefore in Ireland. . . . Ther Women are said to Spine very fine, to Dy, to Tossue, and Embroyder: but whither it is as manuall Operation of substantiall refined Stuffs, with apt and solid Instruments, or only curious Cob-webs, impalpable Rainbows, and a fantastic Imitation of the Actions of more terrestricall Mortalls, since it transcended all the Senses of the Seere to discerne whither, I leave to conjecture as I found it.[112]

Though the dress of the fairies might vary, their essential characteristics and idiosyncrasies remained always the same. In the first place, they were inordinately addicted to dancing. With them, it amounted almost to a natural means of locomotion, especially in England. If they appeared otherwise than tripping, according to most of the representations of them, they were sure to break into a dance before much time elapsed, and to take their departure in a mad whirl of gay steps.

[109] *Shak. Holinshed,* p. 23.

[110] Pitcairn, *Crim. Trials,* Vol. I, pt. 2, pp. 52–53.

[111] *Spald. Club Misc.,* Vol. I, p. 121.

[112] *Sec. Comm.,* pp. 14–15.

These "Paroxisms of antic corybantic Jolity"[113] were the infallible mark of the fairy nationality and an accepted means of identification: "they have so danced, and jingled here, as they had been a set of overgrown fairies";[114] "heigh, how it frisketh! Is't not a fairy?"[115] "Like fairies, dance their night-rounds, without fear";[116] "dancing roundelayes ouer the plesaunt meades."[117] ". . . they dance in rounds in pleasant launds, and greene medowes"[118] was the characterization made of them in 1592, to be repeated in 1621 as "These are they that dance on heaths and greens."[119] And "Enter Fayries dauncing"[120] ushered them on the stage and into the world of mortals.

To record the many dances of the fairies would be but to repeat the number of their appearances. And whatever else happened to their attributes and to their race, they never ceased to dance throughout the length and breadth of Great Britain.

The fairies' dance was not an individual capering but a ceremonial round. "Hand in hand, with fairy grace,"[121] they danced their "Hayes"[122] so frequently and so hard that they left their fairy rings "Whereof

[113] *Ibid.*, p. 16.

[114] Jonson, Morley ed., *Gipsies Met.*, p. 272.

[115] Fletcher, *Pilgrim*, IV, 2.

[116] Beaumont and Fletcher, *Scornful Lady*, III, 2.

[117] C. Middleton, *Chinon of England*, p. 39.

[118] Nashe, *Pierce Penilesse*, Vol. I, p. 232.

[119] Burton, *Anat. of Mel.*, Vol. I, p. 220.

[120] Lyly, *Gallathea*, II, 3. Cf. also James Shirley, Dyce ed., 1833, *Love Tricks*, IV, 2 and *The Witty Fair One*, IV, 4; John Ford, Dyce ed., 1869, *The Sun's Darling*, I, 1; Palingenius, *The Zodiake of Life*, trans. B. Googe, 1588 ed., Lib. II, fig. B. iii.

[121] *M. N. D.*, V, 2.

[122] Drayton, *Nimphidia*, p. 125, l. 63.

the ewe not bites "[123] on nearly every heath of England and in most of the records of their existence:

> Wittness those rings and roundelayes
> Of theirs, which yet remaine;[124]

Also Travellers in the Night, and such as watch their Flocks and Heards, are wont to be compassed about with many strange Apparitions: . . . yet sometimes they make so great and deep impression into the Earth, that the place they are used to, being onely burnt round with extream heat, no gras will grow up there. The Inhabitants call this Night-sport of these Monsters, the Dance of Fayries.[125]

With dancing as their characteristic gesture, it is no wonder that the appearance of the fairies was accompanied " with noyse of musick and minstralsie " and " withall . . . such musicke . . . that Orpheus, that famous Greeke fidler (had hee beene alive), compared to one of these had beene as infamous as a Welch-harper that playes for cheese and onions."[126]

Sometimes they appeared to the " clear sound of ringing bridles," or to " the finest horn in the world,"[127] or circled Windsor forest to the noise of rattles,[128] or danced their ringlets to " the whistling wind,"[129] which changed into the discordance of " ane hiddeous vglie sowche of wind,"[130] and " sic ane dynn as heavin and erd had gane

[123] *Temp.*, V, 1.

[124] Corbet, *Faerye's Farewell*, p. 582.

[125] Olaus Magnus, *De Gentibus Septentrionalibus Historia*, 1658 trans., p. 43.

[126] *Robin Goodfellow; his mad prankes, and merry Jests*, Halliwell rpt., p. 125.

[127] Waldron, *Isle of Man*, p. 33.

[128] *M. W. of W.*, IV, 4.

[129] *M. N. D.*, II, 2.

[130] Pitcairn, *Crim. Trials*, Vol. I, pt. 2, p. 53.

togidder "[131] in the confessions of witches, "And quhene we heir the quhirll-wind blaw in the sey, thay wilbe commounelie with itt, or cumand sone thaireftir."[132]

At other times, and most frequently in Elizabethan England, they sang the measures of their dance in high clear voices, which belated passers-by, once in a while, would hear, "braue musick . . . vnder the green hill"[133] shrilling from the ground or echoing in the breeze from some midnight meadow.

ROD. How sweet these solitary places are! . . .
PEDRO I cannot sleep, friend;
I have those watches here admit no slumbers.
Saw you none yet?
ROD. No creature.
PEDRO What strange music
Was that we heard afar off?
ROD. I cannot guess:
'Twas loud, and shrill; sometimes it shew'd hard by us,
And by and by the sound fled as the wind does.
Here's no inhabitants.
PEDRO It much delighted me.
ROD. They talk of fairies, and such demi-devils;
This is as fine a place to dance their gambols —
PEDRO Methought I heard a voice.
ROD. They can sing admirably; . . .[134]

Few were the times they appeared on the stage in masque or entertainment without a musical accompaniment. In the *Alchemist,* for instance, the line reads, "Bid Dol play music," which, after an interval, is fol-

[131] *Ibid.,* Vol. I, pt. 2, p. 57.

[132] *Ibid.,* Vol. I, pt. 2, p. 164.

[133] *The Wisdome of Doctor Dodypoll,* Act III E, Students' Fac. ed., 1912.

[134] Fletcher, *Pilgrim,* V, 4.

lowed by "Look, the elves are come." [135] In *The Satyr,* to

> the sound of excellent soft music, that was concealed in the thicket, there came tripping up the lawn a bevy of FAIRIES, attending on MAB their queen, who falling into an artificial ring, began to dance a round.[136]

In the plot or platt of *Dead Man's Fortune,* 1593, "after that the musicke plaies & ther Enters 3 antique faires dancynge on after a nother." [137]

> . . . her Majestie was no sooner readie, and at her Gallerie window looking into the Garden [at Elvetham, where she was greeted by a dance of fairies], but there began three Cornets to play certaine fantastike dances, at the measure whereof the Fayery Quene came into the garden, dauncing with her maides about her. . . . the Fairy Quene and her maides daunced about the Garden, singing a Song of sixe parts, with the musicke of an exquisite consort; wherein was the lute, bandora, base-violl, citterne, treble-violl, and flute.[138]

When the fairies sang or their music was heard, the effect both upon their friends and upon their victims was often immediate and violent:

> Than kynge Oberon . . . set hys horne to hys mouth and blewe so melodyous a blast/ that the .xiiii. compaygnyons, beyng vnder the tre, had so parfayte a ioy at there hertes that they al rose vp and begane to synge and daunse; [139]

> Enter the Faieries, singing and dauncing.
>
> . . . .
>
> 1 FAY Will you haue any musick Sir?

[135] Jonson, Gifford ed., III, 2.
[136] Jonson, Morley ed., p. 408.
[137] *Henslowe Papers,* App. II, p. 135.
[138] Nichols, *Prog. of Eliz.,* Vol. III, pp. 118–119.
[139] *Huon of Burdeux,* E. E. T. S. ed., Vol. I, pt. I, p. 66.

2 FAY Will you haue any fine musicke?
3 FAY Most daintie musicke?
MOPSO We must set a face on't now; there's no flying; no, Sir, we are very merrie, I thanke you.
1 FAY O but you shall, Sir.

. . . .

1 FAY Wilt please you daunce, sir.
Io. Indeed, sir, I cannot handle my legges.
2 FAY O you must needs daunce and sing,
Which if you refuse to doe
We will pinche you blacke and blew;
And about we goe.

They all daunce in a ring and sing, as followeth.

Round about, round about, in a fine ring a,
Thus we daunce, thus we daunce, and thus we sing a:
Trip and go, too and fro, ouer this Greene a,
All about, in and out, for our braue Queene a.

Round about, round about, in a fine Ring a,
Thus we daunce, thus we daunce, and thus we sing a:
Trip and go, too and fro, ouer this Greene a,
All about, in and out, for our braue Queene a.

Ye haue daunc't round about in a fine Ring a,
We haue daunc't lustily and thus we sing a;
All about, in and out, ouer this Greene a,
Too and fro, trip and go, to our braue Queene a.[140]

These two attributes of dancing and singing may, in part, account for the fairies' popularity in the age of Shakespeare when rounds and catches, airs and madrigals, corantos and galliards were all the fashion.

It is possible, because of the fairies' numerous appearances in the theatre, that there are fewer records in England than in Scotland, of their other means of locomotion, which was riding. In the translation of *Huon of*

[140] *Maydes Met.*, II, 2.

Burdeux, Oberon and his train appear on horseback, but with this exception [141] the fairies were not represented as mounted until the latter part of the 17th century when they were described in the anonymous *Discourse concerning Devils and Spirits* as "Horse-men . . . to which purpose they do in the night steal hempen stalks from the fields where they grow, to Convert them into Horses as the Story goes"; [142] and in *A Pleasant Treatise of Witches,* 1673, where "they were prancing on their horses round the brims of a large dish of white-broth." [143]

In Scotland, "they naturally rode and went," [144]

Sum bukled on a buinvand, and some one a bene,
Ay trottand in trowpes from the twylycht;
Some saidland a sho aipe all graithid into greine,
Some hobland one ane hempstalk, hovand to þe heicht.
The King of pharie, and his Court, with the elph queine,
With mony elrich Incubus, was rydand that nycht.[145]

If the records of the witchcraft trials of the period are to be believed, riding, not dancing, was their chief means of locomotion:

. . . thair come ane cumpanye of rydaris by, that maid sic ane dynn as heavin and erd had gane togidder; and incontinent, thai raid in to the loich, with many hiddous rumbill. . . . It was the gude wichtis that wer rydand in Middil-zerd; [146]

. . . the Quene of Elphen was their, and vtheris with hir, rydand vpon quhyt haiknayes.[147]

[141] Note that the Queen of the Fayry in *The Queenes Majesties Entertainment at Woodstocke,* appeared in a wagon drawn by six boys: p. 98.

[142] Page 510.

[143] Rpt. in Hazlitt, *Fairy Tales,* 1875, p. 370.

[144] James VI of Scotland, *Daemon.,* p. 132.

[145] Montgomerie, p. 151.

[146] Pitcairn, *Crim. Trials,* Vol. I, pt. 2, p. 57.

[147] *Spald. Club Misc.,* Vol. I, p. 121.

Issobell Gowdie, familiar with the fairies,

> . . . proceidit in hir Confessione, in maner efter following, to wit. . . . I haid a little horse, and wold say, "HORSE AND HATTOCK, IN THE DIVELLIS NAME!" And than ve vold flie away, quhair ve vold, be ewin as strawes wold flie wpon an hie-way. We will flie lyk strawes quhan we pleas; wild-strawes and corne-strawes wilbe horses to ws, an ve put thaim betwixt our foot, and say, "HORSE AND HATTOK, IN THE DIVELLIS nam!" An quhan any sies thes strawes in a whirlewind, and doe not sanctifie them selues, we may shoot them dead at owr pleasour. Any that ar shot be vs, their sowell will goe to Hevin, bot ther bodies remains with ws, and will flie as horsis to ws, als small as strawes.[148]

As late as the last part of the 17th century, according to Aubrey's *Miscellanies,* the fairies were still riding through Scotland preceded by the "noise of a whirlwind" and a sound of voices crying "Horse and Hattock!"[149] Even in 1726, the fairy horsemen were heard in the Manx fields:

> As he [a young sailor] was going over a pretty high mountain, he heard the noise of horses, the hollow of a huntsman, and the finest horn in the world. . . . but he had not time for much reflection before they all passed by him, so near that he was able to count what number there was of them, which he said was thirteen, and that they were all drest in green, and gallantly mounted. He was so well pleased with the sight, that he would gladly have follow'd, could he have kept pace with them; he cross'd the foot-way, however, that he might see them again, which he did more than once, and lost not the sound of the horn for some miles. At length, being arrived at his sister's, he tells her the story, who presently clapped her hands for joy, that he was come home safe; for, said she, those you saw were fairies, and 'tis well they did not take you away with them.

[148] Pitcairn, *Crim. Trials,* Gen. App., pp. 603–604.
[149] 5th ed., 1890, p. 149.

There is no persuading them but that these huntings are frequent in the Island, and that these little gentry being too proud to ride on Manx horses, which they might find in the field, make use of the English and Irish ones, which are brought over and kept by gentlemen. They say that nothing is more common, than to find these poor beasts in a morning, all over in a sweat and foam, and tired almost to death, when their owners have believed they have never been out of the stable. A gentleman of Ballafletcher assured me he had three or four of his best horses killed with these nocturnal journeys.[150]

Who wished to see the fairies riding or dancing or to hear their songs, must be out of doors. With the exception of the water fairies, they held their revels and made their visible appearances in the forests and meadows and on the small green hillocks of a summer England. At no time had they any relish for the houses of mortals, and only entered them on the pressure of important business after their human inmates were asleep, or made their way inside through force of great necessity to steal human children:

They live in wilds and forests, and on mountains, and shun great cities because of the wickedness acted therein.[151]

They danced their " ringlets "

> . . . on hill, in dale, forest or mead,
> By paved fountain, or by rushy brook,
> Or on the beached margent of the sea,[152]

for their " nature is to make strange Apparitions on the Earth in Meddows, or on Mountains." [153]

They were particularly associated with forests, and

150 Waldron, *Isle of Man,* pp. 33–34.
151 *Ibid.,* p. 27.
152 *M. N. D.,* II, 2.
153 *Dis. conc. D. & S.,* p. 510.

16th century playwrights and pageant writers took pains to stage their fairies under an oak in Windsor forest;[154] or against "a dark rock, with trees beyond it, and all wildness that could be presented";[155] or enclosed the company of fairies "in the corner of a field, being defenced with high and thicke bushes."[156]

> . . . would I were out of these Woodes, for I shall haue but wodden lucke, heers nothing but the skreeking of Owles, croking of Frogs, hissing of Adders, barking of Foxes, walking of Hagges,[157]

expressed the usual state of mind of a countryman in a forest.

> . . . goblin, wood-god, fairy, elfe, or fiend,
> Satyr, or other power that haunts the groves,[158]

turned the forest into "Fayry-ground."[159]

They haunted, too, the wells and brooks and streams and lakes of the countryside. Their love for water they may have inherited from the nymphs and naiads with whom they were associated, or from "Pluto, and his quene, Proserpina, and al hir fayërye" who "Disporten hem and maken melodye aboute that welle" of Januarie,[160] or from the fairy ladies of the medieval romances, or from the elves. Whatever the reason, the fairies appeared, poetically at least, almost as many times near water as in a forest.

It is on account of this characteristic that they are invoked in *The Tempest:*

[154] *M. W. of W.*, IV, 6.
[155] Jonson, *Oberon, the Fairy Prince,* Morley ed., p. 143.
[156] Nichols, *Prog. of Eliz.*, Vol. II, p. 211.
[157] Lyly, *Gallathea,* II, 3, p. 442.
[158] Fletcher, *Faith. Shep.*, I, 1.
[159] Corbet, *Iter Boreale,* Chalmers ed., Vol. 5, p. 579.
[160] Chaucer, "The Marchantes Tale," Skeat ed., 1894, ll. 794–797.

Ye elves of hills, brooks, standing lakes, and groves;
And ye, that on the sands with printless foot
Do chase the ebbing Neptune, and do fly him,
When he comes back,[161]

or are represented by Fletcher as dancing their rounds about a "virtuous well,"[162] or by Lodge as

Now near the flood, straight on the mounting hill,
Now midst the woods of youth, and vain desire.[163]

Like the shepherds and shepherdesses of the pastorals, the fairies belonged to a world of green and growing things and, in England, 'the summer did attend upon their state,' to vary a line of Titania's in *A Midsummer Night's Dream.* In Scotland, although their latest recorded appearance was during the month of November,[164] "All-Hallow Evin" seems to have been regarded as the period in which they were most active. According to *The Flyting of Montgomerie and Polwart*, it was in "the hinder end of harvest, on ahallow even, Quhen our good neighboures doth ryd,"[165] while in the Dittay against Andro Man, tried for witchcraft in 1598, occurs the statement of his intention "to have kepit the conventioun on All-Hallow Evin . . . with thame."[166]

In England, there is no record of the fairies' appearance during winter. The first day of May and Midsummer Eve were the two periods when they were most powerful and most enjoyed themselves. He was a brave mortal who wandered out to enjoy the moonlight on the

161 V, 1.

162 *Faith. Shep.*, I, 2.

163 *Phillis,* XXXI, Hunterian Club ed., 1883, Vol. II. In this connection, see Chap. I, pp. 58–59.

164 *Highland Papers,* Macphail ed., 1920, Vol. III, p. 37.

165 *Poems of Alexander Montgomerie,* p. 151.

166 *Spald. Club Misc.,* Vol. I, p. 121.

evening of midsummer, or failed to put primroses (in Ireland, at least) over all the entrances to his house and to his cowbarn on the first of May. The fairies on these two festival days held high revel over the whole land, which, for the time being, became their absolute domain.

Though these two feasts of the year were under their control, the Christmas season, according to Shakespeare, no matter what the weather, was exempt from their power:

> And then, they say, no spirit dare stir abroad;
> The nights are wholesome; then no planets strike,
> No fairy takes, nor witch hath power to charm,
> So hallow'd and so gracious is the time.[167]

The fairies' hour was usually at twelve midnight and noon. Not that they did not appear at other times! One could see them in Scotland "Ay trottand in trowpes from the twylycht," [168] and they were known to be busy in the daytime. But these occasions, in England in the 16th century, were few.

The night, however, was peculiarly the fairies' own. This preference seems to have been emphasized in the 16th century when, according to Nashe, "The Robbin-good-fellowes, Elfes, Fairies, Hobgoblins . . . did most

[167] *Ham.,* I, 1. The fairies experienced another limitation also to their earthly appearances, according to Reginald Scot, for: "The Rabbines, and namely Rabbie Abraham, writing upon the second of Genesis, doe say, that God made the fairies, bugs, Incubus, Robin good fellow, and other familiar or domestical spirits and divels on the friday; and being prevented with the evening of the sabbath, finished them not, but left them unperfect; and therefore, that ever since they use to flie the holinesse of the sabbath, seeking dark holes in mountains and woods, wherein they hide themselves til the end of the sabbath, and then come abroad to trouble and molest men." *Dis. of Witch.,* 1651 ed., p. 364.

[168] Montgomerie, p. 151.

of their merry prankes in the Night," [169] being " another kind of elfes that daunce in darke." [170]

Whenever the fairies appeared, they always appeared together. This idiosyncrasy or racial characteristic or whatever it may be called, was one of the most ancient, and most unique features of their materialization, whether they rushed through the air with Diana in the 12th century, or " Disporten hem and maken melodye " with Proserpina in the fourteenth,[171] or guarded the sleep of Titania in the sixteenth.[172]

In all the records of their history in the 16th century, the number of times they can be discovered as separate individuals are comparatively few. If one appeared, all appeared, as in " The Marchantes Tale," " Ech after other, right as any lyne." [173] A mortal might be mistaken for a fairy, strayed from fairyland, as in *Cymbeline;* or an individual changeling make miserable the life of an unhappy 16th century mother; or a separate lady of the fairy be conjured into a crystal ball; or two Fairies appear to a Knight, as in *The Famous Historie of Chinon of England;* but with rare exceptions like these, the number of the fairies was always plural. Nor was it as an adventitious crowd that they came into sight, but the commonwealth itself, like bees when swarming, appeared with its ruler. " The elf-queen, with hir joly companye "; [174] " the Fayery Quene . . . dauncing with her maides about her "; [175] " fairy Queenes . . . and vnder

[169] *Terr. of the night,* Vol. I, p. 347.

[170] Nichols, *Prog. of Eliz.,* Vol. II, p. 210.

[171] Chaucer, " Marchantes Tale," l. 796.

[172] *M. N. D.,* II, 3.

[173] Chaucer, l. 986.

[174] Chaucer, " The Tale of the Wyf of Bathe," Skeat ed., 1894, l. 4.

[175] Nichols, *Prog. of Eliz.,* Vol. III, p. 118.

them a nacion rough ";[176] " the King of pharie, and his Court, with the elph queine ";[177] a " nation of Faies ";[178] " The king off fary and all hys route ";[179] " a bevy of FAIRIES, attending on MAB their queen ";[180] " the gude nychtbouris and Quene of Elfame "[181] — these are the terms which were used to describe their earthly visitations.

The fairies, in this respect, were unique among the world of supernaturals and spirits. A ghost, a spirit or a demon appeared in his own right and functioned according to his own ability and interest. He was subject, it is true, according to tradition and folk knowledge, to a sovereign, but he acted upon earth as a being under no visible monarchial or imperial guidance. The fairies, on the other hand, functioned as a kingdom or court; in most cases, under the visible and immediate direction of their ruler.

Although the plural number was used to denote the fairy sovereigns, the fairies had but one ruler — a monarch, as old as the race itself, and of the same nationality and being as her subjects, and, like the queen bee, female and nameless except for her royal title. All the other fairy rulers of the 16th century — Mab, Oberon, Aureola, Proserpina, Eambia,[182] Titania, Pluto, Diana, Hecate and Habundia — were the heroes or the heroines of either classical mythology or legendary history and were placed upon the fairy throne by historian or poet, scholar or playwright of the period.

176 T. Phaër, *The eygth booke of Aeneidos,* l. 336.

177 Montgomerie, p. 151.

178 Jonson, *Oberon, the Fairy Prince,* Morley ed., p. 151.

179 " Romance of King Orfeo," rpt. Hazlitt, *Fairy Tales,* l. 289.

180 Jonson, *The Satyr,* Morley ed., p. 408.

181 Pitcairn, *Crim. Trials,* Vol. I, pt. 2, p. 162.

182 *The Queenes Majesties Entertainment at Woodstocke,* p. 120.

But the real ruler of the fairies was neither the creation of poets' imagination nor a figure from classical or Celtic or Christian mythology. She was purely and simply the queen of the fairies, a fact of which the sponsors for the literary and historical sovereigns of the fairy kingdom were as cognizant as the folk.

The country of the fairies was underground — under the mountains or the lakes, or in caves and caverns, or within the hills of both England and Scotland where

> in this same Age, they are some times heard to bake Bread, strike Hammers, and do such lyke Services within the little Hillocks they most haunt.[183]

Although only the fairies themselves knew the way to their country and habitations, the general location of Fairyland was a matter of common knowledge; ". . . the Faeries . . . do principally inhabit the Mountains, and Caverns of the Earth," [184] was the record of *A Discourse concerning Devils and Spirits.* In *Britannia's Pastorals,* the fairy court was found by descending into the earth through

> An arched cave cutt in a rock intire,
> Deepe, hollowe, hideous, overgrowne with grasse,
> With thornes and bryers, and sadd mandragoras.[185]

According to Golding's translation of Ovid's *Metamorphoses,* " a darksome denne forgrowne with busshes hye, . . . was the fayryes bowre "; [186] while in *The Pilgrim*

> yon rocks
> Shew like enchanted cells, where they inhabit.[187]

[183] Kirk, *Sec. Comm.,* p. 6.
[184] Page 510.
[185] Wm. Browne, Vol. II, p. 132.
[186] Book XIV, ll. 584 and 586.
[187] Fletcher, V, 4.

There Bodies of congealled Air are some tymes caried aloft, other whiles grovell in different Schapes, and enter into any Cranie or Clift of the Earth where Air enters, to their ordinary Dwellings,[188]

was the statement of Robert Kirk. "We often use to dwell in some great hill," [189] the fairies informed Robin

[188] *Sec. Comm.*, pp. 6–7.

[189] Halliwell rpt., p. 153. "The consideration of the underground residence of the fairies, as a part of the English mythology, would lead us into long and curious investigations for which now we have not room. The elves have always had a country and dwellings under ground as well as above ground; and in several parts of England the belief that they descended to their subterraneous abodes through the barrows which cover the bones of our forefathers of ancient days is still preserved." Thomas Wright, *Essays,* 1846, Vol. I, pp. 272–273.

"Not more firmly established in this country, is the belief in ghosts, than that in fairies. The legendary records of fancy, transmitted from age to age, have assigned their mansions to that class of genii, in detached hillocks covered with verdure, situated on the banks of purling brooks, or surrounded by thickets of wood. These hillocks are called sioth-dhunan, abbreviated sioth-anan, from sioth, peace, and dun, a mound. They derive this name from the practice of the Druids, who were wont occasionally to retire to green eminences to administer justice, establish peace, and compose differences between contending parties. As that venerable order taught a Saoghl hal, or world beyond the present, their followers, when they were no more, fondly imagined, that seats, where they exercised a virtue so beneficial to mankind, were still inhabited by them in their disembodied state. In the autumnal season, when the moon shines from a serene sky, often is the wayfaring traveller arrested by the musick of the hills, more melodious than the strains of Orpheus, charming the shades, and restoring his beloved Eurydice to the regions of light.

Cantu commotae Erebi, de sedibus imis,
Umbrae ibant tenues.

Often struck with a more solemn scene, he beholds the visionary hunters engaged in the chase, and pursuing the deer of the clouds, while the hollow rocks in long-sounding echoes reverberate their cries.

Chorus aequalis Dryadum, clamore supremos,
Implerunt montes.

Goodfellow in *Robin Goodfellow; his mad prankes, and merry Jests.*

So much were the fairies associated with the hills, that the charms and conjurations "to gett a fayrie" were buried under "some hill, whereas you suppose fayries haunt," and "the flowers or toppes of wild time," which helped to make up a magic medicine, "must be gathered neare the side of a hill where the fayries use to be, and the grasse of a fayrie throne there." [190]

Some hills and smaller mountains, particularly, were known to be inhabited by the fairies,[191] for instance, the downs near Yatton Keynel in Wiltshire,[192] "a hill named Blackdown" near Tanton,[193] and Downiehillis in Scotland.[194] And in Scotland also,

> There be many Places called Fairie-hills, which the Mountain People think impious and dangerous to peel or discover, by taking Earth or Wood from them; superstitiously beleiving the Souls of

There are several now living, who assert that they have seen and heard this aerial hunting; and that they have been suddenly surrounded by visionary forms, more numerous than leaves strewed on the streams of Vallumbrosa in November blasts, and assailed by a multitude of voices, louder than the noise of rushing waters." John Sinclair, *The Statistical Account of Scotland*, 1791–1799, Vol. 12, pp. 461–462.

190 W. C. Hazlitt, *Fairy Tales*, 1875, pp. 276–277.

191 According to Kirk, "They remove to other Lodgings at the Beginning of each Quarter of the Year, so traversing till Doomsday, being imputent and [impotent of?] staying in one Place, and finding some Ease by so purning [Journeying] and changing Habitations. Their chamaelion-lyke Bodies swim in the Air near the Earth with Bag and Bagadge; and at such revolution of Time, SEERS, or Men of the SECOND SIGHT, (Faemales being seldome so qualified) have very terrifying Encounters with them." *Sec. Comm.*, pp. 7–8.

192 Aubrey, "Naturall History of Wiltshire," rpt. Hazlitt, *Fairy Tales*, pp. 349–350.

193 Bovet, *Pandaemonium*, Hazlitt rpt., p. 334.

194 Pitcairn, *Crim. Trials*, Gen. App., p. 611.

their Predicessors to dwell there. And for that End (say they) a Mote or Mount was dedicate beside every Church-yard, to receive the Souls till their adjacent Bodies arise, and so become as a Fairie-hill.[195]

The fairyland within the fairy hills of the 16th and 17th centuries, when the fairies were more domestic spirits than romantic beings, was not the "feyre cunturey" of the preceding centuries. Instead, those mortals who returned from the country of the fairies to recount its wonders, had found themselves in houses, rooms and halls. The human visitor, according to one story, was led by a fairy gentlewoman

to a little Hill and she knocked three times, and the Hill opened, and they went in, and came to a fair hall, wherein was a Queen sitting in great state, and many people about her, and the Gentlewoman that brought him, presented him to the Queen, and she said he was welcom, . . . and so she brought him forth of the Hill, and so they parted. And being asked . . . whether the place within the Hill, which he called a Hall, were light or dark, he said indifferent, as it is with us in the twilight.[196]

The "fairy-boy" mentioned in *Pandaemonium,* who "beat all points" on his drum "every Thursday night" to "a sort of people that use to meet" under "the great hill between Edenborough and Leith," reported that the fairy hill closed with "a great pair of gates that opened to them, though they were invisible to others, and that within there were brave large rooms."[197] When Issobell Gowdie "went in to the Downie-hillis" where she met the Queen of Fairies, "the hill opened, and we cam to an fair and lairge braw rowme, in the day tym."[198]

[195] Kirk, *Sec. Comm.,* p. 23.

[196] Webster, *Disp. of Sup. Witch.,* p. 301.

[197] Bovet, Hazlitt rpt., p. 332.

[198] Pitcairn, *Crim. Trials,* Gen. App., p. 611.

The peasant in *The Wisdome of Doctor Dodypoll* found a company of Fairies "in a caue in the bottome of a fine greene hill," [199] and the fairyland of *Britannia's Pastorals* was situated under a hill in rooms and vaults.[200]

According to Robert Kirk,

> Their Houses are called large and fair, and (unless att some odd occasions) unperceavable by vulgar eyes, like Rachland, and other inchanted Islands, having fir Lights, continual Lamps, and Fires, often seen without Fuel to sustain them. Women are yet alive who tell they were taken away when in Child-bed to nurse Fairie Children, . . . The Child, and Fire, with Food and other Necessaries, are set before the Nurse how soon she enters; but she nather perceaves any Passage out, nor sees what those People doe in other Rooms of the Lodging.[201]

Although the greater consensus of opinion put fairyland within the hills of the countryside, hell was sometimes regarded as the fairies' dwelling place, especially by poets. In hell, they were placed by William Warner at the enthronement of Hecate as "sourantisse of Hell" in *Albion's England:*

> The Elues and Fairies, taking fists,
> Did hop a merrie round:
> . . . .
> The airy sprights, the walking flames,
> And goblins, great and small,
> Had theare good cheere, and company,
> And sport, the Diuell and all.[202]

Hell, too, was made their country by Edward Fairfax

[199] Act III.

[200] Wm. Browne, Vol. II, p. 144. Cf. also C. Middleton, *Chinon of England,* pp. 24–30.

[201] *Sec. Comm.,* pp. 12–13. Cf. also the stage directions in Ben Jonson's *Masque of Oberon,* Morley ed., pp. 143, 147, 151, 155.

[202] Chalmers ed., p. 548.

in his translation of Tasso's *Godfrey of Bulloigne: or The Recovery of Jerusalem,*[203] and by George Peele, whose *Battle of Alcazar* mentions "Fiends, Fairies, hags" as inhabitants of "tormenting hell." [204] And to the unknown author of *Philotus,*[205] and to Sir David Lyndesay,[206] the domains of Satan were synonymous with the realms of the fairy.

As far as the common folk of England were concerned, the fairies were more familiar to them, as inhabitants of England than as citizens of hell. The countryside was surrounded by their hills and bore the marks of their dancing circles. In any forest or at any well, they were apt to materialize with their Queen, either riding on white hackneys or dancing into sight from underground, black, red, green and white, with figures "generally near the smaller size of men," and the fairest of fair faces.

[203] 1687 ed., Stanza 18, p. 97.

[204] IV, 2.

[205] Stanza 132.

[206] *Ane Satyre of the thrie Estaits,* p. 532, ll. 4188–4189, and p. 402, l. 732. Cf. also Thomas Dekker, *Newes from Hell;* and *Comedy of Errors,* II, 2.

CHAPTER III

THE FAIRIES: THEIR LIFE ON EARTH[1]

That the fairies maintained a civilization of their own in a kingdom of their own, from which they issued at intervals for visitations to the earth, was a convention of fairy lore. It was a convention of 16th century fairy lore that the fairies were vitally concerned with the affairs of human beings, and that " a world of Elue work," also, was " walking amongst " mortals in England.

While the spectacle of the fairies' dancing and the sound of their music were aspects of this phenomenon, their Elizabethan existence, if their activities on earth and their intercourse with mortals of the time may be so termed, was bound up with bread and cattle, with new-born babies and brooms, with sixpences and water pails. These homely and domestic interests, which were the particular and unique concern of the Elizabethan fairies, did not proceed wholly from their own whims or desires, but were forced upon them, according to the belief of the 16th century, by their dependence upon mortals for some of the necessities of life, and for the continuation of their race. From this exigency, and, in a lesser degree, from the fairies' own character and idiosyncrasies, originated the activities, the exactions, the benefactions, the prohibitions and the punishments which marked their earthly sojourn.

In the first place, they were beholden to human beings for food. Far from sustaining an ethereal existence on

[1] In this chapter, as in Chapter II, the fairies are treated according to the popular belief of the period, as real and living characters.

air and perfume, like the modern fairy of fancy, the fairies of the 16th and 17th centuries required the beef and bread of mortals, and ate their way through the period, or, as James VI of Scotland stated, they " eate and dranke, and did all other actions like naturall men and women." [2] They were, in fact, addicted to the pleasures of the table and lived in a round of banquets and feasts; " there Food being exactly clean, and served up by Pleasant Children, lyke inchanted Puppets." [3] " I have heard many wonderful Relations from Lunaticks or such as are almost natural fools, who have asserted, That being for many daies together conversant amongst Faeries in Woods, Mountains, and Caverns of the Earth, they have feasted with them, and been magnificently Entertaind with variety of dainties," [4] for " they will have fair coverit taiblis." [5]

The provision for these feasts, they partly supplied themselves, for they were particularly devoted to making cake and bread which they did with so much vigor that the noise of this culinary occupation resounded from their residential hillocks, where, according to Robert Kirk, " they are some times heard to bake Bread," [6] and, as late as 1725, " when they make Cakes (which is a Work they have been often heard at) they are very noisy; and when they have done, they are full of Mirth and Pastime." [7]

[2] *Daemon.*, p. 132.

[3] Kirk, *Sec. Comm.*, p. 11.

[4] *Dis. conc. D. & S.*, p. 505.

[5] *Spald. Club Misc.*, Vol. I, p. 121.

[6] *Sec. Comm.*, p. 6.

[7] Bourne, *Antiq. Vulgares*, p. 83.

The one exception to the general recognition of the fairies' consumption of mortal food is found in *Cymb.*, II, 1:

> " But that it eats our victuals, I should think
> Here were a fairy."

The fairy bread was "the most delicious Bread that ever I did eat, either before or since,"[8] and had the added property of being able to keep people alive without the aid of any other food, if the case of Anne Jefferies be true. She "was fed by these Fairies from that Harvest-time to the next Christmas-Day,"[9] and being arrested on a warrant for having been fed by the fairies,

> she went with the Constable to the Justice, and he sent her to Bodmin Jayl, and ordered the Prison-Keeper that she should be kept without Victuals; and she was so kept, and yet she lived, and that without complaining.[10]

The flour for the fairies' bread, originally, seems to have been made out of the corn which they grew themselves. According to Robert Kirk,

> when severall Countreys were unhabitated by ws, these had their easy Tillage above Ground, as we now. The Print of those Furrous do yet remaine to be seen on the Shoulders of very high Hills, which was done when the champayn Ground was Wood and Forrest.[11]

In the 16th century, there is no record of the actual grain fields of the fairies. Instead, they were believed to subsist, in the main, on mortal crops and mortal food which they obtained by thievery and by terrorism, making

---

Cf. also *The Tempest, The Works of Shakspeare* by Mr. Theobald, 1772, Vol. I, p. 75: "'Where the bee sucks, there suck I.' I have ventured to vary from the printed copies here. Could Ariel, a spirit of a refin'd aetherial essence, be intended to want food!" Changed by Theobald to: "Where the bee sucks, there lurk I."

[8] J. Morgan, *Phoenix Brit.*, p. 549.

[9] *Ibid.*, p. 549.

[10] *Ibid.*, p. 550.

[11] *Sec. Comm.*, p. 7.

. . . fearefull noise in Buttries and in Dairies;

. . . .

And keeping Christmasse gambols all night long.
Pots, glasses, trenchers, dishes, pannes and kettles
They will make dance about the shelues and settles.[12]

There was no householder but labored under the impression that bread must be left for the fairies either upon a clean and well ordered table or upon the hearth, for:

. . . if they spread no Table, set no Bread,
They should haue nips from toe vnto the head.[13]

When the customary bread was forgotten — an omission which must have been very infrequent — the fairies could remedy the deficiency by stealing the grain in the fields:

Some have Bodies or Vehicles so spungious, thin, and defecat, that they are fed by only sucking into some fine spirituous Liquors, that peirce lyke pure Air and Oyl: others feid more gross on the Foyson or substance of Corns and Liquors, or Corne it selfe that grows on the Surface of the Earth, which these Fairies steall away, partly invisible, partly preying on the Grain, as do Crowes and Mice.[14]

Their appetites were not confined wholly to bread or grain. They lived, too, upon beef and brawn, either keeping cattle themselves, or obtaining them by theft from mortals. It is a commonplace of the fairies' history in Ireland and in Wales that the fairy women who married mortal husbands enriched their spouses with great herds of cattle that followed them from the lake or

[12] Heywood, *Hierarchie,* p. 574.

[13] Wm. Browne, *Brit. Pastorals,* Vol. I, p. 67.

[14] Kirk, *Sec. Comm.,* pp. 5–6; cf. also Douce, *Illus. of Shak.,* Vol. I, p. 387.

sea from which they came,[15] and disappeared when their fairy mistresses were forced to depart. In 1662, the fairies in Scotland were reported to have "elf-bullis rowtting and skoylling wp and downe." [16] And in 1691,

> They also pierce Cows or other Animals, usewally said to be Elf-shot, whose purest Substance (if they die) these Subterraneans take to live on, viz. the aereal and aetherial Parts, the most spirituous Matter for prolonging of Life, such as Aquavitae (moderately taken) is among Liquors, leaving the terrestrial behind.[17]

Even, in 1793, the minister of Wick reported,

> Some small stones have been found, which seem to be a species of flint, about an inch long and half an inch broad, of a triangular shape, and barbed on each side. The common people confidently assert, that they are fairies arrows, which they shoot at Cattle, when they instantly fall down dead, though the hide of the animal remains quite entire.[18]

In England, the fairies obtained their beef by another method which Reginald Scot describes as follows:

> You must also understand, that after they have delicately banqueted with the devill and the lady of the faries: and have

[15] *Silva Gadelica,* O'Grady ed., 1892, Eng. trans., pp. 119, 121; Rhys, *Celtic Folklore, Welsh and Manx,* 1901, Vol. I, pp. 8, 10, 23–24.

[16] Pitcairn, *Crim. Trials,* Gen. App., p. 604.

[17] Kirk, *Sec. Comm.,* p. 21.

[18] Sinclair, *Stat. Acct. of Scotland,* Vol. 10, p. 15. Cf. also Collins, *Ode on the Popular Superstitions of the Highlands;* and Kirk, *Sec. Comm.,* pp. 21–22. The possession of a charm to ward off elvish arrows had always been a necessary equipment for a successful farmer, though the cure for such wounds, if one knew it, was surprisingly simple. It consisted "only for a Man to find out the Hole with his Finger; as if the Spirits flowing from a Man's warme Hand were Antidote sufficient against their poyson'd Dairts."

eaten up a fat ox, and emptied a butt of malmesie, and a binne of bread at some noble mans house, in the dead of the night, nothing is missed of all this in the morning. For the lady Sibylla, Minerva, or Diana with a golden rod striketh the vessell and the binne, and they are fully replenished again. Yea, she causeth the bullockes bones to be brought and laid together upon the hide. And lappeth the four ends thereof together, laying her golden rod thereon, and then riseth up the bullocke again in his former estate and condition: and yet at their returne home they are like to starve for hunger.[19]

What the fairies most desired was milk and cream and butter, and their appetite for these commodities was notorious. So much so, that, with Robin Goodfellow, whose propensity for cream amounted to an obsession, they were termed "spirites . . . of the buttry," [20] or "Dairy Sprites"! [21]

For Robin Goodfellow a cream bowl was set out each night by benevolent households. The fairies "enter into the Dairies, and Feast upon the Cream, which they skim from the Milk," [22] or "Drink Dairies dry, and stroke the Cattle." [23] At other times,

What Food they extract from us is conveyed to their Homes by secret Paths, as sume skilfull Women do the Pith and Milk from their Neighbours Cows into their own Chiese-hold thorow a Hair-tedder, at a great Distance, by Airt Magic, or by drawing a spickot fastened to a Post, which will bring milk as farr of as a Bull will be heard to roar.[24]

[19] *Dis. of Witch.*, 1651 ed., p. 36.

[20] *Tarltons Newes out of Purgatorie,* Halliwell ed., 1844, Shak. Soc. Publns., p. 55.

[21] Poole, *English Parnassus.*

[22] Hobbes, *Leviathan,* p. 546.

[23] [James Farewell], *Irish Hudibras,* 1689 ed., p. 122.

[24] Kirk, *Sec. Com.,* p. 11. Cf. also Heywood and Broome, *The Late Lancashire Witches,* where this method of obtaining food is attributed to witches.

The fairies' love for milk and butter and their concern with all dairy operations [25] were recognized as two of their most pronounced traits. Especially was this true of Mab, who was introduced by Ben Jonson in *The Satyr,* as:

> . . . . . . the mistress Fairy,
> That doth nightly rob the dairy,
> And can hurt or help the cherning,
> As she please, without discerning; [26]

and pictured by Milton in *L'Allegro* as the heroine of a folk-tale, "How fairy Mab the Junkets eat." [27]

However the fairies obtained their food, generosity with it was one of their virtues. Not only did they magnificently entertain with "Fairy Dainties" "those mortals conversant amongst them," but they pressed their food upon other mortals with whom they came in contact, "leaving Bread, Butter, and Cheese sometimes with them [" Servants and Shepherds in Country houses "], which if they refuse to eat, some mischief shall undoubtedly befall them by the means of these Faeries." [28]

Issobell Gowdie, tried for witchcraft, in 1662, in Edinburgh, got meat from the Queen of Fairies, "mor

[25] The fairies are believed to have some special affinity for cheese. One of the common methods of appeasing the present day fairy in Ireland and Wales is to drop small pieces of cheese into the various fairy-haunted springs that dot those countries. The one reference I have found in the 16th century which might indicate a knowledge of this love of the fairies for cheese occurs in *M. W. of W.*, V, 5, where Falstaff exclaims:

> "Heavens defend me from that Welch fairy!
> Lest he transform me to a piece of cheese!"

[26] Morley ed., p. 409.

[27] Cambridge ed., 1899, p. 27.

[28] *Dis. conc. D. & S.*, p. 510.

than I could eat,"[29] though she paid for her repletion with her life. And in the Scotland of 1739, the fairies were still given to "stap those they met and are displeased with full of butter and hear awne."[30]

For those mortals to whom they had taken an especial fancy, they were given to providing banquets and feasts, as, for instance, in *The Wisdome of Doctor Dodypoll:*

> Enter Fairies bringing in a banquet.
> O daintie, O rare, a banquet, would to Christ,
> I were one of their guests: Gods ad, a fine little
> Dapper fellow has spyed me: what will he doo?
> He comes to make me drinke. I thanke you sir;[31]

or, in *Robin Goodfellow; his mad prankes, and merry Jests,* where a female friend of "a hee fayrie" every night "for meate . . . had capons, chickins, mutton, lambe, phesant, snite, woodcocke, partridge, quailes. . . . wine had shee of all sorts, muskadine, sacke, malmsie, clarret, white and bastard";[32] or in *Huon of Burdeux,* in which Huon was banqueted as royally at the hands of Oberon.[33]

It was a smaller need but equally as vital a one which bound the fairies a second time to mortal society. With the lakes and springs of England at their command, they seemed unable to obtain bath water without human intervention. This, and the receptacle in which it was contained, they demanded both for their own baths, and especially, for the baths of their small children, a fact which was generally recognized.

[29] Pitcairn, *Crim. Trials,* Gen. App., p. 604.

[30] Robert Heron, *Observations made on a Tour through the Western Highlands of Scotland,* 1793, Vol. II, p. 227.

[31] Act III, E2.

[32] Hazlitt rpt., p. 177.

[33] Vol. I, pt. I, pp. 74–75.

A person would be thought impudently profane who should suffer his family to go to bed without having first set a tub, or pail full of clean water, for these guests to bathe themselves in, which the natives aver they constantly do, as soon as ever the eyes of the family are closed, wherever they vouchsafe to come.[34]

> And further if by Maidens ouer-sight,
> Within doores water were not brought at night:
> . . . .
> They should haue nips from toe vnto the head.[35]

The formula by which the fairies' nightly pail was prepared was well known:

> If ye will with Mab find grace,
> Set each Platter in his place:
> Rake the Fier up, and get
> Water in, ere Sun be set.
> Wash your Pailes, and clense your Dairies.[36]

Sometimes the penalty for the omission of water was very great.

. . . now and then we goe together [was the statement of one of the fairies in *Robin Goodfellow; his mad prankes, and merry Jests*], and at good huswives fires we warme and dresse our fayry children. If wee find cleane water and cleane towels, wee leave them money, either in their basons or in their shooes; but if wee find no cleane water in their houses, we wash our children in their pottage, milke or beere, or what-ere we finde; for the sluts that leave not such things fitting, wee wash their faces and hands with a gilded child's clout, or els carry them to some river, and ducke them over head and eares.[37]

The fairies' need for mortal pails and for bath water, inexplicable as it was, was one of their most pronounced

[34] Waldron, *Isle of Man,* pp. 27–28.

[35] Wm. Browne, *Brit. Pastorals,* Vol. I, pp. 66–67. Cf. also Burton, *Anat. of Mel.,* Vol. I, p. 216.

[36] Robert Herrick, *Hesperides,* Moorman ed., 1915, p. 201.

[37] Hazlitt rpt., p. 206.

characteristics, the tradition of which continued to exist long after the race itself had disappeared from general credence. In the first half of the 18th century, it was reported that

> . . . when the Master and Mistress were lain on their Pillows, the Men and Maids, if they had a Game at Romps, and blundered up Stairs, or jumbled a Chair, the next Morning every one would swear it was the Fairies, and that they heard them stamping up and down Stairs all Night, crying, Waters lock'd, Waters lock'd, when there was no Water in any Pail in the Kitchen.[38]

With their need for mortal bread and water and the necessity put upon them to steal changelings and seduce witches,[39] the dependence of the fairies upon mortals ceased. At no time were they ever regarded as an inferior or a dependent race. Instead, they flourished as domestic tyrants who set up a standard of conduct for the mortals of the 16th century, and established, in their world, a number of prohibitions which had, perforce, to be observed under the penalty either of death or abduction or pinchings.

The latter method of punishment seems to have been the unique invention of the Elizabethan fairies. Whatever its origin (and all trace of its source is lost in the confusion of the characteristics of the devils, hedgehogs, imps and monsters who played one part or another in the fairy genealogy), it was taken up in the 16th century and practised with much vigor from the beginning of Elizabeth's reign.[40]

[38] *Round about our Coal Fire, or, Christmas Entertainments.* Rpt. of 1740 ed., 1883, p. 54.

[39] Discussed in Chap. IV.

[40] Besides the texts used on the following pages, cf. Thomas Campion, *A Booke of Ayres,* Vivian ed., 1909, Poem XIX; Burton, *Anat. of Mel.,* Vol. I, p. 222; *C. of E.,* II, 2; *Maydes Met.,* II, 2; Shirley,

They were no casual, ordinary pinches that were given, but thorough and violent nips of a maximum intensity which had for their avowed purpose a skin "as blue as bilberry."[41] The efficiency and frequency with which this result was achieved is evidenced by the fact that the blueness from the fairy pinches was taken as the standard for a perfect azure:

> HEC. Are the flames blue enough?
> Or shall I use a little seething more?
> STAD. The nips of fairies upon maid's white hips
> Are not more perfect azure.[42]

These nips were not to be lightly dismissed, as the following directions for a fairy pinching show:

> 1 FAIRY. Pinch him blue.
> 2 FAIRY. And pinch him blacke.
> 3 FAIRY. Let him not lacke
> Sharp nailes to pinch him blue and red,
> Till sleepe has rock'd his addle head.
> 4 FAIRY. For the trespasse hee hath done,
> Spots ore all his flesh shall runne.[43]

After such an encounter, the victim was left "more like a Leopard than a man," and could only be relieved of "These spots" "if you rubbe them ouer with this Lunarie."[44]

Dyce ed., 1833, *The Grateful Servant,* I, 1; Jonson, Gifford ed., *Alchemist,* II, 2; Jonson, Morley ed., *The Satyr;* and C. Middleton, *Chinon of England,* p. 30.

The pinching of the fairies seems to have been wholly an English trait. There is no record of their pinching, as far as I have been able to ascertain, in Scotland or Ireland.

[41] *M. W. of W.,* V, 5.

[42] Thomas Middleton, Bullen ed., 1885, Vol. 5, *The Witch,* I, 2.

[43] Lyly, *Endimion,* IV, 3.

[44] *Ibid.*

Yet, in spite of the thoroughness of the fairy pinches and the frequency of their occurrence, there seems to have been, among mortal victims, a certain pride in the characteristic neatness with which they were executed, as, for instance,

> SOLD. . . . .
> . . . I have been so nipt, and pull'd, and pinch'd,
> By a company of hell-cats.
> ARTH. Fairies, sure.
> SOLD. Rather foule fiends, fairies have no such clawes.[45]

Notwithstanding this somewhat questionable advantage, the fairy punishment was not lightly regarded, as the words of Corsites in Endimion indicate:

> I should rather breake into the middest of a maine battaile, than againe fall into the handes of those fayre babies.[46]

The pinchings of the fairies, as well as more dire disasters, could, for the most part, be avoided, by careful observance of the fairy laws and prohibitions.

There was the law which forbade any mortal invasion of that part of the earth the fairies chose to occupy, especially the rings which enclosed their dancing places.[47] So well recognized was the ban which rested upon the latter that any circular spaces in England were, for safety's sake, regarded as fairy property, as in *The Belman of London:*

> It was a Groue set thicke with trees, which grewe in such order, that they made a perfect circle; insomuch that I stood in feare, it

[45] Heywood and Broome, *The Late Lancashire Witches,* 1634 ed., V, 1; rptd. in Halliwell, *The Poetry of Witchcraft,* 1853.

[46] Lyly, IV, 3.

[47] Fletcher, *The Faithful Shepherdess,* III, 1:

> No shepherd's way lies here, 'tis hallow'd ground;
> No maid seeks here her strayed cow, or sheep;
> Fairies and fawns, and satyrs do it keep.

was kept by Fayries, and that I was brought into it by enchantment.[48]

Woe betide the man who put sacrilegious plow or scythe to this ground. The sheep knew better than to take the smallest bite of the fairies' "green-sour ringlets"[49] and only the most incautious of mortals would set foot upon the bare space inside, or fall asleep within the magic confines of the fairies' circles or upon the hillocks they most fancied or in the forests where they had taken up an earthly habitation. If he took this risk, he was either stricken dead, or carried away to fairyland, or left with his body "as many colors as a mackrels backe"[50] from fairy pinches.

The Fayries Daunce of Thomas Ravenscroft would seem to have been written to celebrate this particular prohibition of the fairies:

> Dare you haunt our hallowed greene, none but Fayries
> heere are seene. downe and sleepe, wake and weepe.
> Pinch him blacke, and pinch him blew, that seekes to
> steale a Louer true.
> When you come to heare vs sing, or to tread our Fayrie
> ring, pinch him blacke, and pinch him blew,
> O thus our nayles shall handle you, thus our nayles
> shall handle you.[51]

[48] Thomas Dekker, *Non-Dramatic Works,* Grosart ed., 1884–1886, Vol. III, p. 74.

[49] *Temp.,* V, 1.

[50] *Robin Goodfellow; his mad prankes, and merry Jests,* Hazlitt rpt., p. 203.

[51] Roxburghe Club ed., 1822, No. XXI, p. 20.

According to Robert Chambers' *Popular Rhymes of Scotland,* 1870, p. 324, "Husbandmen used to avoid, with superstitious reverence, to till or destroy the little circlets of bright green grass which are believed to be the favourite ball-rooms of the fairies; for, . . .

Nor were examples lacking on the stage and off of the immediate consequences of an invasion of the fairies' earthly territory. The punishment for an invasion of fairy rings overtook Fortunatus when he fell asleep on haunted ground.[52] And an attempt to be with the fairies and see them on one of their hills was responsible for the lifelong lameness of a "certain man," according to the *Pandaemonium* of Richard Bovet.[53]

It might be mentioned that a fairy abduction could be a vast comfort, however, to thrifty and avaricious Elizabethans, for:

. . . if the destinies, or Fortune, or the Fates, or the Fayries haue stolne him, neuer indite them for the Felonie: for by this meanes

---

He wha tills the fairies' green,
  Nae luck again shall hae;
And he wha spills the fairies' ring,
  Betide him want and wae;
For weirdless days and weary nights
  Are his till his deein' day!

Whereas, . . .

He wha gaes by the fairy ring,
  Nae dule nor pine shall see;
And he wha cleans the fairy ring,
  An easy death shall dee."

Compare also John Leyden, *Scenes of Infancy,* 2d ed., 1811, p. 24:

"Woe to the upland swain, who, wandering far,
The circle treads, beneath the evening star!
His feet the witch-grass green impels to run,
Full on the dark descent, he strives to shun;
Till, on the giddy brink, o'erpower'd by charms,
The fairies clasp him, in unhallowed arms,
Doomed, with the crew of restless foot, to stray
The earth by night, the nether realms by day;
Till seven long years their dangerous circuit run,
And call the wretch to view this upper sun."

52 Dekker, *The Comedie of Olde Fortunatus,* Vol. I, p. 92.

53 Hazlitt rpt., pp. 335–336.

the charges of a Tombe is sau'd, and you being his heyres, may doe as many rich Executors doe, put that money in your purses, and giue out that he dyed a begger.[54]

It was easier to keep away from the fairy haunts and, especially, the fairy rings than it was to observe the fairies' edict against being stared at. For some reason or other, they could not bear to be seen, but followed darkness like a dream, as in *A Midsummer Night's Dream,*[55] and shunned the sun, as in Churchyard's presentation of them in *A Discourse of the Queenes Majestie's Entertainment in Suffolk and Norfolk:*

We shun the Sunne, yet love the Mone, and hate the open light,
We hide our heads amid the reedes in blustring stormy night.
In calmest weather do we play, yet seldome seene we are,
We watch our times, and flee from those that still doe on us stare.[56]

Their resentment at being spied upon was known to be violent. Corsites, in *Endimion,* dared to look at the fairies and obtained many wounds because of his temerity, which were inflicted to the following refrain:

OMNES. Pinch him, pinch him, blacke and blue,
Sawcie mortalls must not view
What the Queene of Stars is doing,
Nor pry into our Fairy woing.[57]

Sir John Falstaff, disguised though he was with a stag's head, refused to gaze at the fairies and threw himself upon his face with the ejaculation, "I'll wink and couch: No man their works must eye."[58] Maria, in *Lusts*

[54] Dekker, *The Comedie of Olde Fortunatus,* Vol. I, p. 124.
[55] V, 2.
[56] Nichols, *Prog. of Eliz.,* Vol. II, p. 210.
[57] Lyly, IV, 3.
[58] *M. W. of W.,* V, 5.

Dominion, could not avoid the sight of their appearance, though she hid herself from their company as soon as she realized who they were.[59]

To escape the consequences of seeing the fairies, as well as for reasons more potently knavish, the clerk who was to seek his fortune with the queen of fairies in *The Alchemist,*[60] was blindfolded when he appeared before her Grace, for:

> . . . if any Superterraneans be so subtile, as to practice Slights for procuring a Privacy to any of their Misteries, (such as making use of their Oyntments, which as Gygef's Ring makes them invisible, or nimble, or casts them in a Trance, or alters their Shape, or makes Things appear at a vast Distance, &c.) they smite them without Paine, as with a Puff of Wind, and bereave them of both the naturall and acquired Sights in the twinkling of ane Eye, (both these Sights, where once they come, being in the same Organ and inseparable,) or they strick them Dumb.[61]

On the occasion of their appearance at Norwich, before Elizabeth, Thomas Churchyard did not fail to have them remind Her Majesty that they had broken a rule of fairyland in appearing:

> Though cleane against the Pharies kind we come in open viewe
> (And that the Queene of Phayries heere presents hirselfe to you)
> Some secret cause procures the same: the gods, at first, ye know,
> In field to honour thee, good Queene, did make a gallant shew.
> Should we that are but sprites of th' aire refuse to do the same? [62]

As late as the 18th century, it was reported of the fairies that "generally they dance in Moon-Light, when Mortals are asleep, and not capable of seeing them," [63]

[59] III, 2.

[60] III, 2.

[61] Kirk, *Sec. Comm.,* p. 13.

[62] Nichols, *Prog. of Eliz.,* Vol. II, p. 212.

[63] Bourne, *Antiq. Vulgares,* p. 83.

for "the moment any one saw them," and took notice of them, "they were struck blind of one Eye." [64]

A third law of the fairies forbade that they should be spoken to. "He who speakes to them shall die," [65] was the formula, as Falstaff states it in *Merry Wives of Windsor*. Huon of Burdeux was reminded of this prohibition of the fairies when he ventured near the haunts of Oberon:

. . . in that wood abydyth a kynge of ye fayrey namyd Oberon/ . . . and ye shall no soner be enteryd in to that wood, yf ye go that way/ he wyll fynde the maner to speke with you/ and yf ye speke to hym ye are lost for euer/ [66]

The same warning was given to Bessie Dunlop, whom the fairies finally seduced as a witch:

The ferd tyme he apperit in hir awin hous to hir, about the xij hour of the day, . . . and he tuke hir apperoun and led hir to the dure with him, and sche followit, and ȝeid vp with him to the kill-end, quhair he forbaid hir to speik or feir for onye thing sche hard or saw; . . . and . . . Thai baid hir sit doun, and said, "Welcum, Bessie, will thow go with ws?" Bot sche ansuerit nocht; becaus Thom had forbidden hir.[67]

On the other hand, if a judicious silence was observed in the presence of the fairies, it, sometimes, had its reward:

Whenas my fellow elves and I
  In circled ring do trip a round;
If that our sports by any eye
  Do happen to be seen or found;
    If that they
    No words do say,

[64] *Round About Our Coal Fire,* p. 52.
[65] V, 5.
[66] *Huon of Burdeux,* E. E. T. S. ed., Vol. I, pt. I, p. 63.
[67] Pitcairn, *Crim. Trials,* Vol. I, pt. 2, pp. 52–53.

But mum continue as they go,
Each night I do
Put groat in shoe,
And wind out laughing, ho, ho, ho! [68]

Not only did the fairies refuse to be spoken to, but they refused to be spoken of, nor would they have any mention made of their favors. Whatever benevolence or fortune they bestowed was immediately accompanied by the reminder, "You must not tell though," or, as Richard Corbet stated:

A tell-tale in theyre company
They never could endure,
And whoe so kept not secretly
Theyre mirth was punisht sure;
It was a just and christian deed
To pinch such blacke and blew.[69]

Alesoun Peirson in 1588 confessed:

. . . quhene scho tellis of thir thingis, . . . scho wes sairlie tormentit with thame: . . . And that thay come verry feirfull sumtymes, and fleit hir verry sair, and scho cryit quhene thay come: And that thay come quhyles anis in the aucht dayes, and quhene scho tauld last of it, thay come to hir and boistit hir, saying, scho sould be war handlit nor of befoir; and that thaireftir thay tuke the haill poistie of hir syde, in sic soirt, that scho lay tuentie oulkis thaireftir: And that oft tymes thay wald cum and sitt besyde hir, and promesit that scho sould newir want, gif scho wald be faithfull and keip promeis: bot, gif scho wald speik and tell of thame and thair doingis, thay sould martir hir.[70]

One of the victims of the Wests, in 1613, or before, thinking "to acquaint these proceedings to some friend," was,

[68] *The Pranks of Puck,* rpt. in Halliwell, *Illus. of Fairy Myth.,* p. 168.

[69] *The Faery's Farewell,* p. 582.

[70] Pitcairn, *Crim. Trials,* Vol. I, pt. 2, p. 163.

as some think, and as by the sequel it appeared, stroke lame by her [Alice West's] sorceries, after which she presently repaired to him, told him his purpose to blab the secrets of the fayries was come to the eares of Oberon, for which he inraged, had inflicted this punishment upon him.[71]

From this prohibition [72] of the fairies, no mortal was considered exempt. In *The Satyr,* the gifts to the queen of England, purporting to have come from the fairies, were accompanied with the usual legend:

> Utter not, we you implore,
> Who did give it, nor wherefore:
> And whenever you restore
> Yourself to us, you shall have more.
>
> Highest, happiest queen, farewell;
> But beware you do not tell.[73]

A strict compliance with the laws which insured the privacy of the fairies' appearance and activities, was not wholly sufficient to protect mortals against fairy interference and fairy punishment. There were certain rules of human conduct which had to be rigorously followed, if the 16th-century house were to remain free from fairy visitations, or the 16th-century citizen to remain untouched by fairy fingers.

Their passion for cleanliness,[74] as characteristic of

[71] *The Cozenages of the Wests,* Hazlitt rpt., p. 227. Cf. also Field, *A Woman is a Weathercock,* I, 1, Dodsley, 1874, Vol. XI; *W. Tale,* III, 3; Wm. Browne, *The Shepheardes Pipe,* Hazlitt ed., 1869, Vol. II, p. 234; Massinger, 1779, Vol. II, *The Fatal Dowry,* IV, 1; *The Honest Man's Fortune,* V, 1.

[72] This prohibition is very old, and is to be found in the romances, etc.

[73] Ben Jonson, Morley ed., p. 412.

[74] It is interesting that Shakespeare, as a compliment to Queen Elizabeth, has the fairies "Search Windsor castle" "within & out" and scour "the several chairs of order" "with juice of balm." *M. W. of W.,* V, 5.

them as their passion for dancing, they expected mortals to share. And two human proclivities they would not tolerate — dirt and disorder; or, to put it in the language of the *Merry Wives of Windsor,* "Our radiant queen hates sluts and sluttery." [75] With such a passion, in such a century, they were kept inordinately busy pinching "maids in their sleep that swept not their houses cleane." [76] When this method proved unavailing, they cured slovenliness by increasing it:

> But where foul sluts did dwell,
>   Who used to sit up late,
> And would not scour their pewter well,
>   There came a merry mate
>
> To kitchen or to hall,
>   Or place where spreets resort;
> Then down went dish and platters all,
>   To make the greater sport.[77]

Some of the fairies were believed to devote their entire existence to the inculcation of cleanliness:

> I, that am called Pinch, do goe about from house to house: sometimes I find the dores of the house open; that negligent servants had left them so, I doe so nip him or her, that with my pinches their bodyes are as many colors as a mackrels backe. Then take I them, and lay I them in the doore, naked or unnaked I care not whether: there they lye, many times till broad day, ere they waken; . . .
>
> Sometimes I find a slut sleeping in the chimney corner, when she should be washing of her dishes, or doing something else which she

[75] V, 5; cf. also Nutt, *Fairy Myth. of Eng. Lit.,* p. 47.

[76] Nashe, *Terr. of the night,* Vol. I, p. 347. Cf. also Burton, *Anat. of Mel.,* Vol. I, p. 220; Drayton, *Nimphidia,* St. 9; and Ben Jonson, *The Satyr.*

[77] Thomas Churchyard, "A Handfull of Gladsome Verses given to the Queen's Majesty at Woodstock this Progress" (1592); rpt. in E. K. Chambers, "Fairy World," p. 164.

hath left undone: her I pinch about the armes, for not laying her armes to her labor. Some I find in their beds snorting and sleeping, and their houses lying as cleane as a nasty doggs kennell; in one corner bones, in another eg-shells, behind the doore a heap of dust, the dishes under feet, and the cat in the cubbord: all these sluttish trickes I doe reward with blue legges, and blue armes. I find some slovens too, as well as sluts: they pay for their beastlinesse too, as well as the women-kind.[78]

After the house, the fairies turned their attention to its human occupants. In this case, their particular detestation was uncared-for hair:

Those that I find with their heads nitty and scabby, for want of combing, I am their barbers, and cut their hayre as close as an apes tayle; or else clap so much pitch on it, that they must cut it off themselves to their great shame. . . . Some I find that spoyle their master's horses for want of currying: those I doe daube with grease and soote, and they are faine to curry themselves ere they can get cleane.

. . . .

Thus many trickes, I, Pach, can doe,
But to the good I ne'ere was foe.[79]

The Mab of *Romeo and Juliet* turned from her state coach and her triumphant journey through lovers' brains, to become " that very Mab "

That plats the manes of horses in the night;
And bakes the elf-locks in foul sluttish hairs
Which, once untangled, much misfortune bodes.[80]

[78] *Robin Goodfellow; his mad prankes, and merry Jests,* Hazlitt rpt., p. 203. Cf. also Herrick, *Hesperides,* p. 201; Martin Llewellyn, *Men-Miracles,* 1646, Song. *At the Holly-Bush Guard,* pp. 35–36.

[79] *Robin Goodfellow; his mad prankes, and merry Jests,* Hazlitt rpt., p. 204.

[80] *R. & J.,* I, 4, ll. 89–91.

And such was the Fairy Queen's insistence upon cleanliness that no one was allowed to come into the royal fairy presence, but

> There must a world of ceremonies pass;
> You must be bath'd and fumigated first.[81]

In spite of their horror of dirt, they did not always use force in inculcating cleanliness. Instead, they rewarded virtue:

> . . . lovingly would they use wenches that cleanly were, giving them silver and other pretty toyes, which they would leave for them, sometimes in their shooes, other times in their pockets, sometimes in bright basons and other cleane vessels.[82]

And,

> . . . if the house be swept,
> And from uncleannesse kept,
> We praise the house and maid,
> And surely she is paid:
> For we do use before we go
> To drop a Tester in her shoe.[83]

This latter method of theirs provided one of the agreeable excitements of dwelling in a fairy-ridden country, and one greatly lamented when the fairies vanished:

> Farewell rewards and Faeries,
> Good houswives now may say,
> For now foule slutts in daries
> Doe fare as well as they.

[81] Jonson, Gifford ed., *Alchemist,* I, 1.

[82] *Robin Goodfellow; his mad prankes, and merry Jests,* Hazlitt rpt., p. 176.

[83] *The Mysteries of Love & Eloquence,* attributed to Edward Phillips: "The Fairies Fegaries," rpt. DeLattre, *English Fairy Poetry,* p. 214.

And though they sweepe theyr hearths no less
Then maydes were wont to doe,
Yet who of late for cleaneliness,
Finds sixe-pence in her shoe? [84]

Of equal intensity with the fairies' passion for cleanliness was their dislike [85] of lust and lechery. For this second human frailty, they had only one method of dealing, — pinching of the severest kind. Unchastity they refused to countenance, and they took few chances of overlooking a sinner. When a human being fell into their power, he was automatically greeted by a series of pinches. In spite of all the precautions of ablutions and immaculate apparel taken by the clerk in *The Alchemist,* the fairy queen appeared to him to the accompaniment of elves' pinches.[86] And the very name fairies in the *Maydes Metamorphosis* brought forth the remark, "Oh we shall be pincht most cruelly." [87]

A similar conviction of sin must have overtaken one of the Dromios in *A Comedy of Errors,* who cried out when he thought himself in Fairyland:

O, for my beads! I cross me for a sinner.
This is the fairy land; — O, spight of spights! —
We talk with goblins, owls, and elvish sprights;
If we obey them not, this will ensue,
They'll suck our breath, or pinch us black and blue.[88]

The fairies' hatred of unchastity was noted in *The Faithful Shepherdess:*

[84] Corbet, *The Faerye's Farewell,* p. 582.

[85] The fairies' dislike of dirt and unchastity cannot be taken as a contradiction of their wicked nature, but is an illustration, like their generosity with food and riches, of the inconsistent qualities with which they were endowed in the 16th century.

[86] Jonson, Gifford ed., III, 2.

[87] II, 2.

[88] II, 2.

Then must I watch if any be
Forcing of a chastity;
If I find it, then in haste
Give my wreathed horn a blast,
And the fairies all will run,
Wildly dancing by the moon,
And will pinch him to the bone,
Till his lustful thoughts be gone,[89]

and used in *Merry Wives of Windsor* with such unmistakable intention that there seems little reason to doubt that it was Shakespeare's knowledge of the fairies' aversion to licentiousness which caused him to expose Falstaff to their mercy as the climax of the comedy. Nowhere is there a better exhibition of the fairies' attitude on the subject than in Act V, Scene 5 of the play:

QUICK. Corrupt, corrupt, and tainted in desire!
About him, fairies; sing a scornful rhyme:
And, as you trip, still pinch him to your time.

. . . .

SONG. Fye on sinful fantasy!
Fye on lust and luxury!
Lust is but a bloody fire,
Kindled with unchaste desire,
Fed in heart; whose flames aspire,
As thoughts do blow them higher and higher.
Pinch him, fairies, mutually;
Pinch him for his villainy;
Pinch him, and burn him, and turn him about,
Till candles, and star-light, and moonshine be out.[90]

[89] Fletcher, III, 1.

[90] There is some small evidence that the fairies were considered patrons of true love. Cf. *M. N. D.*, III, 2; Greene, *James the Fourth,* III, 3; Thomas Campion, *A Book of Ayres,* XIX; and *The Queenes Majesties Entertainment at Woodstocke,* pp. 110–112 ff.

However impeccable the Elizabethan manners and morals, there was little escape from the fairies' one practical joke — that of leading "poore Trauellers out of their way notoriously." [91] This misadventure seems to have been most frequent, judging from the number of times it is referred to, as in *The Pilgrim:*

> I am founder'd, melted; some fairy thing or other
> Has led me dancing; the devil has haunted me
> I' th' likeness of a voice; [92]

or in *If You Know Not Me, You Know No Bodie,* The Second Part:

> HOBSON. Mother a me, what a thick mist is here?
> I walked abroad to take the mornings aire,
> And I am out of knowledge. . . .
>
> . . . .
>
> Ha, ha! I smile at my owne foolery.
> Now I remember mine old grandmother
> Would talk of fairies and hobgoblins,
> That would lead milkmaids ouer hedge and ditch,
> Make them milk their neighbours kine; [93]

or in Clobery's *Divine Glimpses of a Maiden Muse:*

> Thy fairie elves, who thee mislead with stories
> Into the mire, then at thy folly smile,
> Yea, clap their hands for joy; [94]

and the number of times it is represented on the stage, as

[91] Nashe, *Terr. of the Night,* Vol. I, p. 347.

[92] Fletcher, III, 1.

[93] Thomas Heywood, Pearson rpt., 1874, pp. 302–303.

[94] 1659 ed., p. 73: rpt. in Halliwell, *Illustrations of the Fairy Mythology of A Midsummer Night's Dream,* Shak. Soc., 1845, p. xvii.

in *A Midsummer Night's Dream,*[95] *The Tempest,*[96] and *The Valiant Welshman.*[97]

According to Chlorin in *The Faithful Shepherdess,* by one way only could a mortal be safe from the fairies' misleading:

> Yet I have heard (my mother told it me,
> And now I do believe it) if I keep
> My virgin flower uncropt, pure, chaste, and fair,
> No goblin, wood-god, fairy, elfe, or fiend,
> Satyr, or other power that haunts the groves,
> Shall hurt my body, or by vain illusion
> Draw me to wander after idle fires;
> Or voices calling me in dead of night,
> To make me follow, and so tole me on
> Through mire and standing pools, to find my ruin.[98]

Though the fairies were tyrannical and dangerous beings, even in their jokes, it must be counted to their credit that "They do not all the Harme which appearingly they have Power to do."[99] It was easily within their power to seize upon mortals and carry them away. Yet the number of such seizures on record is comparatively few, in spite of the fact that *A Discourse concerning Devils and Spirits* of 1665 insisted that

> . . . many such have been taken away by the sayd Spirits, for a fortnight, or a month together, being carryed with them in Chariots through the Air, over Hills, and Dales, Rocks and Precipices, till at last they have been found lying in some Meddow or Mountain

[95] III, 2.

[96] IV, 1.

[97] II, 5. Cf. also Wm. Browne, *Brit. Pastorals,* Vol. I, Book I, Song 4; *The Little French Lawyer,* II, 3; Ben Jonson, *The Satyr,* Morley ed., p. 409; and *Wit at Several Weapons,* II, 2.

[98] Fletcher, I, 1. Cf. also Milton, *Comus,* ll. 432–438.

[99] Kirk, *Sec. Comm.,* p. 16.

bereaved of their sences, and commonly of one of their Members to boot.[100]

They were able to blast human beings with disease and deformity and to spoil their cattle and blight their crops. They could forespeak mortals into a dazed state, as was apprehended in *Gammer Gurtons Nedle,*[101] or reduce them to a speechlessness incurable by mortal aid, as appeared in the trials for witchcraft, but none of these crimes was overwhelmingly frequent.[102]

Yet had they exercised all their powers for evil consistently and daily, it can be safely assumed that few Elizabethans would have welcomed their banishment from England, for, with all the terrors of their regime, the presence of the fairies added immeasurably to the joys of living.

No one needed to be ill who was in their favor, since the race to which the fairies belonged could " cause and cure most diseases," and knew " the virtues of herbs, plants, stones, minerals, &c. of all creatures, birds, beasts, the four elements, stars, planets " and could " aptly apply and make use of them." [103]

Oberon, Titania, and the fairy train of *A Midsummer Night's Dream* were not acting, therefore, under the inspiration of a poetic imagination when they made use of herbs to cause love and to satisfy it. They were fol-

[100] Pages 510–511.

[101] Brett-Smith ed., 1920, I, 2:

" By gogs soule there they syt as still as stones in the streite
As though they had ben takẽ with fairies or els wt some il sprite "

[102] See *Promptorium Parvulorum,* Camden Soc. ed., p. 138, note 1; Lupton, *Thousand Notable Things,* p. 157; Pitcairn, *Crim. Trials,* Vol. I, pt. 2, pp. 51 & 53, and Gen. App. p. 607; Cockayne, *Leechdoms, Wortcunning, and Star-Craft of Early England,* 1864; Pennant, *Tour of Scotland,* rpt. in J. Pinkerton, *Voyages and Travels,* Vol. III, p. 51; Camden, *Britannia,* Holland trans., p. 147; *Richard III,* I, 3.

[103] Burton, *Anat, of Mel.,* Vol. I, p. 212.

lowing a traditional characteristic of their race which every mortal knew and some favored ones could vouch for, from actual experience — Alesoun Peirsoun, 1588, for instance, who had seen "the guid nychtbouris mak thair sawis, with panis and fyris" and knew "that thay gadderit thair herbis, before the sone rysing, as scho did,"[104] when Shakespeare was but new to poetry.

The cramps and ague, which were caused by the elves and spirits in *The Tempest,* were only a few of the diseases which they had the power of initiating and of relieving. Andro Man, promised by the Quene of Elphen that he "suld help and cuir all sort of seikness, except stand deid," healed the "falling seiknes, barne bed, and all sort of vther seiknes that ever fell to man or beast," "be baptizing thame, reabling thame in the auld corunschbald, and stricking of the gudis on the face, with ane foull in thy hand, and be saying thir words, Gif thow will leiff, leiff, and gif thow will die, die; with sindrie vther orisonis, sic as of Sanct Johne, and of the thrie sillie brethrene, . . . and be geving of blak woll and salt as a remeid for all diseases."[105]

And there was "white powder," "2 or 3 grains" of which, given "to any that were sick" "would heal them,"[106] to be had for the mere going to the fairy hill and knocking; or a "stone that had sundrie vertues"[107] given by the queen of the fairies.

[104] Pitcairn, *Crim. Trials,* Vol. I, pt. 2, p. 163.

[105] *Spald. Club Misc.,* Vol. I, pp. 119–120.

[106] Webster, *Disp. of Sup. Witch.,* p. 301.

[107] James VI of Scotland, *Daemon.,* p. 132. Cf. also Sir Thomas Browne, *Pseudodoxia Epidemica,* Wilkin ed., 1835, p. 356: "Terrible apprehensions, and answerable unto their names, are raised of fairy stones and elve's spurs, found commonly with us in stone, chalk, and marl-pits, which, notwithstanding, are no more than echinometrites, and belemnites, the sea hedge-hog, and the dart-stone, . . . Common opinion commendeth them for the stone, but are most practically used against films in horses' eyes."

More desirable than the possession of the power to heal diseases was the knowledge of the future to be gained by the fairies; ". . . they can foretell future events, and do many strange miracles"[108] having been "indued with knowledge of prophesie by their necromanticall science, bicause euerie thing came to passe as they had spoken."[109]

It was this knowledge which Oberon made use of in determining the future of Huon of Burdeux, which caused him many a "sore wepynge" because he knew "for certen" that Huon had "so myche to suffer/ that therein is none humayne tonge can reherse it."[110] It was this knowledge, too, which Mab possessed, according to *The Satyr:*

> She can start our Franklin's daughters
> In their sleep with shrieks and laughters;
> And on sweet St. Anna's night
> Feed them with a promised sight,
> Some of husbands, some of lovers,
> Which an empty dream discovers.[111]

In Camden's *Britannia,* the future outcome of the disease called Esane was determined by the foreknowledge of the fairies,[112] and, in Sir John Beaumont's *An Historical, Physiological and Theological Treatise of Spirits, Apparitions, Witchcrafts, and other Magical Practices,* a woman who "would generally predict" the death or recovery of "any Person of the Neighbourhood,"

> being ask'd by the Judge, how she came by her knowledge, as to the Death or Recovery of Persons sick; she told him, she could

[108] Burton, *Anat. of Mel.,* Vol. I, p. 208.

[109] *Shak. Holinshed,* p. 24.

[110] *Huon of Burdeux,* E. E. T. S. ed., Vol. I, pt. I, p. 154.

[111] Jonson, Morley ed., p. 410.

[112] Ireland, Holland trans., p. 147.

give no other Account of it, but that when any Person was sick, and she had a Mind to know the Issue, a Jury of Fairies came to her in the Night time, who consider'd of the Matter; and if afterwards they look'd cheerful, the Party would recover; if they look'd sad, he would die.[113]

Sometimes, if the proper procedure was followed, mortals were invested by the fairies with second sight,[114] as was the case with William Lilly, who stated that "Those glorious creatures, if well commanded, and well observed, do teach the master anything he desires";[115] or Christian Lewingstoun, 1597, who possessed foreknowledge of events, and "affermit that hir dochter was tane away with the Farie-folk . . . and that all the knawlege scho had was be hir dochter, wha met with the Fairie";[116] or Bessie Dunlop, 1576, who "culd tell diuerse persounes of thingis thai tynt, or wer stollin away, or help seik persounes," because of her acquaintance with the "gude wychtis that wynnit in the Court of

[113] Pages 104–105.

[114] See J. G. Dalyell, *The Darker Superstitions of Scotland,* 1834, p. 470: ". . . for this faculty, [second sight] . . . came also from supernatural beings,—not so often indeed, in so far as may be collected, because those investigating its later subsistence, seldom advert to such a mode of reception. They are engaged chiefly in describing its extent and consequences. On a question involving life and death, it was alleged against Isobel Sinclair, that during seven years, 'sex times at the reathes of the year, shoe hath bein controlled with the Phairie; and that be thame, shoe hath the second sight: quhairby shoe will know giff thair be any fey bodie in the hous.' (Trial of Issobell Sinclair, ult. Feb. 1633.) The same delinquent's skill in the 'secund sicht' is referred to after her execution, in the trial of Bessie Skebister, whose conviction followed in three weeks. Rec. Ork. f. 86."

[115] *Life and Times,* p. 98.

[116] Pitcairn, *Crim. Trials,* Vol. II, pp. 25–26.

Elfame," [117] as could many of the witches, burned and unburned, in the land.

According to Aubrey's *Miscellanies,*

They generally term this second-sight in Irish Taishitaraughk, and such as have it Taishatrin, from Taish, which is properly a shadowy substance, or such naughty, and imperceptible thing, as can only, or rather scarcely be discerned by the eye; but not caught by the hands: for which they assigned it to Bugles or Ghosts, so that Taishtar, is as much as one that converses with ghosts or spirits, or as they commonly call them, the Fairies or Fairy-Folks.[118]

And they come by it, "Some say by compact with the Devil; some say by converse with those daemons, we call fairies." [119]

But all gifts of the fairies pale into insignificance before the good fortune which they connoted, for "they must be bountifull." [120] There was no need for the common folk to sail the Spanish main or to search for diamonds in New Albion. Every mysterious bundle, by rock or cavern in England, held untold possibilities of a fortune from the fairies, and every waking morning, the excitement of finding shining sixpence pieces in one's shoes.[121]

The mere number of morning testers of "white fairie money, that was all Mill money," [122] must have mounted high. History does not make clear whether these sixpences were an every morning affair or one reserved only for special occasions, but there is reason to believe that the fairies were generous each morning as it rolled round.

[117] *Ibid.,* Vol. I, pt. 2, pp. 51, 53.

[118] Page 192.

[119] *Ibid.,* p. 178. Cf. also Kirk, *Sec. Comm.,* pp. 26–28.

[120] *Cole-Orton,* p. 330.

[121] *The Wisdome of Doctor Dodypoll,* Act I.

[122] *Cole-Orton,* p. 330.

And when one's shoes failed to yield treasure, there were still the basins and cooking vessels to be investigated, and, finally, the bottom of the pail in which the fairies had washed themselves the night before.[123]

There was, too, the chance of being

> . . . of the only best complexion,
> The queen of Fairy loves,[124]

and of having the opportunity to pay court to her, when she might promise to leave the fortunate courtier

> . . . three or four hundred chests of treasure,
> And some twelve thousand acres of fairy land.[125]

If the position of courtier to Her Fairy Majesty was unavailable, one could always " sit naked in a garden a whole cold frostie winters night, with a pot of earth in her lap . . . that ere morning the queene of fayries should turne it into gold." [126]

Each shepherd expected gifts at every turn of the field, though he knew also of the proviso that went with the fairy bounty:

> . . . . if wee impart
> What golden rings
> The Fairie brings,
> Wee loose the Iem: nor will they giue vs more,[127]

> . . . . 'tis Fairies' Treasure;
> Which, but reveal'd, brings on the Blabber's Ruin.[128]

Even in prison, there was still a possibility of good for-

[123] Wm. Browne, *Brit. Pastorals,* Vol. I, p. 67.

[124] Jonson, Gifford ed., *Alchemist,* I, 1.

[125] *Ibid.,* V, 2.

[126] *Cozenages of the Wests,* Hazlitt rpt., p. 229.

[127] Wm. Browne, *Shep. Pipe,* Seventh Eglogve, Vol. II, p. 234.

[128] Massinger, *Fatal Dowry,* IV, 1.

tune, for the fairies haunted their favorites there, leaving unexpected gifts by which they could be recognized. Posthumus, in *Cymbeline,* was well aware of this trait, and accordingly attributed the book of prophecies which he found in his cell to the fairies who "haunt this ground." [129]

The fairies did not confine themselves to money or treasure, but bestowed jewels which they could "fetch . . . from the deep," [130] upon their protegés to such an extent that the recipients sometimes, but most infrequently, complained: ". . . they haunt me like fairies, and give me jewels here"; [131] and any jewels strangely found were fairy donations, for "surely the heauens haue rained thee jewels . . . or else doe Fairies haunt this holy greene." [132]

It was the fairies' well-known generosity with precious stones and other presents that made them so invaluable to generous but shrewd courtiers who wished to present gifts to Elizabeth and her successor without laying themselves liable to a suspicion of bribery. Again and again the fairies were impersonated to make the presentation of a diamond or a ruby for an aspiring mortal, and many a progress or a masque became "a shew representing the Phayries (as well as might be) . . . in the whiche shew, a rich jewell was presented to the Queenes Highnesse," [133] as at Hengrave Hall, or at Apthorpe,[134] or Quarrendon,[135] or as at Woodstocke when "a goune for

[129] V, 4.

[130] *M. N. D.*, III, 1.

[131] Jonson, *The Silent Woman,* Gifford ed., 1846, V, 1.

[132] Chapman, *An Humerous dayes Myrth,* Pearson ed., Vol. I, p. 57.

[133] Nichols, *Prog. of Eliz.*, Vol. II, p. 215.

[134] Jonson, Morley ed., *The Satyr.*

[135] See *The Complete Works of John Lyly,* Bond ed., 1902, Vol. I, p. 453 ff.

her Maiestie of greate price, whereon the imbroderer had bestowed the summe of his conning" was given to Elizabeth by the Queen of the Fayry.[136]

The fairies were so associated with treasure that only to speak of them provoked the sound of money. According to *Saducismus Triumphatus,*

About the latter end of Decemb. 1662. the Drummings were less frequent, and then they heard a noise like the gingling of Money, occasioned, as it was thought, by somewhat Mr. Mompesson's Mother had spoken the day before to a Neighbour, who talkt of Fayries leaving Money, viz. That she should like it well, if it would leave them some to make amends for their trouble. The night after the speaking of which, there was a great chinking of Money over all the House.[137]

Then there was treasure to be found:

These Spirits likewise haue the pow'r to show
Treasures that haue been buried long below:
By Gods permission, all the veins conceald,
Of gold or siluer, are to them reueald.
Of Vnions, Stones, and Gems esteemed high,
These know the place and beds wherein they ly;
Nay ev'ry casket and rich cabinet
Of that vnrifled rocke wherein th' are set.[138]

Any forest, therefore, could be the highway of fairies carrying a treasure trove, and any unexplored cavern in the mountain a mine worked by them. One had only to follow his nose through a sudden crevice in the hillside to discover the fairies enjoying the treasures of the earth,

[136] Publns. of Mod. Lang. Assn., Vol. 26, 1911, p. 99. Attention has already been called to the fact that the fairies were introduced in royal pageants and progresses only in the exercise of their best qualities, especially that of generosity to their favorites.

[137] Joseph Glanvil, London, 1681 ed., Part II, p. 95.

[138] Heywood, *Hierarchie,* p. 570.

and, as likely as not, if he behaved himself according to the rules of fairy etiquette, which he well knew, he would be presented with pieces of gold which multiplied, or with other treasures.

So many opportunities for a fairy fortune had their disadvantages, however, for the credulous Elizabethan was sometimes gulled into believing that impostors were the king and queen of fairies, as happened in *The severall notorious and lewd Cousonages of John West and Alice West,* 1613,[139] by which Thomas Moore and his wife, especially, were ruined. Here the impostor

> takes upon her to bee familiarly acquainted with the king and queene of fairies, two that had in their power the command of inestimable treasure; and . . . communicates [to her victims] a strange revelation, how that the fayrie king and queene had appeared to her in a vision, saying they had a purpose to bestow great summes of gold upon this man and this woman, which . . . if it were revealed to any save them three whom it did essentially concerne, they should not onely hazard their good fortune, but incurre the danger of the fayries, and so consequently be open to great mishapes, and fearefull disasters.
>
> . . . money to performe the due rites of sacrifice to his great patron, the king of fayries [was obtained repeatedly from Thomas Moore], . . . but all this was no charges in regard it should be returned ten-fold; therefore the more they bestowed, the more would be their gaines, in so much that their covetous simplicity so overswayed their understanding, that at several times this Circe had enchanted from them the sum of 40 pounds: and to encourage them the further, they brought him into a vault, where they shewed him two attired like the king and queene of fayries, and by them elves and goblings, and in the same place an infinite company of bags, and upon them written, "This is for Thomas Moore," "This is for his wife."[140]

[139] Hazlitt rpt., pp. 223–238.

[140] *Ibid.*, pp. 226–227.

In contradistinction to these doleful victims of imposture can be set the story of the shepherd, in *The Winter's Tale,* who went forth grumbling to round up his scattered sheep and found himself possessed of a fortune:

> SHEP. Heavy matters! heavy matters! but look thee here, boy. . . . Here's a sight for thee; look thee, a bearing-cloth for a squire's child! Look thee here; take up, take up, boy; open't. So, let's see; It was told me, I should be rich by the fairies: this is some changeling:— open't: What's within, boy?
>
> CLO. You're a made old man; if the sins of your youth are forgiven you, you're well to live. Gold! all gold!
>
> SHEP. This is fairy gold, boy, and 'twill prove so: up with it, keep it close; home, home, the next way. We are lucky, boy; and to be so still, requires nothing but secrecy.— Let my sheep go;— Come, good boy, the next way home.
>
> . . . .
>
> 'Tis a lucky day, boy; and we'll do good deeds on't.[141]

Such was the "world of hel-worke, deuil-worke, and Elue worke"[142] which was "walking amongst" the Elizabethans. Nowhere, as has been said in Chapter I, are most of its features better summed up than in the statement of Robert Burton:

> Some put our Fairies into this rank, which have been in former times adored with much superstition, with sweeping their houses, and setting of a pail of clean water, good victuals, and the like, and then they should not be pinched, but find money in their shoes, and be fortunate in their enterprizes.[143]

And nowhere are the delights of the fairy regime better

[141] III, 3.
[142] Harsnet, *Declaration,* p. 134.
[143] *Anat. of Mel.,* Vol. I, pp. 219–220.

expressed than in the words of a citizeness of *Eastward Hoe:*

GYR. . . . Good Lord, that there are no Faires now a daies, Syn. SYN. Why Madame?

GYR. To doe Miracles, and bring Ladies money. Sure, if wee lay in a cleanly house, they would haunt it, Synne? Ile trie. Ile sweepe the Chamber soone at night, & set a dish of water o' the Hearth. A Fayrie may come, and bring a Pearle, or a Diamond. We do not know Synne? Or, there may be a pot of Gold hid o' the back-side, if we had tooles to digge for't? why may not we two rise earely i'the morning (Synne) afore any bodie is vp, and find a Iewell, i'the streetes, worth a 100 li? . . . for God-sake Syn, let's rise to morrow by breake of day, and see.[144]

[144] *Eastward Hoe*, 1605, Students' Facsimile ed., 1914, IV, 1.

Chapter IV

THE CHANGELING AND THE WITCH

The most important feature of the fairies' earthly activities in the 16th century, as in all the centuries of their existence, was their abduction of human beings.

During the preceding periods, for the most part, according to romance, ballad and folk-tale, men had disappeared with their fairy mistresses, or been forcibly abducted by the elf queen or one of her company. And the king of fairies and his rout had enchanted away noble ladies who were so unwary as to put themselves under the fairies' power. Most of these abductions, however, had proceeded from the fancy or desire of the queen or king of fairies or one of their train, for an especial mortal, or from the love and desire of a mortal for a fairy knight or lady.[1] In the 16th century, the desire for human victims was regarded as characteristic of the whole race of fairies and would seem to have been motivated by necessity rather than by romantic attachment. And the abduction of mortals was accomplished by means of the witch and the changeling.

The reason for the fairies' abduction of mortals has never been definitely settled. According to the confession of Alesoun Peirsoun, in 1588:

. . . quhene we heir the quhirll-wind blaw in the sey, thay wilbe commounelie with itt, or cumand sone thaireftir; than Mr Williame will cum before and tell hir, and bid hir keip hir and sane hir,

[1] In discussing the fairies' abduction of mortals, the question of bewitchment is not taken into account.

that scho be nocht tane away with thame agane; for the teynd of thame gais ewerie ȝeir to hell.[2]

It would seem, from this account, that mortals were used by the fairies to pay their tribute to the devil, an assumption which is warranted also by a passage in *The Romance and Prophecies of Thomas of Erceldoune:*

> Forsoth, Thomas, I wolle the tell,
> thou hast been her iij yere and More;
> And here þou may no lenger dwell,
> I shall the tell A skele wherefore;
> To morowe, a fowle fend of hell,
> A Mongis this folke shall chese his fe,
> And for thou arte long man and hende,
> I lewe wele, he wyll haue þe,[3]

and by a similar statement in the ballad of *Young Tamlane:*

> Then would I never tire, Janet,
> In Elfish land to dwell,
> But aye, at every seven years,
> They pay the teind to hell;
> And I am sae fat and fair of flesh,
> I fear 't will be mysell.[4]

[2] Pitcairn, *Crim. Trials,* Vol. I, pt. 2, p. 164.

[3] E. E. T. S. ed., 1875, Lansdowne MS. (dated before 1500), p. 17.

[4] *The English and Scottish Popular Ballads,* Child ed., 1882–1898, Vol. I, p. 354, No. 39, "The Young Tamlane," Stanza 32. This, as Sir Walter Scott states, in *The Minstrelsy of the Scottish Border,* 1803, Vol. II, p. 237, was "the popular reason assigned for the desire of the fairies to abstract young children, as substitutes for themselves in this dreadful tribute." Cf. also E. S. Hartland, *The Science of Fairy Tales,* 1891, Chap. V; Grimm, *Teutonic Mythology,* Stallybrass trans., 1883, Vol. II, p. 468; and *The English and Scottish*

Beyond these few references, no reason for the fairies' abductions of mortals in the 16th century, as far as can be ascertained, is to be found.

The origins assigned them, however, might account for the belief in their seizure of human beings. As fallen angels, they would entice mortals to sin and to ruin. As ghosts of the dead, they would endeavor to take away the living. As wicked spirits, and as familiar spirits of the devil, they would seek to fill Hell with human souls. And as the British equivalents of nymphs, lamiae, and strygia, they had inherited the tradition of devouring and destroying youths and young children.

The changeling, in particular, seems to have been peculiar to the 16th-century fairies in England. Before 1500 they had bewitched babies and had caused them to become diseased or to die, which is a practice they continued as long as they existed.[5] But, as far as I can discover there are no records in England until the middle of the 16th century, of the exchange of fairy children for mortal offspring which resulted in the disappearance of the human infant and the appearance of a strange and supernatural baby in its stead.

Popular Ballads, Child ed., Vol. I, p. 344, "Young Tom Line," Glenriddell MS., Vol. XI, No. 17, 1791:

> "The Queen of Fairies she came by,
> Took me wi her to dwell,
> Evn where she has a pleasant land
> For those that in it dwell,
> But at the end o seven years,
> They pay their teind to hell."

[5] Witness the fictitious child of Mak and his wife in the Secunda Pastorum of the *Towneley Cycle,* whose true sheep form and figure were accounted for by attribution to fore-speaking by an elf; or the children who were bewitched and "elf grippit" in England and Scotland in the late 17th and 18th centuries. Bewitchment is very different, however, from being exchanged as a changeling.

In the earlier dictionaries, as the *Vulgaria* of Horman,[6] and the *Bibliotheca Eliotae,* reference is made to the fact that the fairies changed children, either altering their "fauour" or "the forme of theym: whyche children be afterwarde called elfes, or taken with the fayrie."[7] These, however, were not changelings.

The true changeling, according to popular belief, was a fairy baby who was exchanged for a human child. The following passage from the play of *Misogonus,* in which one of the earliest and fullest references to fairy changelings is to be found, defines both the process of abduction and the changeling:

CA. To beare witnes yow ar now both toward your landlord trottinge
that his wife of tow children at once [w]as brought to bede
but take hede what yow doe lest yow dame your selves quite
for ye one was not a christen child as yow thought it to be
but a certaine ferye there did dasill yowr sighte
& laid hir changlinge in the infantes cradell trwlye

Hopinge therby your mistrisse child to haue gott
and to leaue hir changlinge there in the stead
which when she saw in a weke she coud nott
she fetcht it away when yow thought it were dede

An overwhart neighboure to of yours now alate
tels him whether twas sent as though trwe it had ben.
but sheis a gayte yow knowe well & a very make . . .
and the fery from that day to this was near se . . .

[6] "The fayre hath chaunged my chylde. Strix, vel lamia pro meo suum paruulum, supposuit." Cf. *Cath. Anglicum,* note p. 113.

[7] Lamiae. L ante A. Florio also refers to "Strega . . . a hag or fairie such as our elders thought to change the fauour of children." *A Worlde of Wordes,* p. 401.

But take yow hede both I giue yow good warnin . . .
least yow be stricken hereby either lame or de . . .
[Yf you] will by cunieratione I will shewe [you] . . .[8]
. . . .

The same definition is given by Puttenham in *The Arte of English Poesie:*

The Greekes call this figure (Hipallage) the Latins Submutatio, we in our vulgar may call him the (vnderchange) but I had rather haue him called the (Changeling) nothing at all sweruing from his originall, and much more aptly to the purpose, and pleasanter to beare in memory: specially for your Ladies and pretie mistresses in Court, for whose learning I write, because it is a terme often in their mouthes, and alluding to the opinion of Nurses, who are wont to say, that the Fayries vse to steale the fairest children out of their cradles, and put other ill fauoured in their places, which they called changelings, or Elfs: so, if ye mark, doeth our Poet, or maker play with his wordes, vsing a wrong construction for a right, and an absurd for a sensible, by manner of exchange.[9]

The definition of Spenser, in the *Faerie Queene,*[10] is

[8] *Early Plays from the Italian,* Bond ed., 1911, III, 3, dated between 1560 and 1577. For discussion of date, see E. K. Chambers, *Eliz. Stage,* Vol. IV, p. 31. This is the earliest account I have found of the fairy changeling. *The New English Dictionary* gives 1561 (cf. John Calvin, *The Institutions of Christian Religion,* trans. by Thos. Norton, 1611 ed., IV, 13) as the date of the first reference to the word changeling used as one person exchanged for another.

[9] Arber rpt., 1869, pp. 183–184.

[10] Book I, Canto X, Stanza LXV. Cf. also Ben Jonson, *The Satyr,* Morley ed.; Warner, *Albions England,* quarto 1612, Chap. 91; Butler, *Hudibras,* Bohn ed., 1859, Part III, Canto 1, ll. 953–954; The Duchess of Newcastle, *Poems and Fancies,* 1653 ed., p. 154; Nashe, *Strange Newes of the Intercepting Certaine Letters,* McKerrow ed., 1904–1910, Vol. I, p. 317; [J. Farewell], *Irish Hudibras,* p. 122; *The Pranks of Puck,* Halliwell rpt., p. 165; and Thoms, *Early English Prose Romances,* 1907: *The pleasant historie of Tom a Lincolne,* p. 608.

equally as explicit:

> For well I wote, thou springst from ancient race
> Of Saxon kinges, that have with mightie hand
> And many bloody battailes fought in place
> High reard their royall throne in Britane land,
> And vanquisht them, unable to withstand:
> From thence a Faery thee unweeting reft,
> There as thou slepst in tender swadling band,
> And her base Elfin brood there for thee left:
> Such men do chaungelings call, so chaungd by Faeries theft.

The idea of the exchange of a fairy child for a mortal child, as Puttenham reminded his readers, was not the invention of the literary imagination, but was an article of faith, common to the English folk of the period, and one which prevailed until the 18th century and, in some parts of Great Britain, well into the 19th.[11]

Reginald Scot enumerates changelings among the terrors of the night in 1584,[12] and Edward Fairfax, in 1621, inveighs against the "strange follies, rooted in the opinion of the vulgar, concerning . . . the changing of infants in their cradles."[13] Hobbes's *Leviathan*, of 1651, mentions as a particular characteristic of the fairies that they "are said to take young Children out of their

[11] Hartland, in *The Science of Fairy Tales,* p. 121, cites the case of two women who were reported as having been arrested May, 1884, at Clonmel, charged with cruelly ill-treating a child three years old, who had not the use of his limbs. They fancied that the child was a changeling and during its mother's absence placed the naked child on a hot shovel under the impression that this would break the charm.

In Tiree, in 1878, a child was exposed on the shore for several hours by its mother, who thought it was a changeling. J. Sands, *Curious Superstitions in Tiree,* The Celtic Magazine, Inverness, VIII (1883), p. 253.

[12] *Disc. of Witch.,* 1651 ed., p. 113.

[13] *Disc. of Witch.,* Preface to Reader, p. 17.

Cradles, and to change them into Naturall Fools, which Common people do therefore call Elves."[14] "Besides, it is credibly affirmed," states *A Discourse concerning Devils and Spirits,* 1665, "and beleev'd by many, That such as are real Changlings, or Lunaticks, have been brought by such Spirits and Hobgoblins, the true Child being taken away by them in the place whereof such are left."[15] According to Waldron, "The old story of infants being changed in their cradles is here in such credit, that mothers are in continual terror at the thoughts of it."[16] I was prevailed upon myself to go and see a child," he continues, "who, they told me, was one of these changelings, and indeed must own was not a little surprized, as well as shocked at the sight."[17]

In Scotland, according to traditional tales and literary records, the fairies were more anxious to obtain mortal nurses for their own children, or mortal children for their offspring, than they were to make any exchange.

According to *Secret Commonwealth* (1691):

Women are yet alive who tell they were taken away when in Childbed to nurse Fairie Children, a lingering voracious Image of their (them?) being left in their place, (like their Reflexion in a Mirrour,) which (as if it were some insatiable Spirit in ane assumed Bodie) made first semblance to devour the Meats that it cunningly carried by, and then left the Carcase as if it expired and departed thence by a naturall and common Death. The Child, and Fire, with Food and other Necessaries, are set before the Nurse how soon she enters; but she nather perceaves any Passage out, nor sees what those People doe in other Rooms of the Lodging.

[14] Page 545.

[15] Page 510.

[16] *Isle of Man,* p. 29.

[17] *Ibid.,* p. 31.

When the Child is wained, the Nurse dies, or is conveyed back, or gets it to her choice to stay there.[18]

Also, the fairies

transgress and commit Acts of Injustice, and Sin, by what is above said, as to their stealling of Nurses to their Children, and that other sort of Plaginism in catching our Children away, (may seem to heir some Estate in those invisible Dominions,) which never returne.[19]

There was no mistaking a fairy changeling. Instead of possessing the usual plumpness and roundness of ordinary babies, the changeling was inordinately thin, "a poor, lean, withered deformed creature." [20] Its emaciation, in fact, reached the point of translucency as in *The Seuen deadly Sinnes of London,* where the coach of candle light is described as "made all of Horne, shauen as thin as Changelings are." [21]

In addition to this abnormal thinness, the changeling was, in most cases, so grossly ill-favored that hideousness was practically its chief attribute, as Puttenham states,[22] and as Ben Jonson mentions in *Underwoods:*

> Be then content, your daughters and your wives,
> If they be fair and worth it, have their lives
> Made longer by our praises: or, if not,
> Wish you had foul ones, and deformed got,

[18] Kirk, pp. 12–13. Cf. also Ramsay, *The Gentle Shepherd,* 1763, II, 3:

> "When last the Wind made Glaud a roofless Barn,
> When last the Burn bore down my Mither's Yarn,
> When Brawny Elf-shot never mair came Hame;
> When Tibby kirn'd and there nae Butter came;
> When Bessy Freetock's chuffy-cheeked Wean
> To a Fairy turn'd, and cou'dna stand its lane;"

[19] Kirk, *Sec. Comm.,* p. 25. [20] Waldron, *Isle of Man,* p. 29.

[21] Dekker, *Non-Dramatic Works,* Grosart ed., 1884–1886, Vol. II, p. 47. [22] *The Arte of English Poesie,* p. 184.

Curst in their cradles, or there chang'd by elves,
So to be sure you do enjoy, yourselves.[23]

What appearance the fairy changeling made under the combined curse of emaciation and ugliness can be seen from the following description in *The Devil's Law-Case:*

CONTIL. The midwife straight howls out, there was no hope
Of the infant's life; swaddles it in a flay'd lambskin,
As a bird hatch'd too early; makes it up
With three quarters of a face, that made it look
Like a changeling; cries out to Romelio
To have it christen'd, lest it should depart
Without that it came for.[24]

The form and figure of the changeling was as unprepossessing as its face. That member of the race seen by Waldron,

tho' between five and six years old, and seemingly healthy, . . . was so far from being able to walk, or stand, that he could not so much as move any one joint: his limbs were vastly long for his age, but smaller than an infant's of six months.[25]

The same infirmity was characteristic of the changeling of *A Pleasant Treatise of Witches,* 1673, for, "after some years, it could neither speak nor go," and its mother "was feign to carry it, with much trouble, in her arms." [26]

Finally, changelings were distinguished by their lack of brains, being "Naturall Fools," [27] "deformes & stupidos," [28] "commonly half out of their wits, and given

[23] Gifford ed., 1846, LX: *An Elegy,* p. 706.

[24] John Webster, Dyce ed., 1859, IV, 2.

[25] *Isle of Man,* p. 29.

[26] Hazlitt rpt., pp. 407–408.

[27] Hobbes, *Leviathan,* p. 545.

[28] Skinner, *Etymologicon Linguae Anglicanae* (under *Elf*): ". . . infantes lepidos & formosos è unis surripiunt, iisque foedos, deformes & stupidos substituunt, nobis ob eam rationem changelings."

to many Antick practices, and extravagant fancies";[29] or like Anne Jefferies, whom "the Extremity of her Sickness, and the long Continuance of her Distemper, had almost perfectly moped . . . so that she became even as a Changeling."[30]

Indeed, so lacking were they in intelligence that the word itself later took on a secondary meaning of half-witted person, as, for instance, in *The Changeling;*[31] *Anything for A Quiet Life;*[32] *The Diary of Samuel Pepys.*[33]

[29] *Dis. conc. D. & S.*, p. 510.

[30] J. Morgan, *Phoenix Brit.*, p. 547.

[31] Thomas Middleton, Bullen ed., 1885, Vol. VI, 2.

[32] *Ibid.*, Vol. V, II, 1.

[33] December 28, 1667: Wheatley ed., 1893–1898. Fable III, "The Mother, the Nurse and the Fairy," of John Gay, Underhill ed., 1893, Vol. II, pp. 56–57, is significant in this connection:

"Give me a son. The blessing sent,
Were ever parents more content?
How partial are their doting eyes!
No child is half so fair and wise.
  Waked to the morning's pleasing care,
The Mother rose, and sought her heir.
She saw the Nurse, like one possess'd,
With wringing hands, and sobbing breast;
  Sure some disaster hath befell:
Speak, Nurse; I hope the boy is well.
  Dear Madam, think not me to blame;
Invisible the Fairy came:
Your precious babe is hence convey'd,
  And in the place a changeling laid.

. . . .

See here, a shocking awkward creature,
That speaks a fool in ev'ry feature.

. . . .

  Just as she spoke, a pigmy sprite
Pops through the key-hole, swift as light;

It is interesting to observe that, in the exchange of offspring, it was the fairy child who suffered most from the transaction. He became superlatively ugly, deformed and stupid in his human estate, and was loathed and resented by his mortal mother. The human baby, on the other hand, suffered neither the disgrace of ill looks nor of idiocy. Instead, he remained beautiful and charming, fit to be chosen as the consort of a queen, as in *The Faerie Queene*,[34] and the most coveted possession of the fairy court in *A Midsummer Night's Dream*.[35]

Far from being shunned and abhorred, the mortal changeling was the object of the most affectionate care and the most untiring attention. In *The Sad Shepherd* of Ben Jonson, the fairies are pictured as carrying their changelings in their arms even when they danced.[36] The "stolen children" of the fairies of *The Faithful Shepherdess* are dipped oftentimes into a consecrated well

> . . . . . so to make them free
> From dying flesh, and dull mortality;[37]

while the "lovely boy" who was a changeling in *A Mid-*

> Perch'd on the cradle's top he stands,
> And thus her folly reprimands:
>   Whence sprung the vain conceited lie,
> That we the world with fools supply?
> What! give our sprightly race away,
> For the dull helpless sons of clay!
> Besides, by partial fondness shown,
> Like you we dote upon our own.
> Where yet was ever found a mother,
> Who'd give her booby for another?
> And should we change with human breed,
> Well might we pass for fools indeed."

[34] Spenser, Book III, Canto III, Stanza XXVI.

[35] II, 1.

[36] Gifford ed., 1846, II, 2.

[37] Fletcher, I, 2.

summer Night's Dream was attended by Titania herself, who

> Crowns him with flowers, and makes him all her joy.[38]

In spite of the loss of human children, and of the trouble and disappointment occasioned by the possession of a fairy baby, the convention of the changeling proved a valuable asset to poet and playwright, and to the common folk. Did " riot and dishonour stain the brow " of the Crown Prince, there was always the hope in the breast of the King

> . . . . that it could be prov'd,
> That some night-tripping fairy had exchang'd
> In cradle-clothes our children where they lay.[39]

Should the suspicion of illegitimacy attach to a royal princess, the child was saved from death by being left in some deserted place with gold near it, and mistaken for a changeling, as was the case with Perdita.[40]

Nor was the changeling less helpful when Elizabeth was to be complimented with a husband:

> The man, whom heavens have ordaynd to bee
> The spouse of Britomart, is Arthegall:
> He wonneth in the land of Fayeree,
> Yet is no Fary borne, ne sib at all
> To Elfes, but sprong of seed terrestriall,
> And whylome by false Faries stolne away,
> Whyles yet in infant cradle he did crall;
> Ne other to himselfe is knowne this day,
> But that he by an Elfe was gotten of a Fay.[41]

Among the English folk the changeling did yeoman service:

[38] II, I.
[39] *Henry IV,* Part I, I, I.
[40] *W. Tale,* III, 3.
[41] Spenser, *F. Q.,* Book III, Canto III, Stanza XXVI.

Thus when a Childe haps to be gott,
Which after prooues an Ideott,
When Folke perceiue it thriueth not,
The fault therein to smother:
Some silly doting brainlesse Calfe,
That vnderstands things by the halfe,
Say that the Fayrie left this Aulfe,
And tooke away the other.[42]

Should a child be missing from the cradle, the nurse, as in *The Tragedie of Dido,* could find legitimate excuse for her lack of care by blaming the fairies:

O Dido, your little sonne Ascanius
Is gone! he lay with me last night,
And in the morning he was stolne from me,
I thinke some Fairies haue beguiled me.[43]

And when a question of twins arose, which involved succession to property, the question of a changeling had only to be raised, as in *Misogonus,*[44] to cause the midwives themselves to doubt the evidence of their own eyes.[45]

Changelings, however, unlike the fairies themselves, were neither a necessary nor an inevitable evil. Their introduction into a mortal family could be prevented by proper precautions, or a reëxchange of fairy baby for human baby effected by methods known to the folk. To bring about the restitution of the mortal child, the mother

[42] Drayton, *Nimphidia,* ll. 73–80.

[43] V, 1, ll. 1620–1623. Cf. also Nathaniel Willis, *Mount Tabor,* p. 92.

[44] III, 3.

[45] Nor must it be forgotten that the fairies were believed to reward the parents upon whom the changeling was foisted, with gifts, "Making the father rich, whose child they keep." — Duchess of Newcastle, *Poems and Fancies,* p. 154. Cf. also *W. Tale,* III, 3.

should make a clear fire, sweep the hearth very clean, and place the child fast in his chair, that he might not fall before it; them break a dozen eggs, and place the four and twenty half-shells before it; then go out and listen at the door, for if the child spoke, it was certainly a changeling.

On this certainty, she "should carry it out, and leave it on the dunghill to cry, and not to pity it, till she heard its voice no more."

That this method proved efficacious can be seen, for the woman,

having done all things according to these words, heard the child say, Seven years old was I, before I came to the nurse, and four years have I lived since, and never saw so many milk-pans before. So the woman took it up, and left it upon the dunghill to cry, and not to be pitied, till at last she thought the voice went up into the air; and, coming out, found there in the stead her own natural and well-favoured child.[46]

Another practice in vogue, in Scotland, in 1703, made it incumbent upon

those who believed that their children were thus taken away, to dig a grave in the fields upon quarter-day, and there to lay the fairy skeleton till next morning; at which time the parents went to the place, where they doubted not to find their own child instead of this skeleton.[47]

If proper charms were used at a child's birth, there could be no exchange with the progeny of the fairies. Bread and cold iron, in this case, were most efficacious:

[46] *Pl. Treatise of Witches,* Hazlitt rpt., p. 408.

[47] M. Martin, "A Description of the Western Islands of Scotland," 2d ed., 1716, p. 116, rpt. in J. Pinkerton, *A Generall Collection of the Best and Most Interesting Voyages and Travels in all Parts of the World,* 1809, Vol. 3, p. 612.

Bring the holy crust of Bread,
Lay it underneath the head;
'Tis a certain Charm to keep
Hags away, while Children sleep; [48]

Let the superstitious wife
Near the childs heart lay a knife:
Point be up, and Haft be downe;
(While she gossips in the towne)
This 'mongst other mystick charms
Keeps the sleeping child from harms.[49]

According to Robert Kirk,

The Tramontains to this Day [1691] put Bread, the Bible, or a piece of Iron, in Womens Beds when travelling, to save them from being thus stollen; and they commonly report, that all uncouth, unknown Wights are terrifyed by nothing earthly so much as by cold Iron. They delyver the Reason to be that Hell lying betwixt the chill Tempests, and the Fire Brands of scalding Metals, and Iron of the North, (hence the Loadstone causes a tendency to that Point,) by ane Antipathy thereto, these odious farscenting Creatures shrug and fright at all that comes thence relating to so abhorred a Place, whence their Torment is eather begun, or feared to come hereafter.[50]

[48] Herrick, *Hesperides,* p. 284.

[49] *Ibid.*

[50] *Sec. Comm.,* pp. 13–14.

In 1703, fire was used to protect mortal babies. Cf. M. Martin, "A Description of the Western Islands of Scotland," rpt. in Pinkerton, *Voyages and Travels,* Vol. 3, p. 612:

"There is another way of the dessil, or carrying fire round about women before they are churched, after child-bearing; and it is used likewise about children until they are christened; both which are performed in the morning and at night. This is only practised now by some of the ancient midwives: I enquired their reason for this custom, which I told them was altogether unlawful; this disobliged them mightily, insomuch that they would give me no satisfaction. But others, that were of a more agreeable temper, told me that fire-round

The fairies' abduction of witches[51] was neither so universal nor so familiar a phenomenon in England as changelings, nor was the association of witches and fairies an idea original to the 16th century.[52] The Elizabethans, however, not only believed that the fairies invested wise women, witches and sorcerers with their supernatural power, but the fairies' practice of seizing mortals and making them their own by turning them into

was an effectual means to preserve both the mother and the infant from the power of evil spirits, who are ready at such times to do mischief, and sometimes carry away the infant; and when they get them once in their possession, return them poor meagre skeletons: and these infants are said to have voracious appetites, constantly craving for meat."

[51] This discussion of the connection between witches and fairies is undertaken only to show that the fairies in the 16th and 17th centuries were believed to take away mortals by converting them into witches, and the examples given are selected solely as proof of that belief. There is no attempt to give a complete or exhaustive treatment of the connection between witches and fairies.

For further discussion of the points of similarity between witches and fairies, see *Hastings Encyclopedia of Religion and Ethics,* Article on *Fairy* by J. A. MacCulloch, Vol. V, pp. 678–689; "Organisations of Witches in Great Britain," M. A. Murray, *Folk Lore,* Vol. 28, No. 3, 1917; *The Witch-Cult in Western Europe,* M. A. Murray, Oxford University Press, 1921, "The Mingling of Fairy and Witch Beliefs in the 16th & 17th Centuries in Scotland," J. A. MacCulloch, *Folk Lore,* Vol. 32, No. 4, 1921; and *Witchcraft in Old and New England,* George Lyman Kittredge, Harvard University Press, 1929. The work of Professor Kittredge appeared after this chapter had been written.

[52] Wright contends that this idea came in the 15th century: "One new circumstance was brought in with the witchcraft of the fifteenth and sixteenth centuries — the power of fairies to enter into people, and 'possess' them. It is not difficult to see whence and how this notion came, and we might point out a hundred instances of it . . ." Thomas Wright, "Essay on the National Fairy Mythology of England," Vol. I, *Essays,* p. 278.

witches was recognized by the laws of England and of Scotland, and was made a crime punishable by the death of the fairies' victims.[53]

The likeness between fairies and witches had early been recognized. In the first dictionaries of the period, it will be remembered, the same Latin terms were applied interchangeably to witches and fairies, and the same function was assigned to both.[54]

Golding's translation of Ovid's *Metamorphoses* of 1567, in Medea's invocation in Booke the Seventh, showed the connection believed to exist between them:

Ye Ayres and windes: ye Elves of Hilles, of Brookes, of Woods alone,
Of standing Lakes, and of the Night approche ye everychone.
Through helpe of whom (the crooked bankes much wondring at the thing)
I have compelled streames to run cleane backward to their spring.
By charmes I make the calme Seas rough, and make ye rough Seas plaine
And cover all the Skie with Cloudes, and chase them thence againe.
By charmes I rayse and lay the windes, and burst the Vipers jaw,
And from the bowels of the Earth both stones and trees doe drawe.
Whole woods and Forestes I remove: I make the Mountaines shake,
And even the Earth it selfe to grone and fearfully to quake.

[53] Though sorcerers and enchanters were tried in ecclesiastical and in civil courts during the 14th century, they were not regarded as witches in the technical sense of the term, as defined by H. C. Lea in *A History of the Inquisition of Spain,* 1907, Vol. IV, p. 206: "The witch has abandoned Christianity, has renounced her baptism, has worshipped Satan as her God, has surrendered herself to him, body and soul, and exists only to be his instrument in working the evil to her fellow-creatures, which he cannot accomplish without a human agent." The parliamentary statute passed 1563, and enforced, was the earliest definite legislation by Parliament against witches. Cf. Wallace Notestein, *A History of Witchcraft in England,* 1911, p. 5.

[54] See Chap. I, pp. 70–71.

I call up dead men from their graves: and thee O lightsome
Moone
I darken oft, though beaten brasse abate thy perill soone
Our Sorcerie dimmes the Morning faire, and darkes ye Sun at
Noone.
The flaming breath of firie Bulles ye quenched for my sake.
And caused there unwieldie neckes the bended yoke to take.
Among the Earthbred brothers you a mortall war did set
And brought a sleepe the Dragon fell whose eyes were never
shet.
By meanes whereof deceiving him that had the golden fleece
In charge to keepe, you sent it thence by Jason into Greece.
Now have I neede of herbes that can by vertue of their juice
To flowring prime of lustie youth old withred age reduce.[55]

The witches' derivation of power from the fairies was early a matter of record in the *Mirror for Magistrates*—the edition of 1578—in the story entitled, "How Dame Elianor Cobham Duchesse of Glocester, for practising of witchcraft and sorcery, suffred open penaunce, and after was banished the realme into the Ile of Man." The soliloquy here leaves little doubt of the evil reputation sustained by the fairies at that time.

The spitefull prieste would needes make mee a witch,
And would to God I had beene for his sake,
I would haue claw'd him where hee did not itche,
I would haue playde the lady of the lake,
And as Merline was, cloasde him in a brake,
Ye a meridian to lul him by day light,
And a night mare to ride on him by night.

The fiery feends with feuers hot and frenzy,
The ayery heggs with stench and carren sauoures,
The watry ghostes with gowtes and with dropsy,
The earthy goblines, with aches at all houres,
Furyes and fayryes, with all infernall powers,

[55] Lines 265–285 incl.

I would haue stir'd from the darke dungeon
Of hell centre, as deepe as demagorgon.[56]

By 1584, in the *Discovery of Witchcraft,* the relationship between witches and fairies was taken for granted:

What is not to be brought to passe by these incantations, if that be true which is attributed to witches? and yet they are women that never went to schoole in their lives, nor had any teachers: and therefore without art or learning; poore, and therefore not able to make any provision of metal or stones, &c. whereby to bring to passe strange matters, by natural magicke; old and stiffe, and therefore not nimble-handed to deceive your eye with legierdemaine; heavy, and commonly lame, and therefore unapt to flie in the aire; or to dance with the fairies.[57]

Camden's *Britannia* of 1586 referred to a woman skillful in curing and prophesying the outcome of the disease, Esane, who, through the fairies, was able to form a better judgment of the disorder than most physicians;[58] while George Giffard in *A Dialogue concerning Witches and Witchcrafts,* of 1593, vouched for the connection of witches and fairies:

There was another of my neighbours had his wife much troubled, and he went to her, and she told him his wife was haunted with a fairie. I cannot tell what she bad him do, but the woman is merrie at this houre. I have heard, I dare not say it is so, that she weareth about her S. Johns Gospell, or some part of it.[59]

[56] Vol. II, Stanzas 30 and 31, p. 121. Cf. also Stanza 14, pp. 115–116:

"Among which sort of those that bare most fame
There was a beldame called the witch of Ey,
Old mother Madge her neighbours did her name,
Which wrought wonders in countryes by here say,
Both feendes and fayries her charming would obay:
And dead corpsis from graue shee could vp rere,
Such an inchauntresse (as) that time had no peere."

[57] Scot, 1651 ed., p. 158. Cf. also Booke III, Chap. II.

[58] See Chap. III, p. 139; also Chap. II, p. 84.

[59] Page 10. Cf. also pp. 35 and 54.

With the accession of James the First in 1603, the recognition of the relationship between the fairies and witches became more definite and more pronounced. This may have been due to the new and sweeping law [60] which brought witchcraft into more prominence, and to the immediate publication of His Majesty's *Daemonologie* in London, in which the creation of witches by fairies was treated as a common occurrence:

PHI. But how can it be then, that sundrie Witches haue gone to death with that confession, that they haue bene transported with the Phairie to such a hill, which opening, they went in, and there saw a faire Queene, who being now lighter, gaue them a stone that had sundrie vertues, which at sundrie times hath bene produced in iudgement?

. . . .

PHI. I would know now whether these kinds of Spirits may onely appeare to Witches, or if they may also appeare to any other.

EPI. They may doe to both; to the innocent sort, either to affray them, or to seeme to be a better sort of folkes nor vncleane Spirits are; and to the Witches to be a colour of safetie for them,

[60] The law of 1603 "repealed the statute of Elizabeth's reign and provided that any one who 'shall use, practise or exercise any Invocation or Conjuration of any evill and wicked Spirit, or shall consult, covenant with, entertaine, employe, feede, or rewarde any evill and wicked Spirit to or for any intent or purpose; or take up any dead man, woman or child, . . . to be imployed or used in any manner of Witchcrafte' should suffer death as a felon. It further provided that any one who should 'take upon him or them by Witchcrafte . . . to tell or declare in what place any treasure of Golde or Silver should or might be founde . . . or where Goods or Things loste or stollen should be founde or become, or to the intent to provoke any person to unlawfull love, or wherebie any Cattell or Goods of any person shall be destroyed, wasted, or impaired, or to hurte or destroy any person in his or her bodie, although the same be not effected and done,' should for the first offence suffer one year's imprisonment with four appearances in the pillory, and for the second offence, death." Notestein, *Hist. of Witch.*, p. 103.

that ignorant Magistrates may not punish them for it, as I told euen now: But as the one sort, for being perforce troubled with them ought to be pitied, so ought the other sort (who may be discerned by their taking vpon them to prophesie by them,) that sort, I say, ought as seuerely to be punished as any other Witches, and rather the more, that they goe dissemblingly to worke.[61]

Whatever the cause, the fairies' abduction of witches was more universally recognized.

On the stage, the connection between the witches and fairies was shown. The weird sisters who had been fairies or goddesses of destiny in Shakespeare's source,[62] appeared in *Macbeth* as witches, practising all the familiar ceremonies of their profession.[63] The witches' power for evil through the aid of the fairies was shown in *The Pilgrim*[64] of Fletcher. The fact of their execution because of their seduction by Robin Goodfellow was mentioned by Ben Jonson in *The Devil is an Ass;*[65] and in *The Sad Shepherd*[66] a witch herself appeared with Puck-Hairy or Robin Goodfellow as the visible source of her power and wickedness.

In courts of justice, the stamp of legal recognition was put upon the fairies' power over witches by the execution of Joan Willimott, following her trial in 1618, and her statement:

That shee hath a Spirit which shee calleth Pretty, which was giuen vnto her by William Berry of Langholme in Rutlandshire, whom she serued three yeares; and that her Master when he gaue it vnto her, willed her to open her mouth, and hee would blow into her a

[61] Pages 132, 133.

[62] Holinshed, *Chronicles of England, Scotland and Ireland,* Vol. 5, pp. 268–269.

[63] I, 3 and IV, 1.

[64] II, 1.

[65] Gifford ed., 1846, I, 1.

[66] Jonson, Gifford ed., III, 1.

Fairy which should doe her good; and that shee opened her mouth, and he did blow into her mouth; and that presently after his blowing, there came out of her mouth a Spirit, which stood vpon the ground in the shape and forme of a Woman, which Spirit asked of her her Soule, which shee then promised vnto it, being willed therevnto by her Master.[67]

This was not the first time, however, that the fairies had been brought into court. As early as 1566, they had figured in legal records as familiar spirits in the crime of witchcraft. In *The Examination of John Walsh:*

He being demaunded how he knoweth when anye man is bewytched: He sayth that he knew it partlye by the Feries, and saith that ther be .iii. kindes of Feries, white, greene, and black. Which when he is disposed to vse, hee speaketh with them vpon hyls, where as there is great heapes of earth, as namely in Dorsetshire. And betwene the houres of .xii. and one at noone, or at mid night he vseth them.[68]

The repeated examinations of William Lilly before Parliament and the courts of England in the 17th century, took place in part because of his own belief and declaration that he owed his power to the fairies.[69] Anne Jefferies was forced to submit to numerous examinations and several months' imprisonment in "Bodmin Jayl" on account of her connection with the fairies.[70] To an association with the fairies, also, was due the trial of "a Man apprehended for suspicion of Witchcraft," mentioned by Durant Hotham, at which John Webster

[67] *A Collection of Rare and Curious Tracts, relating to Witchcraft* . . . p. 17 of "The Wonderfvl Discoverie of the Witchcrafts of Margaret and Philip Flower . . ."

[68] Page 240. Professor Kittredge cites an earlier case of the same kind — that of Joan Tyrrye, 1555. Cf. *Witchcraft in Old and New England,* p. 254. Cf. also *Ibid.,* pp. 145 and 206.

[69] *Life and Times,* p. 98.

[70] J. Morgan, *Phoenix Brit.,* pp. 545–551.

"was both an eye and earwitness." The definite crime of which the accused was charged consisted of performing cures with a "white powder" which he received from the fairy queen and the fairies, "a visible people" to whom he had "access" and with whom he had "converse." [71]

In Scotland, in the 16th and 17th centuries, the recognition of witches as the victims of the fairies was almost a commonplace. And the question, whether the accused witch "hed ony conversatioun with the ffarye-folk" [72] would seem to have been a stock question of witchcraft trials.

Here, as "spretis of the devill," [73] by which term they were defined in law, the fairies accomplished their purpose of abducting mortals in three ways: by means of a mortal inhabitant of fairyland whom them had formerly carried away, who acted as the intermediary between them and their intended victim; by means of the gifts and allurements of the Queen of Elfame who appeared in person; or by the supernatural power of the whole company of fairies.

The dittays against their victims, who were tried for witchcraft from 1576 to 1670 and later, and the confessions of the witches themselves, not only furnish evidence

[71] Webster, *Disp. of Sup. Witch.*, pp. 300–302.

It is significant that Glanvil, 1681, regards the fairies as able to make witches as the Devil. Cf. *Saducismus Triumphatus*, pt. 2, p. 5: ". . . these things [acts of witchcraft] are done by vertue of a Covenant, or Compact betwixt the Witch and an Evil Spirit. A Spirit, viz. an Intelligent Creature of the Invisible World, whether one of the Evil Angels called Devils, or an Inferiour Daemon or Spirit, or a wicked Soul departed; but one that is able and ready for mischief, and whether altogether Incorporeal or not, appertains not to this Question." Cf. also Beaumont, *Treatise of Spirits*, p. 104.

[72] Pitcairn, *Crim. Trials*, Vol. II, p. 537.

[73] *Ibid.*, Vol. I, pt. 2, p. 51.

of the belief in the abduction of human beings by fairies, but give the full details of the process.

There are the dittay and examinations of Bessie Dunlop in 1576,

> Dilatit of the vsing of Sorcerie, Witchcraft, and Incantatioune, with Invocatioun of spretis of the devill; continewand in familiaritie with thame, at all sic tymes as sche thocht expedient; deling with charmes, and abusing the peple with devillisch craft of sorcerie.

For these crimes which were made possible through the power of "ane Thome Reid, quha deit at Pinkye, as he himselff affirmit," who was sent her by the Queen of Elfame and through the power of the fairies, mentioned above as "spretis of the devill," she was "Conuict, and Brynt."[74] The items of the dittay leave no doubt of a belief in the existence and visible appearance of the fairies, nor of the manner by which they obtained possession of mortals, as for instance, Items 5, 6, 16, 20 and 21:

> (5.) ITEM, The ferd tyme he [Thom Reid] apperit in hir awin hous to hir . . . and sche followit, and ȝeid vp with him to the kill-end, quhair he forbaid hir to speik or feir for onye thing sche hard or saw; and quhene thai had gane ane lytle pece fordwerd, sche saw twelf persounes, aucht wemene and four men: . . . and Thome was with thame: And demandit, Gif sche knew ony of thame? Ansuerit, Nane, except Thom. Demandit, What thai said to hir? Ansuerit, Thai baid hir sit doun, and said, "Welcum, Bessie, will thow go with ws?" Bot sche ansuerit nocht; becaus Thom had forbidden hir. And forder declarit, That sche knew nocht quhat purpois thai had amangis thaime, onlie sche saw thair lippis move; and within a schort space thai pairtit all away; and ane hiddeous vglie sowche of wind followit thame: and sche lay seik quhill Thom came agane bak fra thame. — (6.) ITEM, Sche being demandit, Gif sche sperit at Thom quhat persounes thai war?

[74] *Ibid.,* Vol. I, pt. 2, pp. 49–58. "The Dittay, or Indictment, seems to have been an echo of two Declarations, emitted by this ill-fated woman."

Ansuerit, That thai war the gude wychtis that wynnit in the Court of Elfame; quha come thair to desyre hir to go with thame: And forder, Thom desyrit hir to do the sam; quha ansuerit, " Sche saw na proffeit to gang thai kynd of gaittis, vnles sche kend quhairfor! " Thom said, " Seis thow nocht me, baith meit-worth, claith-worth, and gude aneuch lyke in persoun; and (he?) suld make hir far better nor euer sche was? " Sche ansuerit, " That sche duelt with hir awin husband and bairnis, and culd nocht leif thame." And swa Thom began to be verrie crabit with hir, and said, " Gif swa sche thocht, sche wald get lytill gude of him." . . . (16.) . . . Interrogat, Gif euir sche had bene in suspect place with Thom, or had carnell deill with him? Declarit nocht vpoun hir saluatioun and condemnatioun; bot anis he tuke hir be the aproun, and wald haif had hir gangand with him to Elfame. . . . (20.) INTERROGAT, Gif sche neuir askit the questioun at him, Quhairfoir he com to hir mair (than) to ane vthir bodye? Ansuerit, Remembring hir, quhen sche was lyand in chyld-bed-lair, with ane of hir laiddis, that ane stout woman com in to hir, and sat doun on the forme besyde hir, and askit ane drink at hir, and sche gaif hir; quha alsua tauld hir, that that barne wald de, and that hir husband suld mend of his seiknes. The said Bessie ansuerit, that sche remembrit wele thairof; and Thom said, That was the Quene of Elfame his maistres, quha had commandit him to wait vpoun hir, and to do hir gude. — (21.) INTERROGAT, Gif euir sche had spokin with him at ane loich and wattir-syde? Ansuerit, Neuir save anis that sche had gane afeild with hir husband to Leith, for hame bringing of mele, and ganging afeild to teddir hir naig at Restalrigloch, quhair thair come ane cumpanye of rydaris by, that maid sic ane dynn as heavin and erd had gane togidder; and incontinent, thai raid in to the loich, with mony hiddous rumbill. Bot Thom tauld, It was the gude wichtis that wer rydand in Middil-zerd.[75]

There is also the dittay of Alesoun Peirsoun in 1588, " Dilatit of the pointis of Wichcraft eftir specifeit," and " conuict . . . of the vsing of Sorcerie and Wichcraft,

[75] *Ibid.*, Vol. I, pt. 2, pp. 52–53, 56–57.

with the Inuocatioun of the spreitis of the Dewill; speciallie, in the visioune and forme of ane Mr William Sympsoune" (who was with the fairies, having been carried away by them), and

for hanting and repairing with the gude nychtbouris and Quene of Elfame, thir diuers ȝeiris bypast, as scho had confest be hir depositiounis, declaring that scho could nocht say reddelie how lang scho wes with thame; and that scho had freindis in that court quhilk wes of hir awin blude, quha had gude acquentance of the Quene of Elphane, quhilk mycht haif helpit hir: bot scho wes quhyles weill and quhyles ewill, and ane quhyle with thame and ane vthir quhyle away; and that scho wald be in hir bed haill and feir, and wald nocht wit quhair scho wald be or the morne: And that scho saw nocht the Quene thir sewin ȝeir: And that scho had mony guid freindis in that court, bot wer all away now: And that scho wes sewin ȝeir ewill handlit in the Court of Elfane and had kynd freindis thair, bot had na will to visseit thame eftir the end: And that itt wes thay guid nychtbouris that haillit hir vnder God: And that scho wes cuming and gangand to Sanct Androus in hailling of folkis, thir saxtene ȝeiris bypast.[76]

Andro Man, "convictis . . . as a manifest vitche, be oppin voce and commoun fame," and by the "haill assisc," according to the dittay against him, owed his conviction to the "Devill" who came to him "in the liknes and scheap of a woman, quhom thow callis the Quene of Elphen," with whom he continued in familiarity "threttie twa yeris sensyn or thairby." He was most familiar with the company of the Queen of Elfame, among whom were "sindrie deid men," "the kyng that deit in Flowdoun and Thomas Rymour," and affirmed that:

the elphis hes schapes and claythis lyk men, . . . that thay ar bot schaddowis, bot ar starker nor men, and that thay have playing and dansing quhen thay pleas; and als that the quene is verray plesand,

[76] *Ibid.*, Vol. I, pt. 2, pp. 161–162.

and wilbe auld and young quhen scho pleissis; scho mackis any kyng quhom scho pleisis, and lyis with any scho lykis;

and that

the elphis will mak the appeir to be in a fair chalmer, and yit thow will find thy selff in a moss on the morne; and that thay will appeir to have candlis, and licht, and swordis, quhilk wilbe nothing els bot deed gress and strayes; amangis quhom thow art not effrayit to gang, as thow frequentlie all thy dayes hes vsit thair cumpanie and societie.[77]

In like case with Andro Man was Jean Weir, who was hanged in 1670 because of her connection with "the Queen of Farie";[78] and Issobell Haldane (1623), whose "conversatioun with the ffarye-folk" consisted in being "caryit to ane hill-syde: the hill oppynit, and scho enterit in. Thair scho stayit thrie dayis."[79]

Jonet Drever (1616), "indytit and accusit for . . . vseing committing and practizeing of the abhominable and divelishe cryme of witchcraft contened in the particular and severall pointis or dittays," was "banisched the cuntre" for

fostering of ane bairne in the hill of Westray to the fary folk callit of hir our guid nichbouris And in haveing carnall deall with hir And haveing conversation with the fary xxvj zeiris bygane.[80]

Issobel Sinclair, according to the records of her trial, 1633, met her death because "shoe hath bein controlled with the Pharie";[81] and Donald dow McIlmichall was

[77] *Spald. Club Misc.*, Vol. I, pp. 119, 121–122, 123.

[78] George Sinclar, *Satans Invisible World Discovered,* 1871 ed., Supplement, p. xii.

[79] Pitcairn, *Crim. Trials,* Vol. II, p. 537.

[80] *Maitland Club Misc.,* Vol. II, 1840, p. 167: "Curia Capitalis Vicecomitatus de Orknay et Zetland tenta in Kirkwall . . . die vij Junij 1615."

[81] Dalyell, *Darker Superstitions,* p. 470.

"hangit to the death" because he confessed

> judiciallie that on a night in the moneth of November 1676 he travelling betwixt Ardturr and Glackiriska at ane hill he saw a light not knowing quhair he was. And ther a great number of men and women within the hill quhair he entered haveing many candles lighted, and saw ane old man as seemed to have preference above the rest and that sum of them desired to shutt him out and others to have him drawine in And saw them all danceing about the lights and that they wold have him promise and engadge to come ther againe that night eight nights and for a considerable space thereftir. . . . Interrogat with quhom he engadgeit and what he judget them to be . . . Answers . . . that he cannot weill tell quhat persons they wer bot he judges them not to have bein wordlie men or men ordayned of god.[82]

The dittay against Katherene Roiss Lady Fowlis reveals the power of the fairies over her,[83] as do those against Jonet Morisone,[84] Christian Lewingstoun,[85] Isobell Strauthaquhin,[86] and Elspeth Reoch.[87] And the four confessions of Issobell Gowdie, who owed her power to the devil and the Queen of Elfame and her court, furnish full details of the life of a mortal who was also an inhabitant of fairyland.[88]

The examples of witches, made witches by the fairies, and of fairy changelings left in mortal cradles, could be multiplied, but the evidence of the references already cited seems sufficient to warrant the conclusion that the fairies of the sixteenth century were real and powerful beings, who, through the witch and the changeling, gained possession of mortals and carried them away.

[82] *Highland Papers,* Vol. III, p. 37.

[83] Pitcairn, *Crim. Trials,* Vol. I, pt. 2, pp. 192–200.

[84] *Highland Papers,* Vol. III, p. 23.

[85] Pitcairn, *Crim. Trials,* Vol. II, pp. 25–29.

[86] *Spald. Club Misc.,* Vol. I, pp. 177–179.

[87] *Maitland Club Misc.,* Vol. II, pp. 187–191.

[88] Pitcairn, *Crim. Trials,* Gen. App., pp. 602–616.

CHAPTER V

THE FAIRIES OF SHAKESPEARE

Although the Elizabethan fairies continued to exist as realities — both in the belief of the folk and in the literary records of the time — until the end of the 17th century and later, the beginning of their decline as terrible and credible entities took place in the 16th century. This was due, for the most part, not to the curtailment of the power and influence of the Catholic Church in England, as many an Elizabethan scholar was wont to contend, but, indirectly, to the vogue of the fairies in literature and in drama, and, directly, to the influence of the race of fairies created by William Shakespeare in *A Midsummer Night's Dream.*[1]

To these fairies can be traced the change in reputation and appearance which the fairies of tradition and folk belief sustained, and the subsidence of the race from the

[1] Attention has already been called in the Introduction to this essay to the conclusions reached by scholars since the 18th century concerning the fairies of Shakespeare.

Following the conclusions of Thorndike and Neilson in *The Facts about Shakespeare,* 1913, and of Tucker Brooke in *Shakespeare of Stratford,* 1926, all of whom date *M. N. D.* in the year 1594, and of E. K. Chambers who regards the dating of *M. N. D.* in 1594–1595 as fairly certain (cf. *M. N. D.,* Warwick ed., pp. 9–14), I have taken the date of the play as that of 1594. Dated by Alden (*Shakespeare,* 1922), 1593–1595; Adams (*A Life of William Shakespeare,* 1923), 1596; Ward (*A History of English Dramatic Literature to the Death of Queen Anne,* 1899), 1594 or 1595; Malone (*The Plays and Poems of William Shakespeare*), 1594; Fleay (*A Chronicle History of the Life and Works of Shakspere,* 1886), 1595.

position of real and fearful spirits to the present acceptance of them by lettered folk as pleasant myths and fanciful heroines of children's stories.[2]

That the disappearance of the fairies as credible entities should have been hastened by the influence of Shakespeare is one of the greatest ironies of their history. Of all the Elizabethans who made mention of them, there is no one who showed himself more cognizant of the belief in their existence, and no one who featured more prominently their traditional power and activities. In several plays of his, they appear in their own proper person on the stage; in others, mortals are mistaken for them; and in others, space is given to a recital of their activities or a statement of their powers.

Had every source of information been lost concerning the fairies of the period, all the characteristic features of their world and most of the ceremonies consequent on its existence could have been reproduced from his writings. The fairy reputation as "A fiend, . . . pitiless and rough," [3] noted in the *Comedy of Errors,* is substantiated in *Merry Wives of Windsor,*[4] and in *Romeo and Juliet.*[5] Marcellus in *Hamlet* [6] is aware of the fairies' powers of bewitchment, and King Henry, in *Henry IV,*[7]

[2] "Here let me note that not until the peasant belief has come into the hands of the cultured man do we find the conception of an essential incompatibility between the fairy and the human worlds — of the necessary disappearance of the one before the advance of the other. . . . Since his [Shakespeare's] days, fairydom became, chiefly owing to the perfection of his embodiment, a mere literary convention and gradually lost life and savour." Nutt, *Fairy Myth. of Eng. Lit.,* pp. 35 and 53.

[3] IV, 2, l. 39.

[4] V, 5, ll. 51–52.

[5] I, 4, ll. 88–91.

[6] I, 1, l. 178.

[7] I, 1, ll. 86–88.

is familiar with changelings, as is the shepherd in *The Winter's Tale.*[8] In *Cymbeline,*[9] and in *Macbeth,*[10] the fairies appear in their traditional rôles of " tempters of the night," and of familiar spirits of witches. *King Lear,*[11] *Antony and Cleopatra*[12] and *The Winter's Tale*[13] represent them as beautiful and generous to their favorites. *Merry Wives of Windsor*[14] and *Comedy of Errors*[15] reveal their practice of pinching and their insistence on chastity and cleanliness; the *Tempest,*[16] their passion for misleading unwary folk; and *Venus and Adonis,*[17] their obsession for dancing. In *Merry Wives of Windsor,*[18] men, women and children take part in a representation of their race. In *Pericles,*[19] and in *Cymbeline,*[20] mortal women are mistaken for them. And nowhere is the location of fairyland more definitely represented than in the saw-pit of *Merry Wives of Windsor.*[21]

Yet Shakespeare's recognition of the traditional fairies of his time and his representation of the traditional fairy world, complete and detailed as it was, were eventually ignored for his conception of the poetic and imaginary fairyland of *A Midsummer Night's Dream,* and

[8] III, 3, ll. 120–122.
[9] II, 2, ll. 11–12.
[10] IV, 1, ll. 44–48.
[11] IV, 6, ll. 29–30.
[12] IV, 8, l. 59.
[13] III, 3, ll. 25 and 59.
[14] V, 5, ll. 49–51; and V, 5, ll. 100–102.
[15] II, 2, ll. 190–194.
[16] IV, 1, l. 186.
[17] Stanza 25.
[18] IV, 4.
[19] V, 1, ll. 148–150.
[20] III, 6.
[21] V, 3, l. 14.

the native fairies of the folk were ultimately superseded by the fanciful beings that he invented for an appearance in one play.

✱On first acquaintance, there seems but little difference between the fairies of *A Midsummer Night's Dream* and those of native tradition and of Shakespeare's other plays.[22] The train of Titania take their places in a forest as is usual.[23] They materialize as a commonwealth of elves and fairies[24] with their rulers. They come at midnight,[25] and hasten away at sunrise.[26] They break into song at any pretext,[27] and dance their way throughout the play.[28] They can fetch jewels from the deep[29] and are addicted to cleanliness.[30] A human changeling is among their number[31] and a mortal is carried away into their world,[32] and the recollection of the hour of their appearance sends mortals to bed.[33]

On closer study, however, the fairies of *A Midsummer Night's Dream* are seen to be what Oberon calls them,

[22] The exceptions are *The Tempest,* and *Romeo and Juliet.*

[23] *M. N. D.,* II, 2, l. 79.

[24] II, 1, l. 17; III, 1, ll. 158 and 175.

[25] V, 2, l. 9.

[26] V, 2, l. 31.

[27] II, 3, l. 1; III, 1, l. 160; V, 2, l. 26.

[28] II, 2, ll. 27 and 81; II, 3, l. 1; V, 2, l. 26.

[29] III, 1, l. 159.

[30] V, 2, ll. 19–20.

[31] II, 1, l. 23.

[32] III, 1, l. 154.

[33] V, 1, l. 363.

"The fairy of folk-lore in Shakespeare's day is nearly everything that the fairies of *A Midsummer-Night's Dream* are; we may possibly except their exiguity, their relations in love with mortals, and their hymeneal functions. His conception of their size as infinitesimal at least differs from that of the popular stories, where (as far as can be ascertained) they are shown to be about the size of mortal children." Sidgwick, *Sources and Analogues,* p. 65.

"spirits of another sort."[34] Whatever is homely or substantial or dangerous has been removed from the picture of them, which Shakespeare paints, and only their rulers are still invested with formidable powers and uncertain tempers. Diminutive, pleasing, and picturesque sprites, with small garden names and small garden affairs, associated with moon-beams and butterflies, they present themselves as a new race of fairies,[35] as different from the popular fairies of tradition as are those fairies from the fays of the medieval romances.

To create this new conception of fairyland, Shakespeare inaugurated a number of changes in the traditional fairy lore of the period.

Instead of appearing as an active and powerful commonwealth with their traditional ruler, the fairies are given the rôle of innocuous and almost negligible attendants upon two literary or mythological sovereigns, Oberon and Titania.

Oberon, already familiar on the stage as the king of the fairies through *James the Fourth* of Greene and the *Entertainment at Elvetham,* seems to have been taken by Shakespeare directly from *Huon of Burdeux.* With his quick and violent temper, his piety, his devotion to those mortals to whom he took a fancy, his angelic visage, his

[34] III, 2, l. 388.

[35] "The fairies which he [Shakespeare] saw in his imagination in the *Midsummer Night's Dream* are not those of popular English tradition. They are not wild enough, nor unearthly and malicious enough. . . . Remember that many in his audience had seen fairies; those who had, wanted no more of them. Shakespeare gave them gracious romantic inventions, who speak charming verse about the weather." John Masefield, *Shakespeare & Spiritual Life,* The Romanes Lecture, Oxford, 1924, p. 13.

For a different interpretation of the fairies of *M. N. D.,* cf. Floris Delattre, *English Fairy Poetry,* 1912, Chap. IV.

dwarfed stature, his splendid dress and his powers of enchantment — all characteristics of Oberon, the "dwarfe kynge of the fayrey," in the romance — he was admirably adapted to play one of the leading parts in the imaginary and poetic fairy kingdom of a romantic comedy.

The name *Titania* Shakespeare appears to have taken from Ovid's *Metamorphoses*,[36] where it occurs as one of the synonyms of Diana. The precedent for Diana's sovereignty over the fairies is to be found in the *Discovery of Witchcraft*,[37] in Golding's translation of Ovid's *Metamorphoses*,[38] in the *Faerie Queene*,[39] and in *Endimion*.[40] (But the character of the picturesque and romantic queen who rules over the fairies of *A Midsummer Night's Dream* and the plot in which she is involved are Shakespeare's own creation.)

The powers which were attributed to Diana and to Oberon, both in their own persons and in that of the king and the queen of the fairies, are still exercised by the fairy rulers of Shakespeare. Their connection with mortals, however, is revealed as unfailingly beneficent and altruistic, an attitude vastly different from that of Diana, "the goddesse of the Pagans," associated with witches in the *Discovery of Witchcraft*, and from the Oberon of whom Gerames and Huon stood in much fear in *Huon of Burdeux*.

For the first time the fairies themselves are made consistently good.[41] No longer do they function as the

[36] Book III, l. 173. Cf. also E. K. Chambers, "The Fairy World," p. 159; and Sidgwick, *Sources and Analogues*, p. 36.

[37] Scot, 1651 ed., Book III, Chap. XVI, p. 52.

[38] Book IV, l. 304.

[39] Spenser, "A Letter of the Authors."

[40] Lyly, IV, 3.

[41] "Of his [Shakespeare's] unlimited sway over this delightful world of ideal forms, no stronger proof can be given, than that he has

mischievous and dangerous beings they were believed to be, with occasional and erratic lapses into beneficence and the bestowal of good fortune; instead, they become, in actuality, the Good Neighbours which, in flattery and in fear, they had been dubbed by mortals trembling before the idea of their advent. Every aspect of their wickedness and every sign of their devilish connection is omitted from their portrait,[42] and the period of their earthly materialization is devoted to making the world happier and more beautiful,[43] without any of the usual impositions of taboos and without any of the usual demand for worship or payment.

They do not appear from underground or from hell to inspire fear. They travel from the farthest steppe of India [44] to insure for the king of Athens and his bride joy and prosperity, a future of faithful love and fortunate issue.[45]

Notwithstanding their past of spitefulness and malicious meddling, they cannot now bear the slightest disturbance of the peace, but, at the sound of vituperation between Oberon and Titania,

---

imparted an entire new cast of character to the beings whom he has evoked from its bosom, purposely omitting the darker shades of their character, and, whilst throwing round them a flood of light, playful, yet exquisitely soft and tender, endowing them with the moral attributes of purity and benevolence. In fact, he not only dismisses altogether the fairies of a malignant nature, but clothes the milder yet mixed tribe of his predecessors with a more fascinating sportiveness, and with a much larger share of unalloyed goodness. . . .

This love of virtue, and abhorrence of sin, were, as attributes of the Fairies, in a great measure, if not altogether, the gifts of Shakspeare." Drake, *Shak. and His Times,* pp. 502 and 505.

42 III, 2, l. 388.

43 V, 2, l. 30.

44 II, 2, l. 10.

45 II, 2, l. 14.

. . . . all their elves, for fear,
Creep into acorn cups, and hide them there;[46]

while mortal combat so disturbs the soul of Oberon that he overcasts the night when a fight is impending, and takes steps to separate the "testy rivals," "As one come not within another's way."[47]

The fairies' passion for stealing human children from their cradles and their known practice of disfiguring them with withered arms and elvish marks is changed into an excessive solicitude about the welfare of babies.[48] Even the changeling in the fairy kingdom of *A Midsummer Night's Dream* has not been obtained by violence and human woe. He has been adopted by Titania out of friendship for his mother, who, "being mortal, of that boy did die."[49]

In spite, too, of a lifetime devoted to pinchings and kidnappings, both the fairies and their sovereigns refuse to allow any hurt or discomfort to come to the mortals whom they encounter.[50] Bottom the Weaver who, it must be noticed, is changed into an ass and is brought into the fairy world through an individual prank of Robin Goodfellow, and not from any effort of the fairies nor at the command or cognizance of their rulers,[51] is

[46] II, 1, ll. 30–31.
[47] III, 2, ll. 358–359.
[48] II, 1, ll. 21–27; V, 2, ll. 35–44.
[49] II, 2, l. 76.
[50] V, 2, ll. 47–50.
[51] III, 2, ll. 1–3 and 35:

"OBE. I wonder, if Titania be awak'd;
Then, what it was that next came in her eye,
Which she must dote on in extremity.
. . . .
OBE. This falls out better than I could devise."

given fairies to " attend " upon him, to fetch him " jewels from the deep," and to " fan the moon-beams from his sleeping eyes." [52] He is put to sleep on pressed flowers, and sustains no more injury than a diet of

> . . . . apricocks, and dewberries,
> With purple grapes, green figs, and mulberries.[53]

Neither is he returned to human existence deprived of his reason and one of " his members," as was the way of fairies with mortals. He is restored to earth at the exact minute and in the exact place where it is necessary for him to be, able to " discourse wonders," with no other marks of his sojourn with the fairies than the remembrance of a dream.[54]

The fairy queen steps out of a tradition of infernal connections [55] and dark deeds to deplore the fact that the dissensions between her and Oberon have resulted in floods and loss of crops:

> . . . . the green corn
> Hath rotted, ere his youth attain'd a beard:
> The fold stands empty in the drowned field,
> And crows are fatted with the murrain flock.[56]

She is much disturbed over unseasonable temperatures, and " rheumatick diseases " that abound.[57] She is distressed that " human mortals want their winter here," [58] and that " No night is now with hymn or carol blest." [59] And, to quote Drake,

[52] III, 1, ll. 158, 159, 174.

[53] III, 1, ll. 167–168.

[54] IV, 2, l. 29; IV, 1, ll. 205–220.

[55] See Chap. III, pp. 115–116; Chap. IV, pp. 167, 170–175; Chap. V, p. 186.

[56] II, 2, ll. 35–38.

[57] II, 2, l. 46.

[58] II, 2, l. 42.

[59] II, 2, l. 43.

. . . the first fruit of the re-union of Oberon and Titania, is a benediction on the house of Theseus:

" Now thou and I are new in amity;
And will to-morrow midnight, solemnly,
Dance in duke Theseus' house triumphantly,
And bless it to all fair posterity; . . ."

an intention which is carried into execution at the close of the play.[60]

Especially is the change in the character of the fairies emphasized by Shakespeare in his introduction in the fairy kingdom of Robin Goodfellow,[61] who is employed, instead of the fairies, to frighten and mislead mortals, to bewitch Bottom and carry him away into fairyland, to clean the palace of Theseus, and to call attention to the evil reputation and connections of the fairies of tradition.

The difference between these fairies and those of *A Midsummer Night's Dream* is again made apparent in the extravagant attachment for flowers which Shakespeare attributes to his fairies. They had always been connected with hills and wells and green meadows, with now and then a garden in which they had danced and sung, as in " The Marchantes Tale " of Chaucer, and in the *Entertainment at Elvetham*. They had been associated, too, with flowers in Golding's translation of Ovid's *Metamorphoses*,[62] and in *The Queenes Majesties Enter-*

[60] *Shak. and His Times*, p. 504.

Upon this particular evidence of the fairies' attitude toward mortals the observation of Drake is most significant: " How different this from the conduct and disposition of their brother elves of Scotland, of whom Kirk tells us, that 'they are ever readiest to go on hurtfull Errands, but seldom will be the Messengers of great Good to Men.' " *Shak. and His Times*, p. 504.

[61] For a full discussion of Robin Goodfellow's connection with fairies, cf. Chap. VI, pp. 219–221, 253–256.

[62] Book 9, l. 337.

tainment at Woodstocke, where a handmaid of the Fayry Queene presented Elizabeth and her ladies with "many excellente and fine smelling Nosegayes made of all cullers."[63] And in the *Entertainment at Elvetham,* again, the fairy queen had introduced herself to Elizabeth as one

> That every night in rings of painted flowers
> Turne round, and carrell out Elisaes name.[64]

But in *A Midsummer Night's Dream,* the fairies are completely identified with buds and blossoms, dew-drops and butterflies. Their similes are floral; their favors, the gold spots of cowslips; their scent bottles, its freckles.[65] Their occupations, for the most part, consist in watering the fairy ring, in hanging dewdrops in each cowslip's ear,[66] in killing canker in the musk rose buds, in putting spells upon beetles and worms, snails and spiders,[67] and in blessing mortal rooms with "field-dew consecrate."[68] Their names are Cobweb, Mustardseed, Moth, and Peas-blossom.[69] Their changeling and their victim are crowned with flowers,[70] and their charms effected by means of "a little western flower."[71]

The fairy queen who, as Diana, rode over the kingdoms of the earth followed by a multitude of wicked women,[72] now sleeps on

[63] Page 99.

[64] Nichols, *Prog. of Eliz.,* Vol. III, p. 118.

[65] II, 1, ll. 10–13.

[66] II, 1, ll. 9 and 15.

[67] II, 3, ll. 3 and 19–22.

[68] V, 2, ll. 45–48.

[69] III, 1, l. 163.

[70] II, 1, l. 27; IV, 1, ll. 52–53.

[71] II, 2, l. 107.

[72] See "Paenetential" of Bartholomew Iscanus, rpt. *Reliquiae Antiquae,* Wright and Halliwell ed., 1845, Vol. I, p. 285.

> . . . a bank where the wild thyme blows,
> Where ox-lips and the nodding violet grows;
> Quite over-canopied with luscious woodbine,
> With sweet musk-roses, and with eglantine:
> . . . .
> Lull'd in these flowers with dances and delight; [73]

and shows her love by sticking musk-roses in Bottom's "sleek smooth head." [74] And Oberon, whose anger in *Huon of Burdeux* caused

> reyne and wynde/ hayle/ and snowe/ and . . . meruelous tempestes/ with thonder and lyghtenynges/ so that it shall seme to you that all the worlde sholde pereshe,[75]

is melted by the mournful sight of the dew

> . . . . which sometime on the buds
> Was wont to swell, like round and orient pearls,
> Stood now within the pretty flourets' eyes,
> Like tears, that did their own disgrace bewail.[76]

The fourth innovation which Shakespeare made in the popular fairy mythology was the reduction of the fairies' former measurements and figures to those of the most diminutive proportions. So infinitesimal are the fairies of *A Midsummer Night's Dream* that acorn cups become their hiding places,[77] the leathern wings of rere mice or the cast skin of a snake, their coats.[78] The wings of butterflies serve as their fans; [79] the waxen thighs of bumble-bees are their torches,[80] and one of the hazards

[73] II, 2, ll. 190–195.
[74] IV, 1, l. 3.
[75] E. E. T. S. ed., Vol. I, pt. I, p. 64.
[76] IV, 1, ll. 54–57.
[77] II, 1, ll. 30–31.
[78] II, 3, ll. 4–5; II, 2, ll. 196–197.
[79] III, 1, ll. 173–174.
[80] III, 1, ll. 170–171.

of their existence lies in the danger of being drowned by the burst honey-bags of bees.[81]

These diminutive proportions which, slightly modified, less than a century and a half later became the characteristic proportions of the English fairies, would seem to have been the invention of Shakespeare [82] rather than a poetic exaggeration of the diminutive stature of the traditional elves of the period, as has been held. *Before 1594 and *A Midsummer Night's Dream,* as far as can be ascertained, there is no record of any diminutive fairies or elves in the 16th century in England.[83] On the other hand, as has been seen, the fairies before 1594 and throughout the period, with the exception of the fairies of *A Midsummer Night's Dream* and of those fairies who are the literary descendants of Moth and Mustard-seed, are pictured as possessing the statures of boys and maidens, or those of full-grown men and women.[84]

As far as I have been able to discover, also, there are few definite records of any diminutive fairies or elves at any time in England before the fairies of *A Midsummer*

[81] IV, 1, ll. 16–17.

[82] What source, if any, furnished the inspiration for Moth and Mustard-seed has never been discovered. It can be conjectured, with some reason, that the initial idea of infinitesimal fairies came from the Oberon of *Huon of Burdeux,* "ye dwarfe King of ye Fayre," whose stature was commented on as strikingly small. He had already appealed to Greene who had put him on the stage in *James the Fourth,* where his figure is likened to that of the King of Clubs. This play also may have been the source of Shakespeare's Oberon. Local fairy lore in Warwickshire, too, may have been the immediate source of the small fairy. Unfortunately, no records of such sources can be found either in the present day folk tales of that country or in contemporary records, as Dugdale's *Antiquities of Warwickshire,* 1656.

[83] For a discussion of elves and fairies, cf. Introd., pp. 19–22.

[84] See Chap. II, pp. 66–81.

Night's Dream. It has become almost a tradition[85] to point to the Portunes of Gervase of Tilbury, " statura pussili, dimidium pollicis non habentes,"[86] and to the race of little men, " homunculi duo staturae quasi pigmeae,"[87] described by Giraldus Cambrensis, as instances of the diminutive fairies or elves, traditional in England and Wales before Shakespeare. A careful examination of Chapter LXI, " De Neptunis sive Portunis, qui homines illudunt," in the Tertia Decisio of *Otia Imperiale,* and of the subsequent chapters in the same work which treat of supernatural spirits or beings and wood-gods or spirits, will show that Gervase did not identify the Portunes with fays,[88] or lamiae,[89] fauns or satyrs,[90] of whose existence he was cognizant, but pointed out his ignorance of their origin and classification:

> Ecce enim Anglia daemones quosdam habet, daemones, inquam, nescio dixerim, an secretas et ignotae generationis effigies, quos Galli Neptunos, Angli Portunos nominant.[91]

A further examination makes evident that these beings possessed none of the traditional traits of fairies, but, except in stature, are more akin to Puck or Robin Goodfellow, neither of whom traditionally was regarded as a fairy.[92]

There is very little, too, in the account of Elidorus by Giraldus Cambrensis to denote that the two little men

[85] See Ritson, *Dis. of Fairies,* p. 23; E. K. Chambers, " The Fairy World," p. 166; Keightley, *Fairy Myth.,* Vol. II, p. 107.

[86] *Otia Imperialia,* Liebrecht ed., Hannover, 1856, p. 29.

[87] *Itinerarium Cambriae,* Powel ed., London, 1806, p. 65.

[88] D3 C88.

[89] D3 LXXXV and D3 LXXXVI.

[90] D1 XVIII.

[91] Page 29.

[92] See Chap. VI, pp. 219–229.

with whom he was familiar, and the race of men of "staturae minimae" whom he visited, were elves or fairies rather than a race of pigmies. Beyond the fact that they lived underground, they possessed no other traits characteristic of either fairies or elves, and could not have been evil or infernal spirits — in which category the fairies and elves were placed — since it is particularly emphasized that

> Quoties de superiori hemisphaerio revertebantur, ambitiones nostras, infidelitates et inconstantias expuebant. Cultus eis religionis palam nullus: veritatis solum, ut videbatur, amatores praecipui et cultores.[93]

The being, "qui pigmeus videbatur modicitate staturae, que non excedebat simiam," described by Walter Map,[94] may have been the king of pigmies. Except for two characteristic features which his nation possessed in common with the fairies and elves — dwellings underground and a derivation as fallen angels [95] — there is nothing to indicate that he belonged to the fairy race.

The stature and measurements of these beings of Giraldus Cambrensis, Gervase of Tilbury and Walter Map, could not have been regarded as the typical racial proportions of the elves or the fairies during this period since the author of the legend of Saint Michael in the *Early South-English Legendary* described the elves as appearing in the form of women:

> And ofte in fourme of wommane: In many derne weye
> grete compaygnie men i-seoth of heom: boþe hoppie and pleiȝe,
> Þat Eluene beoth i-cleopede; [96]

[93] *Itin. Camb.*, p. 66.
[94] *De Nugis Curialium,* James ed., 1914, p. 13.
[95] *Ibid.*, p. 80.
[96] Page 307, ll. 253–255.

and the *Chronicle* of Robert of Gloucester represented them as possessing the figures of men and women:

And me may hem ofte on erþe in wylde studes y se,
And ofte in monne's fourme wymmen heo comeþ to,
And ofte in wymmen forme þei comeþ to men al so,
Þat men clepuþ eluene, . . . [97]

Neither in Layamon's *Brut* [98] is there evidence of any diminution in the stature of the elves or of Argante, their queen, who is represented as a woman.[99]

[97] Vol. I, p. 130.

[98] Madden ed., London, 1847:
MS. Cott. Calig., A. IX, ll. 19252–19269, Vol. II;
MS. Cott. Otho, c. XIII, ll. 21129–21140, Vol. II;
MS. Cott. Calig., A. IX, ll. 21739–21748, Vol. II;
MS. Cott. Calig., A. IX, ll. 28610–28627, Vol. III.

[99] "It is needless to say that we have no trace of any fairies approaching the minute dimensions of Shakespeare's Queen Mab; for, after all, our fairies are mostly represented as not extravagantly unlike other people in personal appearance — not so unlike, in fact, that other folk might not be mistaken for them now and then as late as the latter part of the fifteenth century. Witness the following passage from Sir John Wynne's *History of the Gwydir Family,* p. 74:

'Haveing purchased this lease, he removed his dwelling to the castle of Dolwydelan, which at that time was in part thereof habitable, where one Howell ap Jevan ap Rys Gethin, in the beginning of Edward the Fourth his raigne, captaine of the countrey and an outlaw, had dwelt. Against this man David ap Jenkin rose, and contended with him for the sovereignety of the countrey; and being superiour to him, in the end he drew a draught for him, and took him in his bed at Penanmen with his concubine, performing by craft, what he could not by force, and brought him to Conway Castle. Thus, after many bickerings between Howell and David ap Jenkin, he being too weake, was faigne to flie the countrey, and to goe to Ireland, where he was a yeare or thereabouts. In the end he returned in the summer time, haveing himselfe, and all his followers clad in greene, who, being come into the countrey, he dispersed here and there among

Whether the diminution of the fairies was the result of the invention or of the poetic exaggeration of Shakespeare, their infinitesimal proportions furthered in no small measure Shakespeare's presentation, in several instances, of the fairies as comic and ridiculous figures. The ceremony of the meeting between Bottom and the fairies, for instance; the incongruity between their figures and his; and the mock heroic form of address adopted toward them by him, made them almost as much figures of fun as Bottom himself. The spectacle of Mustard-seed and Peas-blossom, applying themselves assiduously to the scratching of an ass's head was both humorous and incongruous, especially when viewed with the idea of the traditional fairies of the time in mind.[100] The solicitude of Bottom for Monsieur Cobweb in his assault upon a humble-bee, and the fear he expresses lest the fairy be swept away by a burst honey bag put the proportions and the activities of the fairies in a most ridiculous light. And no more amusing picture of the fairy queen was ever presented than that presented by Titania in love with Bottom, and by the lines with which she expresses her devotion:

> Come, sit thee down upon this flowery bed,
>   While I thy amiable cheeks do coy,
> And stick musk-roses in thy sleek smooth head,
>   And kiss thy fair large ears, my gentle joy.[101]

This treatment of the fairies was as new as it was unusual, and proved of great importance in the subsequent history of the Shakespearean fairies.

---

his friends, lurking by day, and walkeing in the night for feare of his adversaries; and such of the countrey as happened to have a sight of him and his followers, said they were the fairies, and soe ran away.'" Rhys, *Celtic Folklore,* Vol. II, p. 670.

[100] III, 2; IV, 1.

[101] IV, 1, ll. 1–4.

With their dignity thus diminished, their measurements reduced, their characters redeemed, and their association with flowers and insects established, the fairies of *A Midsummer Night's Dream,* as has been said, became a totally new race of spirits. Although they appeared but in one play, introduced by Shakespeare as the creations of a dream,[102] and appeared, too, at a time when the fairies of tradition were most familiar, the charm of their infinitesimal persons caught the fancy of poets and playwrights, and the ultimate adoption of their peculiar and characteristic features as the characteristic features of the English fairies, can be traced to their advent.

Had Shakespeare wished to destroy an ancient belief, he could have found no more effective method than his treatment of the fairies in *A Midsummer Night's Dream.* As long as they were regarded as wicked beings, they survived as powerful and credible entities; but when they became summer sprites and took upon themselves the nature of good spirits, they lost their hold upon the fear of the folk. As long as they occupied dark and mysterious portions of the earth and pursued careers of bewitchment and child stealing as adult and substantial beings, they were perforce characters to be reckoned with. When they became infinitesimal creatures who toyed with dew drops and hid in acorn cups, they vanished from reality.

The influence of the fairies of *A Midsummer Night's*

[102] *M. N. D.,* V, 2, ll. 54–61:

"If we shadows have offended,
Think but this, (and all is mended,)
That you have but slumber'd here,
While these visions did appear.
And this weak and idle theme,
No more yielding but a dream,
Gentles, do not reprehend;
If you pardon, we will mend."

Dream, however, was not immediate. Shakespeare never again put this kingdom of fairies on the stage, and the fairies of native tradition, unreduced in stature and unregenerate of soul, continued to appear in play and pamphlet, in night spells, and in folk tale. Yet the idea of the microscopic miniatures of fairies who hopped in the eyes and gamboled in the walk of Bottom the Weaver, haunted their creator. In 1595,[103] Queen Mab in *Romeo and Juliet,* the fairies' midwife, was described in the same infinitesimal terms as Moth and Mustard-seed:

> In shape no bigger than an agate-stone
> On the fore-finger of an alderman,
> Drawn with a team of little atomies
> Athwart men's noses as they lie asleep:
> Her waggon-spokes made of long spinners' legs;
> The cover, of the wings of grasshoppers;
> The traces, of the smallest spider's web;
> The collars, of the moonshine's watry beams:
> Her whip, of cricket's bone; the lash, of film:
> Her waggoner, a small grey-coated gnat,
> Not half so big as a round little worm
> Prick'd from the lazy finger of a maid:
> Her chariot is an empty hazel-nut,
> Made by the joiner squirrel, or old grub,
> Time out of mind the fairies' coach-makers.[104]

This is the first time that the queen of fairies is represented as diminutive.[105] Nevertheless, this new con-

[103] Date of assignment of play by Tucker Brooke, Thorndike, Chambers; Alden placing date 1593–1595, Adams, 1596.

[104] I, 4, ll. 59–73.

[105] This is the first time, as far as can be ascertained, that Mab appeared in English literature or in folk tale as queen of the fairies. In spite of the number of attempts that have been made to discover the source of Mab as queen of the fairies, nothing is definitely known of her identity or derivation. For a full description of the origins of

ceit of the fairy queen's smallness and that of her elaborate and diminutive state chariot,[106] furthered, no doubt, by the influence of the infinitesimal and picturesque fairies of *A Midsummer Night's Dream,* caught the attention of Shakespeare's contemporaries, and a new and diminutive ruler was introduced into the fairy kingdom who was gradually to usurp the name and office of the traditional fairy queen, while the trappings and appurtenances of her coach initiated a concern with fairy wardrobes and fairy coaches and fairy furniture which eventu-

---

Mab and of the various conclusions in regard to her identity, cf. *Modern Language Notes,* 1902, Vol. 17, No. 1, W. P. Reeves, "Shakespeare's Queen Mab."

A possible reference to the Mab used later by Shakespeare as the fairies' mid-wife, may occur in *The Historie of Jacob and Esau,* S. R. 1557–1558, V, 6, in Esau's remark to Deborah:

"And come out, thou Mother Mab; out, old rotten witch!
As white as midnight's arsehole or virgin pitch.
. . . .
Now, come on, thou old hag, what shall I say to thee?"

The following note from Keightley, *Fairy Myth.,* Vol. II, p. 135, is very interesting:

"'Mab,' says Voss, one of the German translators of Shakespeare, 'is not the Fairy-queen, the same with Titania, as some, misled by the word queen, have thought. That word in old English, as in Danish, designates the female sex.'" In the light of the fact that she is represented as the fairies' mid-wife, and depicted further as the night-mare, and is never represented with any of the attributes of sovereignty, there may be more in the observation of Voss, than Mr. Keightley, who scoffed at his remark, seemed to think.

106 Shakespeare may have derived the idea of the fairy queen's state chariot from *The Queenes Majesties Entertainment at Woodstocke,* where the fairy queen is brought upon the scene in a "waggon" "drawen with 6. children."

ally rendered the fairy world both ridiculous and incredible.[107]

In *Merry Wives of Windsor*,[108] and in *The Tempest*, Shakespeare again reproduced certain features of his fairies of *A Midsummer Night's Dream* or of those of his source, if he had one. The fairies whom he put upon the stage in the former play to frighten Falstaff, pause in their nightly dance to punish those who have forgotten their nightly prayers and to embroider the motto of the garter with "flowers purple, blue and white" [109] upon the earth.[110] And although the spirits, goblins, elves, and fairies in *The Tempest* [111] are bad-tempered and hostile to mortals, the diminutiveness and floral preoccupations of the fairies of *A Midsummer Night's Dream* recur in some measure in the "demy-puppets," "whose pastime is to make midnight mushrooms"; [112] and in the smallness of Ariel and his obsession with flowers, which is featured particularly in his song of Act V, Scene I (if this song is to be taken as autobiographical):

[107] Shakespeare's inconsistency in regard to the fairies, or rather his recognition of the difference between his imaginary fairies and those of tradition, is noteworthy. After emphasizing the diminutive proportions of Mab and picturing her activities in the most poetic and fanciful terms, he identifies her as "This is the hag," etc. The same inconsistency or differentiation is to be found in *A Midsummer Night's Dream* when the fairies are put by Robin Goodfellow among the damned spirits.

[108] Dated 1598 by Thorndike; Alden, 1599–1606; Brooke, 1599–1600; Adams, 1598; Chambers, 1599–1600 (?).

[109] V, 5, l. 72.

[110] The pronouncement, "Fairies use flowers for their charactery" (*M. W. of W.*, V, 5, l. 75), is one unfamiliar to their ears and contrary to their usages.

[111] Date given by Thorndike, Brooke, Chambers, Alden, 1610–1611.

[112] *The Tempest,* V, I, ll. 41, 43–44.

> Where the bee sucks, there suck I;
> In a cowslip's bell I lie:
> There I couch. When owls do cry,
> On the bat's back I do fly,
> After summer, merrily:
> Merrily, merrily, shall I live now,
> Under the blossom that hangs on the bough.[113]

Outside of the works of Shakespeare, the influence of the fairies of *A Midsummer Night's Dream* as literary models is not particularly perceptible until 1600, the date of the publication of the official quarto of *A Midsummer Night's Dream,* and the date found on the Roberts' quarto of the same play.[114]

In the anonymous play, *The Wisdome of Doctor Dodypoll,* dated conjecturally between 1596 and 1599, and entered on the Stationer's Register in 1600,[115] a fairy is described as "a fine little Dapper fellow," and the description of the commonwealth of fairies is as follows:

[113] *Ibid.,* V, 1, ll. 89–95.

[114] The one exception to this statement may occur on p. 30 of *The Famous Historie of Chinon of England* by Christopher Middleton, dated 1597, in which "armies of many little Elues" as "speciall attendants" on Oburam's "traine" are described, "whose busie fingers woulde gladly haue beene pinching" Chinon's and Lancelot's and several other knights' legs, "for higher they coulde not reach." In this case, however, it is probable that the elves so described are copied from the Oberon of *Huon of Burdeux,* from which most of the fairy lore of Chinon is taken (cf. Introd., Mead ed., p. lviii), or are the elves of native tradition of whom this is the first description I have found in English literature which designates them as too small to reach beyond a man's knee (if "leg" be taken to represent the "part of the lower limb between knee and ancle").

[115] Dated by Chambers, 1599 and 1600.

> . . . the light Fairies daunst vpon the flowers,
> Hanging on euery leafe an orient pearle,
> Which strooke together with the silken winde,
> Of their loose mantels made a siluer chime.[116]

The author of *The Maydes Metamorphosis* of 1600 [117] " As it hath bene sundrie times Acted by the Children of Powles," designates the train of fairies again and again by the adjective, little. They are " little vrchins " [118] who trip " Lightly as the little Bee " [119] to " Most daintie musicke." [120] Their names are " Penny, Cricket, and little, little Pricke," [121] and their concerns are with dew-drops, flies and flowers:

> 1 FAY. I do come about the coppes
> Leaping vpon flowers toppes;
> Then I get vpon a Flie,
> Shee carries me aboue the skie,
> And trip and goe.
>
> 2 FAY. When a deaw drop falleth downe
> And doth light vpon my crowne,
> Then I shake my head and skip
> And about I trip.
>
> 3 FAY. When I feele a girle a sleepe
> Vnderneath her frock I peepe.
> There to sport, and there I play,
> Then I byte her like a flea;
> And about I skip.[122]

The most interesting example of the irresistible charm of the figures of the fairies of *A Midsummer Night's*

116 Act III, ll. 349–352.
117 S. R., 1600.
118 Act II, l. 304.
119 Act II, l. 305.
120 Act II, l. 313.
121 Act II, ll. 22, 25, 28.
122 Song, Act II.

Dream occurs in Edward Fairfax's translation of Tasso's *Godfrey of Bulloigne: or The Recovery of Jerusalem,* of the same year. Here, the fairies are given the position of lesser devils under the express domination of Satan yet with diminutive figures and flowery proclivities:

Before his Words the Tyrant ended had,
The lesser Devils arose with gastly rore,
And thronged forth about the World to gad,
Each Land they filled, River, Stream and Shore,
The Goblins, Fairies, Fiends and Furies mad,
Ranged in flowry Dales, and Mountains hore,
  And under every trembling Leaf they sit,
  Between the solid Earth and Welkin flit.

About the world they spread forth far and wide,
Filling the thoughts of each ungodly Heart,
With secret Mischief, Anger, Hate and Pride,
Wounding lost Souls with Sins impoison'd Dart.
. . . .[123]

The incongruity of fairies sweeping from hell with ghastly roar, ranged in flowery dales, and sitting, with the most infinitesimal figures, under every trembling leaf, docs not seem to occur to the translator.

At the same time, approximately, the queen of fairies, influenced by her association with the diminutive fairies of *A Midsummer Night's Dream,* and by her identification with Mab in *Romeo and Juliet,* is made ridiculously decorative and innocuous, and appears in *The Faery Pastorall, or Forrest of Elves* of William Percy as " Chloris stickt with Floweres all her body." [124]

The literary exploitation of the diminutive and florally inclined fairies did not become the fashion until the end of the first quarter of the century. This may have been

[123] Fourth Book, Stanzas 18 and 19, p. 97.

[124] III, 5. Dated 1603. Dated by Chambers 1590?, revised 1599.

due to the accession of James I in 1603, to whom the fairies were devilish and fearful beings, and to the avowal of his belief concerning them and their seduction of witches in the *Daemonologie,* published in London the year of his accession.[125] No doubt the stringent laws against witchcraft passed early in His Majesty's reign and the identification of the fairies as familiar spirits proved a successful obstacle, also, to any playful treatment of them. It is not surprising, therefore, to find that the fairies of Jonson, with one exception,[126] and of Fletcher were the contemporary fairies of common tradition, as were those of Dekker,[127] Heywood, Harsnet and Burton.

Shakespeare's fairies of *A Midsummer Night's Dream* were not without influence during this period, however, as can be seen in the elaborate association of fairies with flowers in *Britannia's Pastorals* of William Browne (1616):

> Sweet Flora, as if rauisht with their sight,
> In emulation made all Lillies white:
> For as I oft haue heard the Wood-nimphs say,
> The dancing Fairies, when they left to play,
> Then blacke did pull them, and in holes of trees
> Stole the sweet honey from the painfull Bees;
> Which in the flowre to put they oft were seene,
> And for a banquet brought it to their Queene.
> But she that is the Goddesse of the flowres
> (Inuited to their groues and shady bowres)
> Mislik'd their choise. They said that all the field
> No other flowre did for that purpose yeeld;
> But quoth a nimble Fay that by did stand:
> If you could giue't the colour of yond hand;

125 See Chap. IV, pp. 167–168.

126 *The Sad Shepherd,* II, 2.

127 *The Whore of Babylon* may be counted an exception.

(Walla by chance was in a meadow by
Learning to 'sample earths embrodery)
It were a gift would Flora well befit,
And our great Queene the more would honour it.
She gaue consent; and by some other powre
Made Venus Doues be equall'd by the flowre.[128]

The last years of James's reign and the third decade of the century proved that the fairies of Shakespeare had influenced the literary conception and idea of fairies more than these scanty records show, for, from this time, the fairies of *A Midsummer Night's Dream*, or copies of them, are to be found in great literary prominence, and are recognized as fairies almost to the exclusion of those of native tradition.

The poets of the earlier part of the century had been influenced by the smallness and prettiness of the Shakespearean fairy. The later poets, inspired by the treatment of the fairies as comic figures, took up the idea of the diminutive costumes of the fairies, and, influenced possibly by the association of the fairies with the wedding of Theseus and Hippolyta, devoted themselves to imaginary pictures of the infinitesimal weddings and banquets of the fairies themselves.

This treatment and development of the fairy world ended the vogue of the fairies in literature as traditional folk fairies, or as any kind of spirits or beings, and aided in bringing about their final repudiation as actual entities. They could, no doubt, have survived with the dimensions fastened upon them in *A Midsummer Night's Dream*, but no spirits with the blackest reputation or the most wicked proclivities (neither of which advantages had been left to them by Shakespeare) could continue a real existence when they were repeatedly appearing on

[128] Book 2, Song 3, ll. 773–793.

the pages of poems in which they were being continually dressed in diminutive garments and fed infinitesimal baked insects. Not the most flagrant crime of witchcraft committed through their power in Scotland, where mortals were being executed because of them, could maintain the race as fearful and credible entities in the face of the ridiculous conceits of Drayton or Browne or Herrick.

That Drayton should have taken up the conceit of diminutive and mock heroic fairies and microscopic fairy costumes is most indicative of the influence of the Shakespearean fairy. In his earlier works, he had mentioned the fairies, and had showed himself familiar with the ordinary fairies of folk tradition. They were referred to in *Idea, The Shepherd's Garland* of 1593,[129] in *Englands Heroicall Epistles* of 1597,[130] and in the first part of the *Poly-Olbion,* published in 1613.[131] And in every instance, the references were to some trait of the folk-fairies, or to the fays of romance.[132]

It is only in the second part of the *Poly-Olbion,* published in 1622, that the ordinary Elizabethan fairies are replaced by fairies who are unmistakably the descendants of the fairies of *A Midsummer Night's Dream,* not only in the reduction of their stature, but also in the reduction of their status to that of playful and ineffectual beings, with a picturesque proclivity for dewdrops, so noticeably a feature of Titania's court:

[129] *Poemes, Lyrick and Pastorall,* Spenser Soc., The Third Eglog, p. 45; The Fourth Eglog, p. 52.

[130] *Poems;* Spenser Soc., No. 46, 1888: "Elinor Cobham to Duke Humfrey," pp. 271 and 272; and "Henry Howard Earle of Surrey to Geraldine," p. 347.

[131] *Poly-Olbion,* Spenser Soc., 1889–1890, The fourth Song, p. 82.

[132] See *Poly-Olbion,* The fourth Song, p. 82.

The frisking Fairy there, as on the light ayre borne,
Oft runne at Barley-breake vpon the eares of Corne;
And catching drops of dew in their lasciuious chases,
Doe cast the liquid pearle in one anothers faces.[133]

Nimphidia, first published in the *Battaile of Agincourt,* of 1627, continues this conception of small fairies who are connected with flowers and insects, and, following Shakespeare's somewhat mock heroic treatment, carries the conceit to the limits of incredible diminutiveness and of ridiculous ineffectualness. Not only are the characteristic features of the fairies of *A Midsummer Night's Dream* reproduced in an exaggerated form but Mab, incongruously enough still identified as the Night-mare, is set upon the fairy throne and for the first time in literature, officiates as the actual and infinitesimal queen of the fairies, and as the consort of Oberon, who is here also given the most infinitesimal dimensions.

The domestic differences between the ruling sovereigns of fairyland, which had formed some part of Shakespeare's fairy plot, furnish the plot of *Nimphidia,* and the fantastic description of the diminutive state chariot of the Mab of Romeo and Juliet serves as the model for Drayton's description of the fairies' palace, their costumes, their means of transportation, and their combats, all of which details occupy the greater part of the poem, and are the chief concern of the poet:

This Pallace standeth in the Ayre,
By Nigromancie placed there,
. . . .[134]
The Walls of Spiders legs are made,
Well mortized and finely layd,

[133] Second part of *Poly-Olbion,* The one and twentieth Song, p. 355, ll. 97–100.

[134] Page 125, ll. 33–34.

He was the master of his Trade
  It curiously that builded:
The Windowes of the eyes of Cats,
And for the Roofe, instead of Slats,
Is couer'd with the skinns of Batts,
  With Mooneshine that are guilded.[135]

The fairies

Hop, and Mop, and Drop so cleare,
Pip, and Trip, and Skip that were,
To Mab their Soueraigne euer deare:
  Her speciall Maydes of Honour;
Fib, and Tib, and Pinck, and Pin,
Tick, and Quick, and Iill, and Iin,
Tit, and Nit, and Wap, and Win,
  The Trayne that wayte vpon her.

Vpon a Grashopper they got,
And what with Amble, and with Trot,
For hedge nor ditch they spared not,
  But after her they hie them.
A Cobweb ouer them they throw,
To shield the winde if it should blowe,
Themselues they wisely could bestowe,
  Lest any should espie them.[136]

The acorn cup for each fairy, provided as a hiding place in *A Midsummer Night's Dream,* is replaced by one hazel nut, " In th' end of which a hole was cut," in which the entire retinue of the queen, and Mab herself, are comfortably housed:

. . . .

Each one may here a chuser be,
  For roome yee need not wrastle:
Nor neede yee be together heapt;

135 Page 125, ll. 41–48.
136 Page 128, ll. 161–176.

So one by one therein they crept,
And lying downe they soundly slept
  As safe as in a Castle.[137]

And Oberon, king of the fairies, is armed as follows:

. . . .
A little Cockle-shell his Shield,
Which he could very brauely wield:
  Yet could it not be pierced:
His Speare a Bent both stiffe and strong,
And well-neere of two Inches long;
The Pyle was of a Horse-flyes tongue,
  Whose sharpnesse nought reuersed.[138]
And puts him on a coate of Male,
Which was of a Fishes scale,
. . . .[139]
His Helmet was a Bettles head,
Most horrible and full of dread,
That able was to strike one dead,
  Yet did it well become him:
And for a plume, a horses hayre,
Which being tossed with the ayre,
Had force to strike his Foe with feare,
  And turne his weapon from him.[140]
Himselfe he on an Earewig set,
Yet scarce he on his back could get,
So oft and high he did coruet,
  Ere he himself could settle.[141]

Important as *Nimphidia* is in showing the influence of the fairies of *A Midsummer Night's Dream*, the extent to which the conceit of small and ornate and some-

[137] Page 134, ll. 363–368.
[138] Page 137, ll. 490–496.
[139] Page 138, ll. 497–498.
[140] Page 138, ll. 505–512.
[141] Page 138, ll. 513–516.

what ridiculous fairies was developed as early as 1627, and the enthronement of Mab as the Queen of the fairies, it is equally important in showing also that a recognition of the fairies of native tradition still prevailed. Side by side, with the absurdities of the court of Mab and of Oberon on grasshoppers and earwigs, are set down the homely features of the traditional fairy world; the pinching of mortals black and blue, the reward for cleanliness, and the stealing of changelings.[142]

The three years which elapsed between the publication of *Nimphidia* and *The Muses Elizium,* saw the coarse and country fairy, as far as Drayton was concerned, completely supplanted by those created by Shakespeare's imagination. In the second Nimphall of the latter poem, the alliance of a Rivelet and a Fay is noted.[143] In the third Nimphall, devoted to "Poetick Raptures" and impossibilities, the "Countrey of the Fayries" is cited as an imaginary place invented by human imagination, and the fairies are described as follows:

> NAIJS. The Faires are hopping,
> The small Flowers cropping,
> And with dew dropping,
> Skip thorow the Greaues.
>
> CLOE. At Barly-breake they play
> Merrily all the day,
> At night themselues they lay
> Vpon the soft leaues.[144]

In the sixth[145] and in the tenth[146] Nimphalls, the "Fayry" designated by the adjectives *frisking* or *wanton*

142 Page 126, ll. 65–80.

143 Drayton, *The Mvses Elizivm,* rpt. of 1630 ed., Spenser Soc., 1892, p. 20.

144 Pages 35–36.

145 Page 60.

146 Page 91.

are given a place. In "The Eight Nimphall," the ornaments and costumes, the jewels and furniture necessary for the wedding of a fairy, so much a descendant of the fairies of *A Midsummer Night's Dream* that

> . . . by her smalnesse you may finde,
> That she is of the Fayry kinde,[147]

occupy the entire attention of the poet.

All the wealth of the insect kingdom and the vegetable kingdom is exhausted to furnish the trousseau of Tita, a subject of Queen Mab, under which name the Titania of *A Midsummer Night's Dream* may be conjectured to have reached a final diminution. One needs only to observe the wedding buskins and the bride's bed to discover to what lengths Drayton has carried the floral and garden connections of Shakespeare's fairies. The former

> . . . shall be of the Lady-Cow:
> The dainty shell vpon her backe
> Of Crimson strew'd with spots of blacke;
> Which as she holds a stately pace,
> Her Leg will wonderfully grace.[148]
> But for the Bride-bed, what were fit,
> That hath not beene talk'd of yet.
>
> Of leaues of Roses white and red,
> Shall be the Couering of her bed:
> The Curtaines, Valence, Tester, all,
> Shall be the flower Imperiall,
> And for the Fringe, it all along
> With azure Harebels shall be hung:
> Of Lillies shall the Pillowes be,
> With downe stuft of the Butterflee.[149]

[147] Page 75.
[148] Page 78, ll. 100–105.
[149] Page 79, ll. 121–130.

In the poems of William Browne of Tavistock, a change, similar to that of Drayton, from the fairies of native tradition to those of *A Midsummer Night's Dream,* can be traced. The first [150] and second [151] books of *Britannia's Pastorals,* and *The Shepheard's Pipe* [152] contain references to the activities and characteristics of fairies who, though in their more benevolent aspects, were the fairies of tradition; and the fourth Song of the first Booke of the *Pastorals* represents the fairies as of the size of mortal maidens,[153] or of Venus.

By 1616, however, in the second Booke of *Britannia's Pastorals,* as has been noted,[154] the fairies of tradition are endowed by Browne with marked and extravagant floral proclivities which were one of the outstanding features of the fairies of *A Midsummer Night's Dream.* The third Booke of the *Pastorals* [155] is a monument to

[150] Booke 1, Song 2, ll. 389–404; and Booke 1, Song 4, ll. 277–292. Dated 1613. Vol. I.

[151] Booke 2, Song 4, ll. 699–702 and 747–750. Dated 1616. Vol. II.

[152] The First Eglogue, ll. 754–763; The Seventh Eglogve, ll. 110–114. Dated 1614. Vol. II.

[153] See Chap. II, p. 72.

[154] See Chap. V, p. 200.

[155] Date of composition unknown. Ascribed by F. W. Moorman in Chap. IV of *William Browne His Britannia's Pastorals and the Pastoral Poetry of the Elizabethan Age,* 1897, to the years between 1624–1628; not published until 1852. Browne's death, 1643 or 1645.

The question of the exact date of composition of the fairy poems of Drayton, of Browne, and of Herrick, has never been determined. *Nimphidia,* as has been stated, appeared in a volume of poems in 1627. The poems of William Browne were in manuscript form until the 19th century. The poems of Herrick appeared in the *Hesperides,* 1648, and *Oberon's Feast* appeared separately, 1635. Moorman would give the poems of Browne precedence over the poems of Herrick. Bullen dates the poems of Browne 1635, the year of the appearance of *Oberon's Feast.*

the ridiculous diminutiveness and floral connections of the descendants of the Shakespearean fairies and to the prevailing mode of fairy poems, set going by the picture of the fairy world in *A Midsummer Night's Dream* and by the description of Mab and her chariot in *Romeo and Juliet*. Here the smallness of the fairies is carried almost to the vanishing point, in the description of

> . . . . a little elfe
> (If possible, far lesser then itselfe);[156]

while the entire book is too short to contain an adequately detailed description of the king of fairies' costumes and the courses of his banquet.

Oberon, who had been able in *A Midsummer Night's Dream* to overcast the night and to change the course of mortal love, is ushered into being

> Cladd in a sute of speckled gilliflowre.
> His hatt by some choice master in the trade
> Was (like a helmett) of a lilly made.
> His ruffe a daizie was, soe neately trimme,
> As if of purpose it had growne for him.
> His points were of the lady-grasse, in streakes,
> And all were tagg'd, as fitt, with titmouse beakes.
> His girdle, not three tymes as broade as thinne,
> Was of a little trouts selfe-spangled skinne.
> His bootes (for he was booted at that tyde),
> Were fittly made of halfe a squirrells hyde,
> His cloake was of the velvett flowres, and lynde
> With flowre-de-lices of the choicest kinde.[157]

His activities consist in dining upon minute dishes:

> The first dish was a small spawn'd fish and fryde,
> Had it been lesser, it had not been spyde;

[156] Booke 3, Song 1, Vol. II, p. 145.

[157] Wm. Browne, *Brit. Pastorals,* Booke 3, Song 1, ll. 815–827, Vol. II.

The next, a dozen larded mytes; the third,
A goodly pye fill'd with a lady-bird.
Two roasted flyes, then of a dace the poule,
And of a millers-thumbe a mighty joule;
A butterfly which they had kill'd that daye,
A brace of ferne-webbs pickled the last Maye.
A well-fedd hornet taken from the souse,
A larkes tongue dryde, to make him to carowse,[158]

and listening to small music

. . . . with a dynne
Of little hautboys, whereon each one strives
To shewe his skill; they all were made of syves,
Excepting one, which pufte the players face,
And was a chibole, serving for the base.[159]

The fairy poems of Robert Herrick, though taking note both of the existence of the changeling[160] and of Mab's punishment of sluttery,[161] are written to celebrate the feasts, the palaces, and the furniture of the most diminutive Oberon and

His Moon-tann'd Mab, . . .
. . . . tender as a chick.
Upon six plump Dandillions, . . .
. . . .
Whose woollie-bubbles seem'd to drowne
Hir-Mab-ship in obedient Downe.[162]

The small appointments of their temple, the "Fairie-Psalter,"

[158] *Ibid.,* Booke 3, Song 1, ll. 904–913.
[159] *Ibid.,* Booke 3, Song 1, ll. 779–783.
[160] "Charmes" and "Another," p. 284.
[161] *The Fairies,* p. 201.
[162] *Oberons Palace,* p. 167, ll. 84–89.

Grac't with the Trout-flies curious wings,
Which serve for watched Ribbanings;[163]
An Apples-core . . .
With ratling Kirnils, which is rung
To call to Morn, and Even-Song;[164]

and the saints,

Saint Tit, Saint Nit, Saint Is, Saint Itis,
Who 'gainst Mabs-state plac't here right is.
Saint Will o'th' Wispe (of no great bignes)
But alias call'd here Fatuus ignis.
Saint Frip, Saint Trip, Saint Fill, S. Fillie,[165]

show the depths of insignificance and of absurdity to which the fairy world since *A Midsummer Night's Dream* has been reduced, as does the poem of Sir Simon Steward, of the same period, entitled "King Oberon's Apparel," which emphasizes the fairy buttons:

. . . . . . a sparkling eye
Ta'ne from the speckled adders frye,

[163] *The Fairie Temple: or, Oberons Chappell,* p. 92, ll. 71–73.
[164] *Ibid.,* p. 93, ll. 126–128.
[165] *Ibid.,* p. 91, ll. 28–32.
The following statement of Edmund W. Gosse is significant: "And with him [Robert Herrick] the poetic literature of Fairyland ended. He was its last laureate, for the Puritans thought its rites, though so shadowy, superstitious, and frowned upon their celebration, while the whole temper of the Restoration, gross and dandified at the same time, was foreign to such pure play of the imagination. But some of the greatest names of the great period had entered its sacred bounds and sung its praises. Shakespeare had done it eternal honour in *A Midsummer Night's Dream,* and Drayton had written an elaborate romance, *The Court of Faerie.* Jonson's friend Bishop Corbet had composed fairy ballads that had much of Herrick's lightness about them. It was these literary traditions that Herrick carried with him into the west." *Seventeenth Century Studies,* London, 1883, p 131.

Which in a gloomy night, and dark,
Twinckled like a fiery spark.[166]

Amid this profusion of buttons and apparel, diets and dishes, the power and personality of the fairies disappeared as a matter of literary record. In the *Amyntas* of Thomas Randolph, of 1638, "the bevy of Fairies attending on Mab their queen," once invoked by Ben Jonson to welcome the Queen of England to Apthorpe, is itself entertained by a "rare device,"

An anti-masque of fleas, . . . taught
To dance corantoes on a spider's thread.[167]

And the status of the fairies under the sovereignty of Oberon and Mab is fittingly epitomized as follows:

Marry a puppet? wed a mote i' th' sun?
Go look a wife in nutshells? woo a gnat,
That's nothing but a voice? No, no, Jocastus,
I must have flesh and blood, and will have Thestylis.
A fig for fairies! [168]

More conclusive still of the influence of the Shakespearean fairies is the stature of the fairies in *The Sad Shepherd,* in which the usual consistent and painstakingly accurate presentations of the folk fairy by Ben Jonson show the effect of the prevailing literary fashion, and "span-long elves," "With each a little changeling in

[166] Ascribed to Sir Simon Steward and found in the *Musarum Deliciae,* London, 1656; rpt. Halliwell, *Fairy Myth.,* p. 313.

[167] Hazlitt ed., 1875, Vol. I, I, 3, ll. 47, 49–50.

[168] I, 3, ll. 8–12.

In the *Amyntas* is to be found also a number of characteristics of the fairies of the folk, utterly inconsistent with the fairies described above.

their arms,"[169] appear instead of the native fairies of tradition.[170]

By 1651, the Shakespearean fairies were firmly established in literature as the English fairies, their measurements as miniatures of themselves in *A Midsummer Night's Dream* regarded as their racial proportions, and their existence in consequence denied. Witness the Duchess of Newcastle, who not only devotes page after page of her *Poems and Fancies,* published that year, to diminutive and ornate fairy palaces, fairy embellishments and the fairy queen "for whom gnats do sing for her delight,"[171] but prefaces her work with an insistence on the fairies' reality in spite of their diminution:

> I wonder any should laugh, or think it ridiculous to heare of Fairies, and yet verily beleeve there are spirits; and witches, yet laugh at the report of Fairies, as impossible; which are onely small bodies not subject to our sense, although it be to our reason. Shall we say Dwarfes have lesse soules, because lesse, or thinner bodies? And if rational souls, why not saving souls? So there is no reason in Nature, but that there may not onely be such things as Fairies, but these be as deare to God as we . . .[172]

or later Milton who in *Paradise Lost* uses the figures of the faery "less than smallest dwarfs" as a standard for smallness:

[169] II, 2, Gifford ed. First published folio 1640. Dated conjecturally a few years before Jonson's death, 1637. Cf. p. XX, Greg ed., 1905.

[170] This description of Jonson shows the usual inconsistency apparent in the Shakespearean fairies. Here, elves a span long are represented with changelings who are mortal babies, several times longer than a span.

[171] Page 148.

[172] Preface, pp. 139–140.

Of Satan and his peers . . .
. . . .
In bigness to surpass Earth's giant sons,
Now less than smallest dwarfs, in narrow room
Throng numberless — like . . .
. . . . faery elves,
Whose midnight revels, by a forest-side
Or fountain, some belated peasant sees,
Or dreams he sees, . . .
. . . .
Thus incorporeal Spirits to smallest forms
Reduced their shapes immense, . . .[173]

The early part of the 18th century continued to regard the excesses of the fairies' diminution, their infinitesimal banquets, and minute quarrels, as their only claim to literary fame, as may be seen in William King's poem, *Orpheus and Euridice,* 1704, in which, in contradistinction to the powerful and fearful fairies of the *Romance of King Orfeo* several centuries before, the fairies were pictured as small enough to dance around a mortal hat, and as giving banquets of "Things to be Eat by Microscopes";[174] and in the *Kensington Garden* of Thomas Tickell whose concern with the fairies' diminutive figures led him into a description of the dietary measures taken to secure their inches:

Each supple Limb she swath'd, and tender Bone,
And to the Elfin Standard kept him down;
She robb'd Dwarf-elders of their fragrant Fruit,
And fed him early with the Daisy's Root,
Whence through his Veins the powerful Juices ran,
And form'd in beauteous Miniature the Man.[175]

173 Cambridge ed., 1899, Book First, ll. 757, 778–784, 789–790.
174 *Miscellanies in Prose and Verse,* 1704, pp. 380 and 383.
175 The Works of Celebrated Authors, Vol. II, 1750, ll. 113–118.

Not only in plays and poems, however, was the influence of the Shakespearean fairies, especially the feature of their smallness, felt. In popular belief, also, the fairies of tradition tended, it would seem, to become contaminated by the fairies of *A Midsummer Night's Dream*. *Robin Goodfellow; his mad prankes, and merry Jests,* less than forty years after the appearance of *A Midsummer Night's Dream,* contained a characterization of the fairies for the first time in popular history as "harmlesse spirits called fayries." [176]

In the record of a contemporary encounter with the fairies in the year 1630–1634, the smallness of the fairies was emphasized:

> Comming over the downes, it being neere darke, and approaching one of the faiery dances, as the common people call them in these parts, viz. the greene circles made by those sprites on the grasse, he all at once sawe an innumerable quantitie of pigmies or very small people dancing rounde and rounde, and singing, and making all maner of small odd noyses. He, being very greatly amaz'd, . . . fell down scarcely knowing what he did; and thereupon these little creatures pinch'd him all over, and made a sorte of quick humming noyse all the time.[177]

By 1648, the fairies of *A Midsummer Night's Dream,* might well have sat as the models for the fairies mentioned in the *Cosmographie* of Peter Heylyn, where they are defined as "a pretty kind of little Fiends or Pigmey-Devils, but more inclined to sport than mischief." [178] In 1653, in an *Antidote against Atheism* by Henry More, the fairies are referred to as "those little Puppet-Spirits,

[176] Dated 1628. This date is assigned the tract according to the findings of most scholars. Halliwell rpt., p. 122.

[177] John Aubrey, *Naturall History of Wiltshire,* and in Wiltshire collections of Aubrey, Oxford; Hazlitt rpt., pp. 349–350.

[178] App., p. 161.

which they call Elves or Fairies." [179] And, in 1673, in *A Pleasant Treatise of Witches,* the fairies are represented as follows:

It happened one day, as this admirable seamstress sate working in her garden, that . . . she saw, as she thought, a little gentleman, yet one that shewed great nobility by his clothing, come riding toward her from behind a bed of flowers; thus surprised how any body should come into her garden, but much more at the stature of the person, who, as he was on horseback, exceeded not a foot's length in height, she had reason to suspect that her eyes deceived her. But the gallant, spurring his horse up the garden made it not long, though his horse was little, before he came to see her: then greeting the lady . . . he acquaints her with the cause of his bold arrival; that, forasmuch as he was a prince amongst the fairies, and did intend to celebrate his marriage on such a day, he desired she would work points for him and his princess against the time he appointed. . . . The hour wherein she had promised the fairy-prince some fruits of her needle, happened to be one day as she was at dinner with many noble persons, having quite forgot her promise; when on a sudden, casting her eye to the door, she saw an infinite train of fairies come in: so that fixing her eyes on them, and remembering how she (had) neglected her promise, she sate as one amazed, and astonished the whole company. But at last, the train had mounted upon the table, and, as they were prancing on their horses round the brim of a large dish of white-broth, an officer that seemed too busy in making way before them, fell into the dish, which caused the lady to burst into a sudden fit of laughter, and thereby to recover her senses. When the whole

[179] Page 121.

By 1677, according to John Webster, the smallness of the fairies was made a characteristic feature of the race: "In a few ages past when Popish ignorance did abound, there was no discourse more common (which yet is continued amongst the vulgar people) than of the apparition of certain Creatures which they called Fayries, that were of very little stature, and being seen would soon vanish and disappear." *Disp. of Sup Witch.,* p. 283.

fairy company was come upon the table, that the brims of every dish seemed filled with little horsemen, she saw the prince coming toward her, (who) hearing she had not done what she promised, seemed to go away displeased. The lady presently fell into a fit of melancholy, and, being asked by her friends the cause of these alterations and astonishments, related the whole matter; but, notwithstanding all their consolations, pined away, and died not long after.[180]

By the end of the first quarter of the 18th century, the proportions given by Shakespeare to Titania's court were the native measurements of the traditional fairy in popular belief and in folk tale. In one of the earliest collections of the folklore of the time, Henry Bourne's *Antiquitates Vulgares, or The Antiquities of the Common People,* in Chapter X of The Country Conversations on a Winter Evening:

Another Part of this Conversation generally turns upon Fairies. These, they tell you, have frequently been heard and seen, nay that there are some still living who were stollen away by them and confined seven Years. According to the Description they give of them, who pretend to have seen them, they are in the Shape of Men, exceeding little: . . .

Now in all this there is really nothing, but an old fabulous Story, which has been handed down even to our Days from the Times of Heathenism, . . .[181]

The subsequent history of the fairies in the 18th and 19th centuries, at least in scholars' dissertations and treatises, has been traced.[182] Nor is it necessary to recall the fact that the fairies of Shakespeare were regarded, during the former century, as the fairies of England, and during both periods, as small creatures whose

[180] Hazlitt rpt., pp. 369–371.

[181] Pages 82–83.

[182] See Introd.

name, popularly, stood for loveliness, etherealness, and an imaginary fabrication. It would be a work of supererogation to recall the modern conception of English fairies. These are the fairies, not of Shakespeare's time, but of his mind, who were invented to play a part in a midsummer night's dream, and have found themselves cast forever in the rôle of English fairies.[183]

[183] The difference between the fairies of the 16th century and of the 20th, is at once perceptible in the difference attached to the meaning of *fairy-like,* as used in *M. W. of W.,* IV, 4:

"And, fairy-like, to-pinch the unclean knight,"

and the meaning associated with fairy-like, today.

CHAPTER VI

ROBIN GOODFELLOW

When *A Midsummer Night's Dream* was put upon the stage, there appeared among the fairies Robin Goodfellow, who was given, in the play, two other names also — Hobgoblin and Puck. The " merry wanderer of the night," as he called himself, might well have uttered a protest, had he been able to speak in his real and accepted capacity, both against the company in which he was put and against the names, especially that of Puck, which were bestowed upon him. He was no fairy, if the records of his history before 1594 be true, and this was his first inclusion in fairyland. And the term *Puck* or *pouke* was a generic term applied to a class of demons or devils and to the devil himself, with whom, before *A Midsummer Night's Dream,* he had never been classified.[1]

For himself, he had no need for any identification. In his own person and with the title of Robin Good-

[1] " Their choral dances were enlivened by the introduction of the merry goblin Puck, for whose freakish pranks they exchanged their original mischievous propensities." Scott, *Minstrelsy,* Vol. II, pp. 222–223.

" Puck is perhaps the same with the old word Pouke, the original meaning of which would seem to be devil, demon, or evil spirit. . . . The truth perhaps is, that the poets, led by the inviting conciseness of the term, applied it to the house-spirit, or hob-goblin. Shakespeare appears to have been the original offender." Keightley, *Fairy Myth.,* Vol. II, pp. 118 and 120.

One of the earliest discussions of Robin Goodfellow is to be found in Drake's *Shakspeare and His Times.* Cf. also William Bell, *Shakespeare's Puck, and His Folkslore,* 1852–1864.

fellow, this "great and antient bull-begger" was the most famous and the most esteemed of all the spirits and supernatural beings who haunted England.

Such has been the powerful influence, however, of the Shakespearean sponsorship, that, notwithstanding the facts of his previous history and reputation and the fact that he had never been represented either as a fairy or a puck before 1594, he has been known to the popular mind, since *A Midsummer Night's Dream,* as Puck, and as a happy, frisky fairy of moonlit nights and summer evenings, owing his existence to the genius of Shakespeare.[2]

That Robin Goodfellow was not a native of fairyland, Shakespeare seems to have been well aware, since he

[2] "In the character of Puck Shakespeare has embodied almost every attribute with which the imagination of the people has invested the Fairy race; and has neither omitted one trait necessary to give brilliancy and distinctness to the likeness, nor sought to heighten its effect by the slightest exaggeration. . . . And that this was done designedly and of aforethought can scarcely be doubted, when it is borne in mind that Shakespeare has designated this personification of the fairy tribe not by any imaginary title, but simply as Puck. For though 'Puck' is now only applied to designate the 'merry wanderer of the night,' it was originally a name applied to the whole race of fairies, and not to any individual sprite." Thoms, *Three Notelets on Shakespeare,* 1865, pp. 48 and 50.

"In order to complete the picture of fairy superstition, as given us by Shakespeare, it remains to consider his description of Puck or Robin Good-fellow, the confidential servant of Oberon, an elf or incubus of a mixed and very peculiar character. This quaint, frolicksome, and often mischievous sprite, seems to have been compounded of the qualities ascribed by Gervase of Tilbury to his Goblin Grant, and to his Portuni, two species of demons whom he describes, both in name and character, as denizens of England; of the benevolent propensities attributed by Agricola to the Guteli, Cobali, or Brownies of Germany, and of additional features and powers, the gift and creation of our bard." Drake, *Shak. and His Times,* p. 508.

takes pains to show that he is unknown to the fairies of *A Midsummer Night's Dream,* and to identify him to them and to the audience in the traditional way by which Robin Goodfellow was identified — by his figure and appearance and by a recital of his exploits and characteristics:

> FAI. Either I mistake your shape and making quite,
> Or else you are that shrewd and knavish sprite,
> Call'd Robin Good-fellow: are you not he,
> That fright the maidens of the villagery;
> Skim milk; and sometimes labour in the quern,
> And bootless make the breathless housewife churn;
> And sometime make the drink to bear no barm;
> Mislead night-wanderers, laughing at their harm?
> Those that Hobgoblin call you, and sweet Puck,
> You do their work, and they shall have good luck:
> Are not you he? [3]

Though the presentation of Robin Goodfellow as a member of the fairy race may have gone counter to the accepted canons of folk belief, Shakespeare's introduction of him among his fairies of *A Midsummer Night's Dream* gave evidence both of his knowledge of folklore and of his genius. Of all the spirits who were believed to haunt England, there was not one whom he could have better chosen to give a sense of reality to his fairy plot, or to furnish, to an audience, the immediate assurance of boisterous gayety and of harmless fun.

So accepted was Robin Goodfellow's reality that faith in his existence was made the standard of common credulity.

> To you that are wise and discreet [wrote Reginald Scot in 1584, in an endeavor to disprove the existence of witches] few words may suffice: . . . But to make a solemn suit to you that are partial readers, desiring you to set aside partiality, to take in good part my

[3] *M. N. D.,* II, 1, ll. 32–42.

writing, and with indifferent eies to looke upon my book, were labour lost, and time ill imployed. For I should no more prevaile herein, then if a hundred years since I should have intreated your predecessors to beleeve, that Robin good-fellow, that great and antient bull-begger, had been but a cousening merchant, and no devil indeed. . . . And know you this by the way, that heretofore Robin good-fellow, and Hob-gobblin were as terrible, and also as credible to the people, as hags and witches be now: . . . And in truth, they that maintain walking spirits, with their transformation, &c. have no reason to deny Robin good-fellow, upon whome there have gone as many and as credible tales, as upon witches.[4]

So cherished were his person and his presence that he was offered every inducement of hospitality[5] by the country folk who found the house "sonsier"[6] for his presence, and "famozed in every olde wives chronicle" for his mad and merry pranks.[7]

There were a number of reasons for Robin Goodfellow's fame and popularity. He was a native British spirit, as far as can be ascertained, bound up with the traditions of the country and the customs and beliefs of the people.[8] Of all the spirits and terrors of the night, he was never known to possess or to make use of any supernatural powers fatal to mankind.[9] Finally,

[4] *Dis. of Witch.*, 1651 ed., "To the Readers," B; and p. 97.

[5] *Ibid.*, p. 66; *Grim, the Collier of Croydon,* Dodsley ed., 1780, Vol. XI, V, 1.

[6] James VI of Scotland, *Daemon.*, p. 127.

[7] *Tarltons Newes,* p. 55.

[8] "He [Oberon] is totally unlike Puck, his lieutenant, 'the merry wanderer of the night,' who springs from purely English superstition." *Huon of Burdeux,* E. E. T. S. ed., Introduction by S. L. Lee, p. li. Cf. also C. H. Herford, *Studies in the Literary Relations of England and Germany in the Sixteenth Century,* 1886, p. 306; and E. K. Chambers, "Fairy World," p. 160.

[9] Note in the list of spirits given in *The Buggbears,* Robin Goodfellow is not placed among those who are evil, but among those amiable.

he occupied the unique position of the national practical joker whose presence furnished an excuse for any untoward domestic accident and connoted every mad prank and merry jest that could be devised.

Yet, in spite of his position and fame, he could more easily be included among the fairies, especially the fairies created by Shakespeare, than most of the native spirits, for beyond the fact that he was a walking spirit, nothing definite seems to have been known in the 16th century concerning his race or his original name.[10]

The term, Goodfellow, was not a family name, nor a proper name, but a propitiatory term bestowed upon him, in accordance with a universal belief that such complimentary appellations, as good fellow and good neighbor, would propitiate any anger and render the spirit addressed both agreeable and kind.

When he first came into literary mention, he was apparently already so well known as an individual hero that any identification of him or enumeration of his characteristics was considered superfluous. This is at once obvious in the earliest record of the name Robin Goodfellow, which occurred in a letter of William Paston to Sir John Paston, May, 1489. Here, commenting on the anonymity and lack of authenticity of an unofficial proclamation of rebellion, William Paston added significantly, " And thys is in the name of Mayster Hobbe Hyrste, Robyn Godfelaws brodyr he is, as I trow." [11]

[10] See Sidgwick, *Sources & Analogues*, p. 38.

[11] *The Paston Letters*, Gairdner ed., 1900–1901, Vol. III, p. 362. A similar use of " Robin Goodfellow " to denote lack of authenticity and authority, or a fabrication or joke, is to be found in Gabriel Harvey's *Pierces Supererogation or A New Prayse of the Old Asse*, 1593, Grosart ed., 1884–1885, Vol. II, p. 53: " Robin Good-fellow the meetest Autor for Robin Hoodes Library." Cf. also *Memoirs of The Life and Times of Sir Christopher Hatton* by Sir Nicholas

In the early part of the 16th century, he was treated as a known and accepted folk hero by William Tyndale, who, in *The Exposition of the First Epistle of St. John*[12] and in *The Obedience of a Christian Man*,[13] recounted his exploits but failed to mention his race. In *The Buggbears* of 1564 (c.),[14] he was added as an English spirit, with no further specifications — except his title of Robin Goodfellow — to the spirits enumerated in the Italian original,[15] and in the translation of the *Popish Kingdome* of Naogeorgus by Barnabe Googe in 1570,[16] he was cited as an individual with neither introduction nor classification.

Not until 1584 does any attempt seem to have been made to define or classify him. In the *Discovery of Witchcraft* of that year, he was spoken of as a devil,[17] and specifically classified as a cousin of Incubus,[18] and as the English counterpart of "Virunculi terrei," who "are

Harris Nicolas, London, 1847; and *The Historie of Tithes* by John Selden, 1618 ed., Chap. V, p. 51, for the use of Hobgoblin similar to that of Hobbe Hyrste of the Paston letters.

Halliwell in his introduction to his *Illus. of the Fairy Myth. of M. N. D.*, p. xi, states that a story, found in a manuscript of the 13th century in the Bodleian Library, has been pointed out by Sir Frederick Madden as apparently introducing "Robin Goodfellow both in name and action at that early period." The name given here is Robinet and the characteristic represented is not the most striking or most familiar of those attributed to Robin Goodfellow.

[12] *Expositions and Notes,* Parker Soc. ed., 1849, Vol. 37, p. 139.

[13] *Doctrinal Treatises,* Parker Soc. ed., 1848, Vol. 32, p. 321.

[14] For date, cf. Introd. to *Early Plays from the Italian,* Bond ed., p. 83.

[15] Page 117.

[16] Hope ed., 1880, The third Booke, p. 33.

[17] Scot, 1651 ed., "To the Reader," B. This reference may have furnished the inspiration for Shakespeare's "Puck."

[18] Scot, 1651 ed., p. 66.

such as . . . Robin Goodfellow, that would supply the office of servants, specially of maids." [19]

Tarltons Newes out of Purgatorie of 1588, likened "Hob Thrust, Robin Goodfellow and such like spirites, as they tearme them of the buttry, famozed in every olde wives chronicle for their mad merrye prankes" to "Familiares Lares that were rather pleasantly disposed then endued with any hurtfull influence"; [20] while Nashe, in 1592, regarded "Robbin-good-fellowes,[21] Elfes, Fairies, Hobgoblins of our latter age" as the native equivalents of "Fawnes, Satyres, Dryades, & Hamadryades." [22]

With the exception of these three somewhat general classifications of Robin Goodfellow in terms of classical mythology, he was treated as an individual folk spirit until 1594; and identified, as in *Tell-Trothes New-Yeares Gift* of 1593, as a "merry mate" "who neuer did worse harme then correct manners, and made diligent maides"; who had "by nature giuen him, that he should bee subiect to no inferiour power whatsoeuer, either ruling or inhabiting vnder the highest elemente," and who was invested "with a generall priuiledge to search euery corner, and enter any castell to a good purpose." [23]

In *A Midsummer Night's Dream,* he was given a number of classifications and names. Besides being presented as the jester of Oberon and as a member of the fairy band,[24] he was made to call himself a goblin,[25] an

[19] *Ibid., A Discourse upon divels and spirits,* p. 374.

[20] Page 55.

[21] This is one of the few occurrences of the name of Robin Goodfellow used in the plural. There are no occurrences in literature or folk tale of more than one Robin Goodfellow.

[22] *Terr. of the Night,* Vol. I, p. 347. Cf. also *Ibid.,* pp. 367–368 for a further description of Robin Goodfellow.

[23] New Shak. Soc., 1876, Ser. 6, No. 2, pp. 3–4.

[24] II, 1, l. 44; and III, 2, l. 110.

[25] III, 2, l. 399.

honest Puck [26] and the Puck,[27] and was referred to also as Hobgoblin,[28] none of which terms had been applied to him before, with the possible exception of goblin. His subsequent identification, therefore, as a fairy and as Puck rests, ironically enough, more upon Shakespeare's uncertainty in regard to his origin [29] than upon the facts of his history.

What authority, beyond the general classification of the two beings as supernatural or devilish spirits, Shakespeare had for identifying Robin Goodfellow as a puck or as the Puck is not known.[30]

[26] V, 2, l. 62.

[27] V, 2, l. 66. Cf. also Sidgwick, *Sources and Analogues,* p. 37.

[28] II, 1, l. 40.

[29] The Portuni and the Grant, both of which are described by Gervase of Tilbury as English spirits, *Otia Imp.,* D3 lxi and lxii, have by many critics been regarded as beings similar to Puck or Robin Goodfellow, or possibly the original Puck or Robin Goodfellow. The Portuni, in particular, show many of the attributes and characteristics which are later those of Robin Goodfellow, but the antiquated countenance, wrinkled face, diminutive stature and the diet of little broiled frogs which distinguished the Portuni, have never occurred as characteristics of Puck or Robin Goodfellow.

[30] The following note on the subject by William Bell is most entertaining:

"The English seem conscious that Robin Goodfellow, by which name the sprite was distinguished, Halliwell says, 'in the thirteenth century,' was but a circumlocution, perhaps, of the real ineffable appellative, that, like the tetragrammaton of the Hebrews, was too sacred to be lightly pronounced. I think the following is an allusion to the loss of the original denomination, or its restriction to the priesthood:

> 'In briefe christened hee was, at the which all this good cheare was doubled, which made most of the women so wise, that they forgot to make themselves ready, and none of them next day could remember the child's name but the clarke, and hee may thanke his booke for it, or else it had beene utterly lost.'

As far as can be seen from an examination of the early use of the word, and of a number of references to pucks, in the 13th and 14th centuries, the name of Robin Goodfellow was not associated or connected with the race or with any member of the race previous to 1594. This is true of the first mention of "larbula, puca," in the Glosses of Aldhelm's *Aenigmata*;[31] of the use of the word in the romance of *Richard Coer de Lion* attributed to the 12th century, where a mysterious and superhumanly strong knight is referred to as a puck;[32] and of a number of references in several poems of the 13th[33]

Would the resuscitation of the name of Puck by Shakespeare be a discovery of this lost denomination? or was that only generic, and the secret have to be still farther traced back through Pez and Per, to the Percunnus and Percullos of the Wends? I think it must." *Shak. Puck,* Vol. I, pp. 190–191. Cf. also Sidgwick, *Sources and Analogues,* footnote on p. 64.

[31] Napier, *Old English Glosses,* 1900, No. 23, p. 191.

[32] H. Weber, *Metrical Romances,* 1810, Vol. II, pt. I, ll. 565–566:

"I wis, sere kyng — quod ser Fouke, —
I wene that knyght was a pouke."

[33] *Old English Miscellany,* E. E. T. S. ed., 1872, *Sinners Beware!* p. 76, ll. 115–120:

"Þes Munekes weneþ summe.
Þat gedereþ gersumme.
Þat heo hit schulle bruke.
Ah hwen deþ schal cume.
Al hit wurþ heom bi-nume.
And he bitauht þe puke."

See also "St. Gregory" or "Gregorius auf dem Steine," Herrig, *Archiv,* Vol. 57, p. 62, ll. 241–248:

"Þþo ȝeo hadde hit ȝeue ones souke,
Ȝeo mad þe croiȝ uppon his brest,
fforte hit saue fram þe pouke.
Þþo hit was in þe cradel fest,

and 14th [34] centuries, where the puck is used to denote the Biblical devil or Satan.

Neither in the early 16th century was the name of Robin Goodfellow given to pucks. In the enumeration of spirits in *The Buggbears, puckes* and *puckerels* are cited with Robin Goodfellow, but the terms are used to denote separate and distinct spirits.[35] A distinction between the two spirits is to be noted in the *Discovery of Witchcraft,* where the *puckle* is mentioned with Robin Goodfellow and Tom Thumb, but as a different personage.[36]. The name, Robin Goodfellow, is not connected with the "pouke bugs" of Stanyhurst's translation of the *Aeneid,*[37] nor with "that same pooke" with

> ȝeo toke a somme of seluer & golde
> And leide hit under þe cradel heued:
> ffor som man scholde hit biholde
> And helpe þt hit were nouȝt ded."

[34] Langland, *The Vision of William concerning Piers the Plowman,* Skeat ed., 1886, Vol. I, pp. 494 and 496 (MS. Laud 851 [Bodleian Library], B Passus XVI, ll. 254–266):

> "For in his bosome he bar a thyng · that he blissed euere.
> And I loked on his lappe · a lazar lay there-inne
> Amonges patriarkes and profetes · pleyande togyderes.
> 'What awaytestow?' quod he · 'and what woldestow haue?'
> 'I wolde wyte,' quod I tho · 'what is in ȝowre lappe?'
> 'Loo!' quod he, and lete me se · 'lorde, mercy!' I seide,
> 'This is a present of moche prys · what prynce shal it haue?'
> 'It is a preciouse present,' quod he · 'ac the pouke it hath attached,
> And me there-myde,' quod that man · 'may no wedde vs quite,
> Ne no buyrn be owre borwgh · ne bryng vs fram his daungere;
> Oute of the poukes pondfolde · no meynprise may vs fecche,
> Tyl he come that I carpe of · Cryst is his name,
> That shal delyure vs some daye · out of the deueles powerè."

Cf. also B Passus XIII, ll. 157–164; A Passus X, ll. 62–67; A Passus XI, ll. 151–159.

[35] Page 117.

[36] Scot, 1651 ed., p. 113.

[37] Book III, l. 89.

"Goatish body, Lions head and brist, and Dragons tayle" of Golding's translation of Ovid's *Metamorphoses.*[38] Nor is there any reference to Robin Goodfellow as a puck in the *Epithalamion* of Spenser:

> Ne let the Pouke, nor other evill sprights,
> Ne let mischivous witches with theyr charmes,
> Ne let hob goblins, names whose sense we see not,
> Fray us with things that be not.
> Let not the shriech oule, nor the storke be heard,
> Nor the night raven that still deadly yels,
> Nor damned ghosts cald up with mighty spels,
> Nor griesly vultures make us once affeard:
> Ne let th' unpleasant quyre of frogs still croking
> Make us to wish theyr choking.
> Let none of these theyr drery accents sing;
> Ne let the woods them answer, nor theyr eccho ring.[39]

Hobgoblin also, which is a term applied to Puck in *A Midsummer Night's Dream,* would seem to be the name of another being, at least early in the century. In the various enumerations of spirits and bugbears occurring in the *Discovery of Witchcraft,*[40] and in *The Buggbears,*[41] both appear as separate beings. In *Gammer Gurtons Nedle,*[42] in Stanyhurst's translation of *Thee First Fovre Bookes of Virgil His Aeneis,*[43] in Spenser's

[38] Book IX, ll. 766–767.

[39] Cambridge ed., 1908, ll. 341–352.

[40] Scot, 1651 ed., p. 113.

[41] Page 117. Hobgoblin here is made a bad spirit.

[42] V, 2.

[43] Thee Fovrth Booke, ll. 301–305:

> "With gagd rocks coompast, then vaynely, Dido, reciting,
> Thow shalt bee punnisht. Ile with fyre swartish hop after.
> When death hath vntwined my soule from carcas his holding,
> I wyl, as hobgoblin, foloa thee: thow shalt be soare handled:
> I shal hyre, I doubt not, thy pangs in lymbo related."

Epithalamion,[44] and in *Fidele and Fortunio*,[45] where the names, hobgoblin, and Robin Goodfellow, or Hobgoblin occur, each term is used to denote a separate spirit, as for example, " Robin goodfellowe, Hobgoblin, the deuill and his dam." [46]

Especially is the difference between the two beings apparent in Churchyard's *Handfull of Gladsome Verses* which celebrates in the same poem old Hobgobling, " That walked like ghost in sheets," and " Rude Robin Goodfellow, the lout." [47]

Although Shakespeare's designation of Robin Goodfellow as a fairy and as Puck, both in *A Midsummer Night's Dream* and in *Merry Wives of Windsor*, was of the utmost influence upon Robin Goodfellow's subsequent literary career and final degradation, and ultimately, accepted as the proper name and race of Robin Goodfellow,[48] in the main, in the 16th and early 17th centuries, he was given no special racial name or connection, but as goblin, or satyr, or devil, or mortal, was known and represented, as Reginald Scot and the anonymous author of *Tarltons Newes out of Purgatorie* had represented him — as an individual hero and country spirit given to domestic occupations and " pleasantly disposed."

No writers of the period have better reproduced the spirit in which he was regarded and the personality with which he was invested than have Ben Jonson and

[44] Line 343.

[45] [Anthony Munday], Malone Society Reprints, 1909, l. 566.

[46] *Fidele and Fortunio*, l. 566.

[47] Rpt. in E. K. Chambers, " Fairy World," p. 164. Cf. also R. G. White, *Works of William Shakespeare*, 1865, Vol. IV, Introd., p. 13.

[48] See Jonson, Greg ed., *Sad Shepherd*, Cast of characters; Heywood, *Hierarchie*, Book 9; Butler, *Hudibras*, p. 371; Drayton, *Nimphidia;* Corbet, *Iter Boreale; Die Maske von Cole-Orton.*

Samuel Rowlands. In the masque of *Love Restored* of the former, he boasts himself " the honest plain country spirit, and harmless; Robin Goodfellow, he that sweeps the hearth and the house clean, riddles for the country maids, and does all their other drudgery," and continually shows himself full of good humor and jokes and honest morality.[49] In *More Knaues Yet? The Knaues of Spades and Diamonds* of the latter, he becomes

> . . . . a good fellow deuill,
> So called in kindnes, cause he did no euill,
> Knowne by the name of Robin (as we heare)
> And that his eyes as bigge as sawcers were,
> Who came a nights, & would make Kitchins cleane
> And in the bed bepinch a lazie queane.
> Was much in Milles about the grinding Meale,
> (And sure I take it, taught the Miller steale,)
> Amongst the creame bowles, & milke pans would be
> And with the country wenches, who but hee.
> To wash their Dishes for some fresh-cheese hier:
> Or set their Pots and Kettles bout the fier.
> T'was a mad Robin, that did diuers prancks,
> For which with some good Cheere, they gaue him thanks
> And that was all the kindnes he expected,
> With gaine (it seems) he was not much infected.[50]

The Anatomy of Melancholy, treating hobgoblins and Robin Goodfellows as identical spirits, defines them as a " bigger kind " of terrestrial devils, " called with us

[49] Morley ed., 1890, pp. 167 and 168.

[50] Vol. II, pp. 40–41. Cf. also Fletcher, *The Night-Walker,* III, 2:

> " My aunt has turned me out a-doors; she has,
> At this unchristian hour; and I do walk
> Methinks like Guido Faux, with my dark lanthorn,
> Stealing to set the town a-fire; i' th' country
> I should be ta'en for William o' the Wisp,
> Or Robin Goodfellow."

Hobgoblins, & Robin Goodfellows, that would in those superstitious times grind corn for a mess of milk, cut wood, or do any manner of drudgery work "; [51] and *A Discourse of Witchcraft* makes Robin Goodfellow a domestic deity of the Saxons.[52]

Thomas Heywood, evincing much uncertainty in regard to the exact distinction between Robin Goodfellow and other spirits, assigns him to the race of " Kibaldi ":

> In Iohn Milesius any man may reade
> Of Diuels in Sarmatia honored,
> Call'd Kottri, or Kibaldi; such as wee
> Pugs and Hob-goblins call. Their dwellings bee
> In corners of old houses least frequented,
> Or beneath stacks of wood: and these conuented,
> Make fearefull noise in Buttries and in Dairies;
> Robin good-fellowes some, some call them Fairies.[53]

In two instances Robin Goodfellow is set down as a mortal, endowed with supernatural powers. In *Wily Beguiled* of 1606, he is stated to be the son of a witch who possessed him after death and made him her instrument on earth:

> At length not finding any one so fit
> To effect her diuelish damned charge as I:
> She comes to me, as to her onely childe,
> And me her instrument on earth she made,
> And by that meanes I learnd this diuellish trade.[54]

In the popular history of *Robin Goodfellow; his mad prankes, and merry Jests,* he is the son of King Obreon, " a hee fayrie; whether he was their king or no I know not, but surely he had great government and commaund

[51] Burton, Vol. I, p. 220.

[52] Edward Fairfax, p. 18.

[53] *Hierarchie,* p. 574.

[54] Malone Soc. rpt., 1912, ll. 2043–2047.

in that country," and "a proper young wench." At his christening the wine flowed so freely that "none of them next day could remember the child's name, but the clarke, and hee may thanke his booke for it, or else it had been utterly lost. So much for the birth of little Robin." [55]

In Scotland, a spirit similar to Robin Goodfellow, or Robin Goodfellow himself, under the more prosaic name of Brownie, was cherished by the folk and perpetuated in literature. In *The Proloug of the Saxt Buke* of the translation of the *Aeneid* of Virgil by Gawin Douglas, Hades is pictured "Of browneis and of bogillis ful." [56] John Major, in his *Exposition in Matthew,* has the following account of these spirits:

[55] Hazlitt rpt., pp. 176–177.

The uncertainty in regard to Robin Goodfellow's place in the world of spirits can be seen in the dictionaries. In the *Worlde of Wordes* of Florio, 1598, with "a hag," "an elfe," "a ghost," "the riding hagge, or mare," Robin Goodfellow is given as the English equivalent of Folletto and Fantasma. In *A Dictionarie of the French and English Tongves* compiled by Cotgrave in 1611, Robin Goodfellow is rendered as "Fantasme," "Loup-garou," "Gobelin," "Follet" and "Lutin: . . . a spirit which playes reakes in mens houses anights."

Note also this account of Robin Goodfellow's origin and history from a ballad of the seventeenth century:

> "Of Robin Goodfellow also,
> Which was a seruant long agoe,
> The Queene of Fairies doth it know,
> and hindered him in fashion:
> She knew not what she did her selfe,
> She chang'd him like a Fairie elfe,
> For all his money, goods, and pelfe,
> she gull'd him."

No. 79, A Monstrous Shape, A Pepysian Garland, *Black-Letter Broadside Ballads of the Years 1595–1639,* Rollins ed., 1922, p. 452.

[56] Page 298.

Dubitatur adhuc: Isti Fauni et vocati brobne (brownies) apud nos domi qui non nocent, ad quod propositum talia faciunt. Respondetur: multa referuntur de talibus: ut proterere tantum tritici in una nocte vel sicut xx. viri terere possunt. Projiciunt lapillos inter sedentes prope ignem ruri, ridere videntur, et similia facere. Insuper dubitatur: an possunt futura predicere; et movetur dubitatio. Sunt aliqui apud nostrates Britannos qui more prophetico futura predicunt utpote de morte et homicidio aliquorum.[57]

James VI of Scotland in the *Daemonologie,* makes special mention of Brownie:

And yet the Diuell for confirming in the heades of ignorant Christians, that errour first maintained among the Gentiles, he whiles among the first kind of spirits that I speake of, appeared in time of Papistrie and blindnesse, and haunted diuers houses, without doing any euill, but doing as it were necessarie turnes vp and downe the house: and this spirit they called Brownie in our language, who appeared like a rough-man: yea, some were so blinded, as to beleeue that their house was all their sonsier, as they called it, that such spirits resorted there;[58]

as does Robert Kirk in *Secret Commonwealth:*

. . . some whereof of old, before the Gospell dispelled Paganism, and in some barbarous Places as yet, enter Houses after all are at rest, and set the Kitchens in order, cleansing all the Vessels. Such Drags goe under the name of Brownies.[59]

Save for the unanimous agreement in regard to the Brownie in Scotland, and for the various connections and affiliations and identities assigned to Robin Goodfellow in literature after *A Midsummer Night's Dream,* in which he is made a citizen of the fairy kingdom, a lesser

[57] 1518 ed., fol. xlviii. Cf. Major, *A History of Greater Britain,* Constable ed., 1892, Life of the Author, p. xxx, footnote 2.

[58] Page 127.

[59] Page 6.

devil of Hell and the familiar spirit of witches, his origin and race were never determined. In spite of the various names [60] bestowed upon him or invented to fit his nature, his real name remained a matter for conjecture to the end of his history, as the following stanza indicates:

Some call him Robin Good-fellow,
 Hob-goblin or mad Crisp,
And some againe doe tearme him oft
 by name of Will the Wispe;
But call him by what name you list,
 I have studied on my pillow,
I think the best name he deserves
 is Robin the Good Fellow.[61]

Contrary to the usual case of a nameless hero of obscure origin, Robin Goodfellow's absence of a family name and of racial identity proved a boon rather than a disgrace. For with no known or traditional attributes, he became the embodiment of his own flattering nickname, and was cherished and remembered for the gen-

[60] The list of names and affectionate titles which were attached to Robin Goodfellow is almost as long and as varied as are the accounts of his origin and his race. He was known as Puck, Hobgoblin, Goblin, Lob of spirits (*M. N. D.*); Pug (Jonson, *The Devil is an Ass*); Puckerel (Giffard, *Dial. conc. Witches and W. cr.*); Puckling (Heywood and Broome, *Late Lanc. Witches*); Puck-hairy (Jonson, *Sad Shep.*); Pug-robin (Butler, *Hudibras*); Hob (Drayton, *Nimphidia*); Lubbar fend (Milton, *L'Allegro*); Lob-lie-by-the-fire (Beaumont, *Knight of the Burning Pestle*); Crisp (*The merry pranks of Robin-Goodfellow*); William o' the Wisp (Fletcher, *Night-Walker*); Pixie (Clobery, *Divine Glimpses;* and Mrs. Bray, *A Description . . . of Devonshire*); Willy Wispe (*Robin Goodfellow; his mad prankes, and merry Jests*); Hodgepoke (Churchyard, *A Handfull of Gladsome Verses*). Cf. also E. K. Chambers, "Fairy World," p. 165; and Thoms, *Three Notelets,* p. 165.

[61] *The merry pranks of Robin-Goodfellow;* rpt. Halliwell, *Fairy Mythology,* 1845, p. 164.

erous qualities and agreeable personality with which the propitiatory term of a once fearful folk invested him.

In order to obtain a true idea of Robin Goodfellow as he flourished in the 16th century therefore, the characteristics, attributes, idiosyncrasies and antipathies which went to make up his unique personality, must be known. Nor is this knowledge difficult to obtain, since, as in *A Midsummer Night's Dream,* he was invariably identified by his jokes and exploits or recognized by his "shape and making."

And in no case, except in the final stages of his literary career, did he lose his unique identity. In fact, instead of becoming confused with other spirits, or losing, as did they, many of his individual traits, he was invested with the various names and proclivities of contemporary folk heroes, as Friar Rush, Will-o-the-Wisp, and Robin Hood. An example of this latter process is to be found in *Misogonus,* in which an unexpected encounter between Misogonus and the fool causes the following identification:

MIS. Bodye of god stande backe what monster haue we heare
an antike or a munke a goblinge or a finde
some hobbye horse I thinke or some tumblinge beare
Yf thou canst speake & declare me the kinde.

CA. My yonge master ho ho ho

MIS. Passion of me it is robin hoode I thinke verelye
I will let flye at him if he speake not furthwith
speake lubber speake or Ile kill the presentlye
Nay then haue at the shalt near dye other death.

Act I, Scene 3.[62]

The characteristics which struck Misogonus were, for the most part, the essential characteristics of Robin

[62] See also C. H. Herford, *Lit. Rel. between Eng. & Ger.,* Chap. V; and Thomas Wright, *Essays,* Vol. II, Essay X.

Goodfellow. His sense of humor and his propensity for jokes were always in evidence, as was his laugh. He never outgrew his strength and breadth of body, or the lubberliness of his figure, which caused him more than once to be taken for a performing bear. His wearing apparel was never standardized. He could not refrain from good-natured meddling in human affairs, nor could he resist the allurements of a bowl of cream and white bread.

Thanks to these unfailing attributes and the atmosphere of affection and amusement, sometimes fearful, which surrounded him, he became for all time, but more especially in the 16th century, a universally recognized member of English country life and an accepted figure in literature and on the stage, where his existence was referred to as frequently and as casually as that of the moon or the stars. To laugh like Robin Goodfellow became a proverb which was in evidence as late as the 19th century.[63] The saying, " Robin Goodfellow has been with you " had taken on, by the middle of the 16th century, a proverbial significance also, in allusion to the victim of a practical joke or a person who had been visited with some annoyance, as may be seen in Harman's *A Caueat or Warening for Commen Cursetors,*[64] and in several of Tyndale's works.[65] In the *Apophthegms* of Francis Bacon can be read the statement:

> Sir Fulke Grevill had much and private access to Queen Elizabeth, which he used honourably, and did many men good; yet he would say merrily of himself; That he was like Robin Goodfellow; For when the maids spilt the milkpans, or kept any racket, they

[63] Robert Forby, *The Vocabulary of East Anglia,* 1830, Vol. II, p. 431.

[64] E. E. T. S. ed., 1869, p. 30.

[65] *Expos. of the 1st Epistle of St. John,* p. 139; *Obedience of a Christ. Man,* p. 321.

would lay it upon Robin; So what tales the ladies about the Queen told her, or rather bad offices that they did, they would put it upon him.[66]

Nor were pictures of Robin Goodfellow lacking! On the title-page of *Robin Goodfellow; his mad prankes, and merry Jests*, 1628, is to be found a rough woodcut of him.[67] Here, in the midst of a circle of diminutive men and women, hand in hand, presumably in this case fairies, bulks the figure of a strong and heavy man. "On the opposite flyleaf is another figure of a sort of wild hunter, with a staff on his arm, and a horn at his side." [68]

As his portraits and the proverbs concerning him would indicate, he played his part in the 16th century in two capacities — as a forest spirit and, more frequently, as a "spirit domesticall."

In his capacity of forest spirit or "merry wanderer of the night," Robin Goodfellow was a trifle more mischievous than as a domestic spirit, and would seem to have been more delighted with himself and his performances. His chief functions, as a forest spirit, consisted in misleading unwary travellers, and in frightening unprotected mortals. In his domestic capacity, he took up his sojourn with some particular family. Here, if he found everything to his taste, he aided in the domestic labors, doing in one night, according to Milton,[69] ten men's work. For these labors he expected a mess of

[66] *The Works of Francis Bacon:* Spedding, Ellis and Heath ed., Boston 1860, Vol. 13, p. 377.

[67] See Bell, *Shak. Puck,* Vol. I, p. 156. See frontispiece to this volume.

[68] J. P. Collier, *A Bibliographical and Critical Account of the Rarest Books in the English Language,* 1866, Vol. III, p. 327.

[69] *L'Allegro,* ll. 107–109. Cf. also John Major, *Expos. in Matt., op. cit.,* p. 234 of this essay.

white bread and cream. If, however, his surroundings or the diligence of the maids did not meet his approval, he punished the family and servants by pinching and exposure, and went laughing away.

In either case, he was a plain country spirit and frequented the fields and woods and dairies and cottages of plain country folk. Never was he known to take up his residence in castles or palaces, or to ally himself voluntarily with lords or ladies. "Are these your court sports?" he is represented as blurting out in the masque of *Love Restored.* "Would I had kept me to my gambols o' the country still, selling of fish, short service, shoeing the wild mare, or roasting of robin-redbreast." [70]

This contempt for polite society and joy in rustic company were among his most enduring and most individual traits, and ones which he never lost, whether he appeared as a folk spirit or folk hero, or was represented in literature as a fairy or as a devil. The most significant instance of his passion for rustic society is to be found in *Grim, the Collier of Croydon,* where, though playing the rôle of a devil, he escapes from the high society to which he was sent, to live among the country folk, remarking,

> These silken girls are all too fine for me:
> My master shall report of those in hell,
> Whilst I go range amongst the country-maids,
> To see if home-spun lasses milder be
> Than my curs'd dame, and Lacy's wanton wife.
> Thus therefore will I live betwixt two shapes.[71]

Though this statement and that of *Love Restored* may have been written to satirize court ladies and court sports, they kept true to the traditional characteristic of Robin Goodfellow.

[70] Jonson, Morley ed., p. 167.

[71] IV, 1, ll. 5–10.

His figure and person, if nothing else, would have marked him as a country spirit, or would have kept him one. He was both tall and broad, of the size of a full grown man or bigger, with nothing ethereal or graceful about his proportions. His bigness particularly set him apart from other terrestrial spirits, as Robert Burton noted when he classified him as a " bigger kind " of terrestrial devil,[72] and as Ben Jonson knew when he represented him in *Love Restored* as saying

> I am none of those subtle ones, that can creep through at a keyhole, or the cracked pane of a window. I must come in at a door.[73]

So much were his shape and making different from the fairies of *A Midsummer Night's Dream* that he was identified there by his figure, and so well known were his measurements that in *Merry Wives of Windsor,* his rôle was not entrusted to any of the Windsor children, not even to one of the boys who was big enough and tall enough to be mistaken for Mistress Anne Page, but was played by Pistol.[74]

In *Albions England* he stood out as " of bigger bulke and voyce " than the " round of Fairie-elves, and Larrs of other kind " that appeared with him.[75] The ghost of Richard Tarlton took Robin Goodfellow's shape and appeared full grown as in the days of his human existence.[76] In *Grim, the Collier of Croydon,* where Robin Goodfellow had the part of servingman, he needed only to change his face and clothes to become himself again;[77]

[72] *Anat. of Mel.,* Vol. I, p. 220.

[73] Page 168.

[74] V, 5.

[75] William Warner, *Albions England,* 1612 quarto, Chap. 91, rpt. Hazlitt, *Fairy Tales,* p. 363.

[76] *Tarltons Newes,* p. 54.

[77] IV, 1.

while in *Robin Goodfellow; his mad prankes, and merry Jests,*[78] as in *The Midnight's Watch*[79] and in *Wily Beguiled,*[80] he moved among men with no noticeable discrepancy between his size and that of the company. Even among the ultra diminutive and mock-heroic fairies of Drayton, he seems to have retained his own measurements and clumped his way through *Nimphidia.*

There was nothing smart, or brisk, or trim, or graceful about his figure to recommend it. Drayton represented him as

> . . . . . a dreaming dolt,
> Still walking like a ragged Colt.[81]

James VI of Scotland described him as a "rough-man."[82] To Churchyard he appeared as "Rude Robin Goodfellow, the lout."[83] In *Love Restored,* he was mistaken for a "fighting bear of last year,"[84] as in *Misogonus,*[85] and in *L'Allegro*

> Then lies him down, the lubbar fend,
> And, stretched out all the chimney's length,
> Basks at the fire his hairy strength.[86]

He possessed, however, if the later records of his history are to be believed, the power of transformation,[87]

[78] Hazlitt rpt., pp. 173–207.

[79] Rpt. in Halliwell, *Fairy Myth.,* pp. 273–279.

[80] Pages 17 and 18.

[81] *Nimphidia,* ll. 289–290.

[82] *Daemon.,* p. 127.

[83] *A Handful of Gladsome Verses,* rpt. in Chambers, "Fairy World," p. 164.

[84] Jonson, Morley ed., p. 168.

[85] I, 3.

[86] Milton, ll. 110–112.

[87] According to *Robin Goodfellow; his mad prankes, and merry Jests* (Hazlitt rpt., p. 180), this power was only given to Robin Goodfellow on condition that, "transformed thus," he should see that he harmed none "but knaves and queanes."

and could change his shape to that of any animal or mortal which the exigencies of the occasion demanded, as, for instance, in *The Pranks of Puck:*

Sometimes I meet them like a man,
  Sometimes an ox, sometimes a hound;
And to a horse I turn me can,
  To trip and trot about them round;
    But if, to ride,
    My back they stride,
More swift than wind away I go;
  O'er hedge, o'er lands,
  Through pools, through ponds,
I hurry laughing, ho, ho, ho! [88]

or in *A Midsummer Night's Dream:*

I'll follow you, I'll lead you about a round,
  Through bog, through bush, through brake, through brier;
Sometime a horse I'll be, sometime a hound,
  A hog, a headless bear, sometime a fire;
And neigh, and bark, and grunt, and roar, and burn,
Like horse, hound, hog, bear, fire, at every turn.[89]

Nothing about him betrayed his folk origin or his country manners more than his wardrobe. Although this was never standardized and he possessed no traditional or national costume, his taste in wearing apparel could only pass muster in field or forest, or in country kitchen or servants' hall.

Many times he wore nothing at all, as in *Albions England,*[90] the *Discovery of Witchcraft,*[91] and *Robin Goodfel-*

[88] Halliwell rpt., pp. 166–167.

[89] III, 1, ll. 107–112. Cf. also Scot, *Dis. of Witch.,* 1651 ed., p. 97; and Jonson, *Love Restored,* Morley ed., pp. 168–169.

[90] Warner, 1612 quarto, Chap. 91, Hazlitt rpt., p. 363.

[91] Scot, 1651 ed., p. 66.

low; his mad prankes and merry Jests.[92] In *L'Allegro,*[93] in *The Satyr,*[94] and in the *Sad Shepherd,* in which he was called Puck-hairy,[95] he was covered with a thick pelt of hair. At other times his clothing must have consisted of a suit of russet, since the ghost of Tarlton who was mistaken for him, appeared " attired in russet, with a buttond cap on his head, a great bag by his side, and a strong bat in his hand." [96]

What he wore when he appeared among the fairies is not known, except in *The Satyr,* where he was referred to as a satyr; [97] but when he was put on the stage in the rôle of a lesser devil, he affected a close fitting suit of calfskin, with the exception of his appearance in *The Devil is an Ass,* where the red roses on his shoes and his stolen suit caused the final disaster that befell him.

It was as a devil, and as a devil only, that Robin Goodfellow was represented as particularly concerned about his appearance. In *Grim, the Collier of Croydon,* he twice changed his costume, and discarded the tawny coat of a servant for his own choice of a suit of leather close to his body, with the face and hands colored russet color.[98] In *Wily Beguiled,* he was continually gloating over his clothes:

> Ile put me on my great carnation nose
> And wrap me in a rowsing Calueskin suite,
> And come like some Hob goblin or some diuell.[99]

92 Hazlitt rpt., p. 185.
93 Milton, l. 112.
94 Jonson, Morley ed.
95 Jonson, Gifford ed.
96 *Tarltons Newes,* p. 54.
97 Jonson, Morley ed.
98 IV, 1.
99 Lines 1037–1039.

Not content with this enumeration, he mentioned his costume five times over until he finally appeared in his "Christmas Calues skin sute." [100] And the question of his earthly wardrobe brought about a deal of discussion between him and Satan in *The Devil is an Ass.*[101]

Wearing apparel for some reason, either unknown or forgotten in the 16th century, must originally have been invested with a particular and important significance in regard to Robin Goodfellow. On his own part, any notice of his nakedness or any change suggested in his costume was the one insult which caused him mortal offense:

> . . . and you have also heard that he would chafe exceedingly, if the maid or good-wife of the house, having compassion of his nakednesse, laid any clothes for him, besides his messe of white bread and milke, which was his standing fee. For in that case he saith; What have we here? Hemton hamten, here will I never more tread nor stampen.[102]

This idiosyncrasy of Robin recurs again and again in his subsequent history, and is to be found in modern folk tales of England and Scotland concerning him. The formula, "Hemton hamten," connected, it would seem, in some way with hemp or hemp stalks of superstitious associations, invariably accompanied the expression of anger with which he repudiated a proffer of clothes, even a waistcoat, and was never omitted or forgotten.[103]

On the part of the folk themselves, in the 16th century a singular superstition prevailed that turning the coat or some other garment would protect a mortal from

[100] *Ibid.*, l. 1256.

[101] Jonson, Gifford ed., I, 1. Cf. also V, 4.

[102] Scot, *Dis. of Witch.*, 1651 ed., p. 66.

[103] Warner, *Albions England,* quarto, 1612, Hazlitt rpt., p. 364. *Robin Goodfellow; his mad prankes, and merry Jests,* Halliwell rpt., pp. 131–132.

the practical jokes of Robin Goodfellow, especially from being misled by him. In Tyndale's *Exposition of the First Epistle of St. John,* this belief is set down as follows:

> . . . the scripture is locked up and become so dark unto them, that they grope for the door, and can find no way in; and is become a maze unto them, in which they wander as in a mist, or (as we say) led by Robin Goodfellow, that they cannot come to the right way, no, though they turn their caps;[104]

while the *Iter Boreale* of Bishop Corbet of nearly a century later contains the admonition

> . . . . "Turne your cloakes,"
> Quoth he, "for Puck is busy in these oakes."[105]

However Robin Goodfellow's clothes might vary, one item of his costume never changed. This was the broom or threshing flail which he habitually carried. Find him in whatever company you may, his broom especially is in easy reach. In *Love Restored,* he "e'en went back, and stuck to this shape . . . of mine own, with my broom and my candles, and came on confidently."[106] In *Grim, the Collier of Croydon,*[107] and in *L'Allegro,*[108] he carries a flail. One of his chief occupations, according to Jonson,[109] Scot,[110] and Tyndale,[111] was sweeping. And

[104] *Expositions and Notes,* p. 139.

[105] Page 579. It is interesting to note in this connection that the small screech owls whose habit it is to appear at twilight and dart down upon the head of any unwary pedestrian are called in some counties of England *Puckridge,* and that the superstition still prevails among the negroes of the South that turning one's cap or some portion of wearing apparel inside out will drive away screech owls.

[106] Jonson, Morley ed., p. 169.

[107] IV, 1.

[108] Milton, l. 108.

[109] *Love Restored,* Morley ed., p. 167.

[110] *Dis. of Witch.,* 1651 ed., p. 66.

[111] "Obed. of a Chr. Man," in *Doctrinal Treatises,* p. 321.

Shakespeare in *A Midsummer Night's Dream,* though placing Robin Goodfellow in a poetic and etherealized fairy court, as messenger and jester of Oberon, does not take away his broom. In Act V, Scene 2, he not only appears with a broom, but calls public attention to it, remarking complacently,

> I am sent, with broom, before,
> To sweep the dust behind the door.[112]

That Robin Goodfellow survived the 16th and 17th centuries without losing his broom or his candlestick, would argue well for the universality and minuteness of the knowledge concerning him, and would furnish ample proof of his folk origin, the recollections of which continued to exist.

It was surely this origin which would account for one of his most emphasized traits: namely, his desire for bread and cream. According to the *Discovery of Witchcraft,* a mess of white bread and cream had been recognized for a hundred years as Robin Goodfellow's standing fee.[113]. And from the "crummed mess of milke" bestowed upon him in *Albions England* [114] and the milk pans which he raided in Rowlands' *More Knaues Yet?* [115] to the last years of the 18th century in Scotland when he was presented with a dish of cream which he sometimes "eat till he bursted," [116] Robin Goodfellow's appetite

[112] Lines 19–20.

[113] Scot, 1651 ed., p. 66.

[114] Warner, quarto, 1612, Chap. 91, Hazlitt rpt., p. 364.

[115] Vol. II, p. 40.

[116] Heron, *Observations made in a Journey through the Western Counties of Scotland,* Vol. II, p. 227.

In Scotland in 1792, "They had an universal custom of pouring a cow's milk upon a little hill, or big stone, where the spirit called Browny was believed to lodge: this spirit always appeared in the

never varied. Harsnet, in the *Declaration of egregious Popish Impostures,* calls attention to " the bowle of curds and creame . . . set out for Robin Good-fellow " [117] in no uncertain terms; as does the author of the *Masque at Cole-Orton,*[118] and the author of *The Cobler of Canterburie,* who deplored the disappearance of Robin Goodfellow with the disappearance of hospitality toward him:

> This makes Robin Good fellow that was so merrie a spirite of the butterie, to leaue all, and keep himselfe in Purgatorie, for Hospitalitie is so cleane runne out of the countrie, that he needes not now helpe the maides to grinde their mault, for the drinke is so small, that it needs little corne: and if he should helpe them, where he was wont to finde a messe of creame for his labour, scarce get a dish of floate milke.[119]

Even when he was represented as a lesser devil, his desire for cream and bread was still a predominant characteristic. In *The Devil is an Ass,* Satan is to be found in Hell reminding Pug of his interest in cream.[120] And in *Grim, the Collier of Croydon,* Robin cannot keep his spoon out of the cream bowl, but states frankly:

> I love a mess of cream as well as they.[121]

It must have been this passion that prompted the superstition that bread carried about the person was a talisman

---

shape of a tall man, having very long brown hair. There was scarce any the least village in which this superstitious custom did not prevail. I enquired the reason of it from several well-meaning women, who until of late had practised it; and they told me that it had been transmitted to them by their ancestors successfully, who believed it was attended with good fortune." M. Martin, *Desc. of West. Isles,* Pinkerton rpt., p. 610.

[117] Page 134.

[118] Page 330.

[119] Appendix, *Tarltons Newes,* p. 110.

[120] Jonson, Gifford ed., I, 1.

[121] V, 1.

against the tricks of Robin Goodfellow or Puck. According to Clobery's *Divine Glimpses of a Maiden Muse,*

> Old countrey folk, who pixie-leading fear,
> Bear bread about them to prevent that harm,[122]

a belief which is also mentioned by Robert Herrick in *Hesperides.*[123]

Robin Goodfellow's standing fee, however, was not forced from a reluctant householder, nor was it obtained usually by robbery or terrorism. In return for his favorite dish, he applied himself to all the domestic operations which went on in the house. Nothing pleased him better than to "make a fier in the morning, sweepe the house, grind mustard and malt, drawe water," [124] and "helpe the maydes to breake hempe, to bowlt, to dresse flaxe, and to spin," [125] "cut wood, or do any manner of drudgery work." [126]

> And with the country wenches, who but hee.
> To wash their Dishes for some fresh-cheese hier:
> Or set their Pots and Kettles bout the fier.[127]

In all his domestic occupations, he was very earnest and very noisy, and would "rumble in houses, drawe latches, go up and downe staiers," [128] "locking and unlocking of dores, tinckling amongst the fier-shouels and the tonges, ratling uppon the boards, scraping vnder their beds, and blowing out the candels, except they were halowed." [129]

[122] Rpt. Halliwell, *Fairy Myth.,* p. xvii.

[123] Page 323.

[124] Scot, *Dis. of Witch.,* 1651 ed., p. 437.

[125] *Robin Goodfellow; his mad prankes, and merry Jests,* Hazlitt rpt., p. 184.

[126] Burton, *Anat. of Mel.,* Vol. I, p. 220.

[127] Rowlands, *More Knaues Yet?,* Vol. II, p. 40.

[128] Scot, *Dis. of Witch.,* 1651 ed., p. 437.

[129] Harsnet, *Declaration,* p. 14.

There were two conditions upon which, in addition to his fee, Robin Goodfellow's domestic services were given. He required of the mistress or maid whom he served that she did not, as he put it, " sluttish lie "; nor would he lend his aid to men or women unless they conformed to his standard of morality in regard to love. If they were true lovers, he took a tremendous interest in their affairs, in which he meddled, until he brought about a happy consummation. So well known were his match-making instincts and his devotion to the cause of true love that his endeavors in this regard were recognized as one of his functions.

In the masque of *Love Restored,* he was chosen to throw out " that impostor Plutus, the god of money, who has stolen Love's ensigns, and in his belied figure rules the world," and to restore true love " in despight of this insolent and barbarous Mammon." [130]

In *Grim, the Collier of Croydon,* he took a great hand in furthering the cause of love:

> I like this country-girl's condition well;
> She's faithful, and a lover but to one;
> Robin stands here to right both Grim and her; [131]

and in punishing attempts against virtue:

> What, priest, still at your lechery?
> Robin beats the priest.
> I'll thresh you for your knavery;
> If any ask who beat thee so,
> Tell them 'twas Robin Goodfellow.[132]

In *Nimphidia,* he endeavored to restore the erring Mab to her husband; while in *A Midsummer Night's Dream*

[130] Jonson, Morley ed., pp. 170 and 171.
[131] IV, 1.
[132] *Grim, the Collier,* IV, 1.

he lamented the fortunes of the love-lorn Hermia, and the knavishness of Cupid

Thus to make poor females mad.[133]

But of all the idiosyncrasies and characteristics attributed to Robin Goodfellow, those that most insured his immortality and most endeared him to his time were his sense of humor and his infectious laugh.

Wherever in Elizabethan literature or folk tale Robin Goodfellow is met, his laugh is heard — a loud and boisterous guffaw of " ho, ho, ho! " — which only ceased to identify him when he ceased to appear. Yet for all its frequency, Robin Goodfellow's laugh was never cruel or malicious, but was always the sign of unfailing good humor and of the successful achievement of a merry prank. The gaiety and fun which Robin Goodfellow's laugh connoted are a marked indication of his reputation among the folk, since his particular ho, ho, ho's had formerly been the distinctive property of the devil in the miracle plays and moralities, and were still associated with him in 1616, in *The Devil is an Ass,* when Satan opens the play with the " Hoh, hoh, hoh, hoh, hoh, hoh, hoh, hoh! " of his infernal mirth,[134] as they were in the earlier part of Elizabeth's reign when the great black

[133] III, 2, l. 441. Cf. also *Robin Goodfellow; his mad prankes, and merry Jests;* and Henry Austin, Grosart ed., 1876, *The Scovrge of Venvs: or, The wanton Lady,* Stanza 117:

" Their bed doth shake and quauer as they lie,
As if it groan'd to beare the weight of sinne,
The fatall night-crowes at their windowes flie,
And cries out at the shame they do liue in:
And that they may perceiue the heauens frowne,
The Poukes & Goblins pul the couerings down."

[134] Jonson, Gifford ed., I, 1. Cf. also *The Devil is an Ass,* W. S. Johnson, Introd., p. xxiii and notes.

devil in *Gammer Gurtons Nedle* "cryed ho, ho, he roared and he thundred."[135]

Robin Goodfellow's laugh, common in Elizabethan England, has not survived, but the sense of humor which called it forth is as much an attribute of the modern conception of Puck as it was of Robin Goodfellow. To point out the references to this characteristic is almost unnecessary, for Robin Goodfellow's jokes tally, with few exceptions, with every mention of him, and fill the pages of his history which is entitled "his mad prankes, and merry Jests."

It was in his capacity as a practical joker that the name Robin Goodfellow was first mentioned, and it was in this capacity that he was known by 1562:

I was credebly informed that a hoker came to a farmers house in the ded of the night, and putting back a drawe window of a low chamber, the bed standing hard by the sayd wyndow, in which laye three parsones (a man and two bygge boyes), this hoker with his staffe plucked of their garments which lay vpon them to kepe them warme, with the couerlet and shete, and lefte them lying a slepe naked sauing there shertes, and had a way all clene, and neuer could vnderstande where it became. I verely suppose that when they wer wel waked with cold, they suerly thought that Robin goodfelow (accordinge to the old saying) had bene with them that night.[136]

In *A Midsummer Night's Dream,* a large part of the fun is due to Robin Goodfellow's ruling passion for jokes, and the well-known episode of Bottom the Weaver and the ass's head is a device of his own contriving. His pranks provide both the occasion and the plot for two of the gayest court masques of Jonson, furnish most of the comedy in the *Sad Shepherd, Grim, the Collier of Croy-*

[135] III, 2.

[136] Thomas Harman, *Caveat,* p. 69.

don, and *Wily Beguiled,* and are the subject of the tracts and ballads of which he is the hero.

Few jokes were omitted from his repertoire. As a specimen page of his history shows,

Robin Good-fellow would many times walke in the night with a broome on his shoulder, and cry chimney sweepe, but when any one did call him, then would be runne away laughing ho, ho, hoh! Somtime hee would counterfeit a begger, begging very pitifully, but when they came to give him an almes, he would runne away, laughing as his manner was. Sometimes would hee knocke at mens doores, and when the servants came, he would blow out the candle, if they were men; but if they were women, hee would not onely put out their light, but kisse them full sweetly, and then go away as his fashion was, ho, ho, hoh! Oftentimes would he sing at a doore like a singing man, and when they did come to give him his reward, he would turne his backe and laugh.[137]

But all of these inventions faded into insignificance in comparison with his chief joke of misleading night wanderers, "Laughing at their harmes," a prank in which he indulged so frequently that pucks have gone down in history as

Ambulones, that walk about midnight on great heaths and desert places, which (saith Lavater) draw men out of the way, and lead them all night a by-way, or quite bar them of their way. These have several names in several places; we commonly call them Pucks. In the deserts of Lop in Asia, such illusions of walking spirits are often perceived, as you may read in Marco Polo the Venetian, his

[137] *Robin Goodfellow; his mad prankes, and merry Jests,* Halliwell rpt., pp. 142–143. Cf. also Dekker, *The Seuen deadly Sinnes of London,* Vol. II, p. 46: "When the Bell-man for anger to spie (such a Purloyner of Cittizens goods) so many, hath bounced at the doore like a madde man. At which (as if Robin Good-fellow had been coniur'd vp amongst them) the Wenches haue falne into/ the handes of the Greene-sicknesse, and the yong fellowes into cold Agues, with verie feare least their maister . . . shoulde come downe."

travels. If one lose his company by chance, these devils will call him by his name, and counterfeit voices of his companions to seduce him.[138]

These, then are the qualities, attributes and exploits which went to make up the character and personality of Robin Goodfellow as he was known in the 16th and 17th centuries.

Had he been allowed to remain in the customs of the country and in the tales of the folk, untouched by literary fancy or literary phrase, he would no doubt still be found, the identical Robin Goodfellow portrayed in Scot's *Discovery of Witchcraft,* haunting the countryside, drinking cream and lending a gay and good-natured hand to domestic affairs. But he could not survive the literary and dramatic vogue he enjoyed after *A Midsummer Night's Dream,* and the fact that instead of being presented as an individual hero in his own right, he was either numbered among the members of a particular race of spirits as a fairy, or devil, or familiar spirit, or his name of Puck or Robin Goodfellow and a number of his characteristics were given to characters who were represented as fairies, or devils, or familiar spirits.

As has been noted, he owed his literary career and his classification as a fairy, as a puck, and as Hobgoblin, to Shakespeare who put him on the stage for the first time in his history as Puck, in company with the diminutive fairies of *A Midsummer Night's Dream.* To his position and associations here can be traced the beginning of two features, at least, which marked many of his later appearances in literature and in drama, both of which tended to diminish his prestige and his reality:

[138] Burton, *Anat. of Mel.,* Vol. I, pp. 222–223. Cf. also Nashe, *Terr. of the Night,* Vol. I, p. 347; Corbet, *Iter Boreale,* p. 579; and Drayton, *Nimphidia,* Stanza 37.

namely, an incongruity which rendered him ridiculous, and a subserviency to a higher power which reduced him from his traditional position as an independent spirit [139] to that of a vassal and servant.[140]

Among the diminutive and ethereal fairies of *A Midsummer Night's Dream,* Robin Goodfellow's uncouth shape and figure are stressed,[141] and the rusticity of his affections and his devotions to his broom [142] are emphasized. He is unable to see things which Oberon can see,[143] and, in contradistinction to the fairies, at least in this play, he is in terror lest daylight find him on earth.[144] In addition, he is reduced to the position of jester and messenger of Oberon whose commands he must obey. Although, in this situation, he is able to carry out any mad pranks which come into his head, he is forced to

[139] Cf. Chap. VI, p. 225.

[140] The position of Robin Goodfellow among the fairies, and the devastation wrought upon him, are especially illustrated in the following stanza:

> " Of Robin Goodfellow also,
> Which was a seruant long agoe,
> The Queene of Fairies doth it know,
> and hindered him in fashion:
> She knew not what she did her selfe,
> She chang'd him like a Fairie elfe,
> For all his money, goods, and pelfe,
> she gull'd him."

No. 79, A Monstrous Shape, A Pepysian Garland, p. 452.

Other records of the association of Robin Goodfellow with the fairies occur in Heywood, *Hierarchie,* p. 574; in Rowlands, *More Knaues Yet?* Vol. II, p. 40; in the quarto ed. of Warner, *Albions England,* Chap. 91; and in *The Midnight's Watch,* rpt. Halliwell, *Fairy Myth.,* pp. 273–279.

[141] II, 1.

[142] V, 2.

[143] II, 2.

[144] III, 2.

explain his mistakes and to suffer a sharp reproof from Oberon because of his jokes.[145]

His position in *Merry Wives of Windsor* is similar to his position in *A Midsummer Night's Dream*.[146] In *Nimphidia* his incongruity is magnified, and his powerlessness before the charms of the fairy, Nimphidia, is exaggerated until he becomes a most ridiculous and ineffectual figure. In *The Satyr* of Ben Jonson, though possessed of an intimate knowledge of the fairies and a tongue which divulges all their secrets, he is made curiously fearful of their pinches and powerless against their banishment. *The Masque at Cole-Orton* of 1618 represents him in some sort of subserviency to the fairies, as does the ballad, *The Pranks of Puck*. In *Robin Goodfellow; his mad prankes, and merry Jests,* he owes all of his powers and fame to "King Obreon," and takes his orders from him:

> Doe thus, and all the world shall know
> The prankes of Robin Good-fellow;
> For by that name thou cald shalt be
> To ages last posterity.
> If thou observe my just command
> One day thou shalt see Fayry Land!
> This more I give: who tels thy prankes
> From those that heare them shall have thankes.[147]

In spite of the fact that Robin Goodfellow lost his independence and much of his power as a member of the fairy kingdom, his own personality and his own individual characteristics remained intact in the plays and poems where he was represented as a fairy. In folk

[145] III, 2.

[146] V, 5. The word, Puck, is applied to Sir Hugh in the quarto, and Hobgoblin to Pistol in the folio.

[147] Hazlitt rpt., p. 180.

tale and in folk belief he was never regarded as a fairy, and his connection with the fairy kingdom seems to have been one of association rather than one of blood kinship.

His second classification — that of a lesser devil — which occurred in the plays concerning Satan and the devil,[148] proved more detrimental to the preservation of his personality and his reputation. In them, he is presented, at least in two cases, in Hell, in subjection to Satan and to Beelzebub, and is sent to earth, disguised as a servant, to further human wickedness and to bring about human disaster.

In both capacities — as a devil in Hell and as a devil on earth — he is represented as a failure. He is by no means clever enough to gain preference in Hell, or

[148] *Wily Beguiled;* Jonson, *The Devil is an Ass;* and *Grim, the Collier.*

In *Wily Beguiled,* as Mr. W. S. Johnson notes, "Robin Goodfellow is a malicious intriguer, whose nature, whether human or diabolical, is left somewhat in doubt." He appears as a well-known ale companion, wicked and evil and interested in injuring mortals, claims to practise a devilish trade, plays the part of an arrant coward and ends in disgrace, desiring to live in Hell as a reward for his acts. He possesses, however, a number of the traditional characteristics of Robin Goodfellow, and can be taken as a somewhat distorted representation of Robin Goodfellow as a devil. (Introd. by W. S. Johnson to *The Devil is an Ass.*)

Mr. Johnson states that one of the leading ideas of the Jonson comedy, *The Devil is an Ass,* is derived from the legend of Friar Rush, which, according to Mr. Johnson's statement again, had become by this time already partially identified with that of Robin Goodfellow. Mr. Johnson adds further that Jonson's character of Pug was certainly influenced in some degree both by the popular and the literary conception of this lubber fiend who appears in the mysteries in the shape of Titivillus. Introd., *The Devil is an Ass.* Cf. also Herford and Simpson, *Ben Jonson,* Vol. II, pp. 154–161.

In *Grim, the Collier of Croydon,* the devil, Akercock, is introduced as Robin Goodfellow in II, 1, and in the prologue.

wicked enough to hold his own on earth. As Satan states, in *The Devil is an Ass,*

> What wouldst thou do on earth?
> . . . .
> . . . . the laming a poor cow or two,
> Entering a sow, to make her cast her farrow,
> Or crossing of a market-woman's mare
> 'Twixt this and Tottenham? these were wont to be
> Your main achievements, Pug: You have some plot now,
> Upon a tunning of ale, to stale the yeast,
> Or keep the churn so, that the butter come not,
> Spite of the housewife's cord, or her hot spit:
> . . . .
> . . . Foolish fiend!
> Stay in your place, know your own strength, and put not
> Beyond the sphere of your activity:
> You are too dull a devil to be trusted
> Forth in those parts, Pug, upon any affair
> That may concern our name on earth. It is not
> Every one's work. The state of hell must care
> Whom it employs, in point of reputation,
> Here about London.[149]

More humiliating than Robin Goodfellow's or Pug's failure in his rôle of devil is the change in his character. All his old defiance of public opinion in the matter of clothes disappears.[150] He takes on a multitude of " sirs " and acts as valet or page with the most obsequious footman's bearing.[151] His mad and merry spirit is subdued to a cowardice that thrives on a broken head at the hands of ladies, or of a bleeding back from the cudgels

149 Jonson, Gifford ed., I, 1.

150 Jonson, *Devil is an Ass,* Gifford ed., V, 2; *Wily Beguiled,* ll. 715–718; *Grim, the Collier,* I, 3.

151 *Devil is an Ass,* Gifford ed., I, 2, and II, 1; and *Grim, the Collier,* II, 1.

of country men and the canes of gentlemen.[152] And his amused contempt for mortals, and the jokes and pranks which had marked his progress for a hundred years or more, are replaced by a dense stupidity which makes him the butt of servants and fools.[153]

Instead of going laughing away, as had been his traditional method of departure, in both plays, he bursts into prayers for an immediate transportation to Hell because of his inability to compete with human intelligence.[154]

No better illustration of the distance which lies between Robin Goodfellow, "that great and antient bull-begger," and Robin Goodfellow, a lesser devil in the plays of the 17th century, can be found than in the representation of him in *Grim, the Collier of Croydon.* Here, as a devil, he undergoes all the humiliations noted above, but when he deserts his devilish companions, puts on his native habit and runs away to pursue his usual career of a plain and honest country spirit, he becomes a dominant and forceful personality among mortals, upon whom he enforces his idea of decency and of true love.

Whatever qualities or character remained to Robin Goodfellow after the representation of him as a minor devil, vanished in the final rôle assigned him as a familiar spirit of witches. He had earlier been associated with them both in the *Discovery of Witchcraft,*[155] and in the *Daemonologie.*[156] But his connection with them had consisted, in the first case, in the fact that his reputation had been as terrible and credible as that of witches, and that he was associated with familiar spirits and devils;

[152] *Devil is an Ass,* Gifford ed., II, 1; *Wily Beguiled,* ll. 2008–2012, and ll. 2015–2020; *Grim, the Collier,* II, 1, and III, 1.

[153] *Devil is an Ass,* Gifford ed., III, 3; *Grim, the Collier,* II, 1.

[154] *Devil is an Ass,* Gifford ed., IV, 1; *Wily Beguiled,* ll. 2066–2070.

[155] Scot, 1651 ed., pp. 97 and 364.

[156] James VI of Scotland, p. 127.

and, in the second case, that he was, as were witches, an illusion or instrument of the devil. Giffard's *A Dialogue concerning Witches and Witchcrafts* of 1593 had, moreover, definitely connected witches and "puckerels," [157] into which class Robin Goodfellow was put after *A Midsummer Night's Dream.*

In *The Devil is an Ass* of 1616, Pug is introduced as numbering among his most successful exploits:

> . . . some good ribibe, about Kentish Town
> Or Hogsden, you would hang now for a witch,
> Because she will not let you play round Robin.
> And you'll go sour the citizens' cream 'gainst Sunday,
> That she may be accused for't, and condemn'd,
> By a Middlesex jury, to the satisfaction,
> Of their offended friends, the Londoners wives,
> Whose teeth were set on edge with't; [158]

and Lancashire, famous for contemporary witch trials, is recommended to him as the particular field for his especial endeavors.[159]

In *The Sad Shepherd,* in the cast of which he is described as "Puck-hairy, Or Robin-Goodfellow, their Hine," [160] he is presented as the familiar of Maudlin, the witch, but as a spirit superior to her and the source of her power: [161]

[157] Page 9.

[158] Jonson, Gifford ed., I, 1.

[159] *Ibid.*

[160] Jonson, Greg ed., p. 117.

[161] On page 234, Vol. II, of Herford & Simpson's *Ben Jonson,* the statement is made that Puck-hairy is "No kinsman of the impish Puck, hardly even of Jonson's own hapless outwitted Pug." A knowledge of Robin Goodfellow's and of Puck's history and antecedents, and of Ben Jonson's knowledge and use of folklore forces me to dissent from this statement.

The fiend hath much to do, that keeps a school,
Or is the father of a family;
Or governs but a country academy:
His labours must be great, as are his cares,
To watch all turns, and cast how to prevent them.
This dame of mine here, Maud, grows high in evil,
And thinks she does all, when 'tis I, her devil,
That both delude her, and must yet protect her.
She's confident in mischief, and presumes
The changing of her shape will still secure her;
But that may fail, and divers hazards meet
Of other consequence, which I must look to,
Nor let her be surprised on the first catch.
I must go dance about the forest now,
And firk it like a goblin, till I find her.[162]

But with the second act of *The Sad Shepherd,* any vestige of self-respect or dignity which attached to Robin Goodfellow as a witch's familiar, ceases to be recorded, and from his last jibe at Maudlin,

I do love, madam,
To shew you all your dangers, — when you're past them! [163]

he never speaks upon the stage again as a merry spirit or as an individual hero.

One degradation after another overwhelms him, and the former proud and popular personality of Robin Goodfellow is turned into that of an imp, Robin; and the Puck of *A Midsummer Night's Dream* becomes a disreputable Pug or an obsequious Puggy, or worse still, as in one instance, an indecent female spirit, old Puckle.[164] Instead of shouting songs of his own along the country

[162] Gifford ed., III, 1.

[163] Gifford ed., III, 2.

[164] Middleton, *The Witch,* I, 2, and V, 2; Shadwell, *The Lancashire Witches,* Halliwell ed., 1853, Act III, pp. 80–81; Heywood and Broome, *The Late Lancashire Witches,* IV, 1.

side, or waking a sleeping village with his loud guffaws, he figures as Puckey or as Robin in a witches' "Charm-Song about a Vessel":

> Black spirits and white, red spirits and gray,
> Mingle, mingle, mingle, you that mingle may!
> Titty, Tiffin,
> Keep it stiff in;
> Firedrake, Puckey,
> Make it lucky;
> Liard, Robin,
> You must bob in.
> Round, around, around, about, about!
> All ill come running in, all good keep out![165]

In place of the cream bowls which had been set out for Robin Goodfellow for hundreds of years, he is allowed, as Puckling, a drop or two of witch's blood as a recompense for labor:

> Come Mawsy, come Puckling,
> And come my sweet suckling,
> My pretty Mamillion, my Joy,
> Fall each to his duggy,
> While kindly we huggie,
> As tender as nurse over boy,
> Then suck our blouds freely, and with it be jolly,
> While merrily we sing hey, trolly, lolly.
>
> We'l dandle and clip yee,
> We'l stroke yee, and leape yee,
> And all that we have is your due;
> The feates you doe for us,
> And those which you store us
> Withal, tyes us onely to you.
> Then suck our blouds freely, and with it be jolly,
> While merrily we sing hey, trolly, lolly.[166]

[165] T. Middleton, *The Witch,* V, 2.

[166] Heywood and Broome, *The Late Lancashire Witches,* Song, p. 238.

To leave Robin Goodfellow as the disreputable familiar spirit of a witch would be unfair to his memory. Although his literary career ended with his appearance in witch plays, he has survived in the echoes of his own chuckles and in the smile which his name evokes, as the synonym for mischief and for mirth. And no more fitting epitome of himself and his career can be found, with which to close his life, than the exclamation of Grim, the collier of Croydon:

> Master Robert you were ever one of the honestest
> merry Devils that ever I saw.

LIST OF AUTHORITIES AND TEXTS CONSULTED

ADAMS, W. H. DAVENPORT, Witch, Warlock, and Magician. London, 1889.

ADAMS, JOSEPH QUINCY, A Life of William Shakespeare. Boston and New York, 1923.

ADDISON, JOSEPH, The Spectator; with introduction and notes by George A. Aitken. London, 1898, 8 vols.

AIKIN, LUCY, Memoirs of the Court of Elizabeth, Queen of England. New York, 1870, 2 vols. in 1.

——— Memoirs of the Court of King James the First. London, 1822, 2 vols.

ALDEN, RAYMOND MACDONALD, Shakespeare. New York, 1922.

Antiquary, The. A magazine devoted to the study of the past. Published by Elliott Stock, London, 1880–1915, 51 vols.

ARBOIS, MARIE HENRY DE JUBAINVILLE D', Le Cycle mythologique irlandais et la mythologie celtique, Vol. 2 of Cours de littérature celtique. Paris, 1883–1902, 12 vols.

ARONSTEIN, B., Ben Jonson. Berlin, 1906.

ASCHAM, ROGER, The Whole Works of Roger Ascham, edited by Dr. Giles. London, 1864, 2 vols.

ATKINSON, J. C., A Glossary of the Cleveland Dialect. London, 1868.

ATKINSON, ROBERT, The Book of Ballymote, edited by Robert Atkinson. Dublin, 1887.

——— The Book of Leinster, edited by Robert Atkinson. Dublin, 1880.

AUBREY, JOHN, Miscellanies upon Various Subjects. London, 1890.

——— Naturall History of Wiltshire. Fairy Tales, Legends and Romances Illustrating Shakespeare, edited by W. Carew Hazlitt. London, 1875.

——— Remaines of Gentilisme and Judaisme, edited by James Britten. Folk Lore Soc. Publns., Vol. 4, London, 1881.

AUSTIN, HENRY, The Scourge of Venus, edited by A. B. Grosart, Lancashire, 1876.

AYDELOTTE, FRANK, Elizabethan Rogues and Vagabonds. Oxford, 1913.

Bacon, Francis, Works, collected and edited by Spedding, Ellis and Heath, Vols. 4, 5, 13. Boston, 1860–1864, 15 vols.

Bailey, Nathan, A New Universal Etymological English Dictionary, originally compiled by Nathan Bailey & others. London, 1764.

Baldwin, Thomas Whitfield, The Organization and Personnel of the Shakespearean Company. Princeton, 1927.

Bale, John, The Dramatic Writings of John Bale, edited by John S. Farmer. London, 1907.

Ballads & Broadsides Chiefly of the Elizabethan Period, edited by Herbert L. Collmann. Oxford, 1912.

Bandello, Certain Tragical Discourses of Bandello, translated into English by Geffraie Fenton, 1567, with introduction by Robert L. Douglas. London, 1898, 2 vols.

Barclay, Alexander, Certayne Egloges. Spenser Society Publns. No. 39, Manchester, 1885.

——— The Cytezen and Uplondyshman, edited by F. W. Fairholt. Percy Society Publns. Vol. 22, London, 1847.

——— The Mirrour of Good Manners. Spenser Society Publns. No. 38, Manchester, 1885.

——— The Ship of Fools, translated by Alexander Barclay, edited by T. H. Jamieson. Edinburgh and London, 1874, 2 vols.

Barksted, William, Poems, edited by A. B. Grosart. Manchester, 1876.

Barnes, Barnabe, The Devil's Charter, edited by R. B McKerrow. Louvain, 1904.

——— Poems, edited by A. B. Grosart. Lancashire, 1825.

Barnfield, Richard, Complete Poems, edited by A. B. Grosart. Roxburghe Club Publns. London, 1876.

Baskervill, Charles Read, The Genesis of Spenser's Queen of Faerie. Modern Philology, Vol. 18, May 1920, Chicago, 1920–1921.

Bastian, Adolf, Zeitschrift für Ethnologie, edited by Adolf Bastian and R. Hartman. Berlin, 1869.

Baxter, Richard, The Saint's Everlasting Rest. The Practical Works of the Rev. Richard Baxter, edited by William Orme, Vol. 22. London, 1830, 23 vols.

Beauford, William, The Antient Topography of Ireland. No. XI of Vol. 3 of Vallancey, Collectanea de Rebus Hibernicis, Dublin, 1783.

Beaumont, Francis and John Fletcher, The Works of Beaumont and Fletcher, with introduction by George Darley. London, 1851, 2 vols.

Beaumont, John, An Historical, Physiological and Theological Treatise of Spirits, Apparitions, Witchcrafts and other Magical Practices. London, 1705.

Bekker, Balthazar, Le Monde Enchanté ou Examen des communs seulements touchant les Esprits. Rotterdam, 1694, 4 vols.

Bell, William, Shakespeare's Puck, and His Folkslore. London, 1852–1864, 3 vols.

Birch, Thomas, Memoirs of the Reign of Queen Elizabeth from the Year 1581 till Her Death. London, 1754, 2 vols.

Blount, Thomas, Glossographia. London, 1656.

Boas, Frederick S., University Drama in the Tudor Age. Oxford, 1914.

Boece, Hector, The History and Chronicles of Scotland, translated by John Bellenden. Edinburgh, 1821, 2 vols.

——— Scotorvm historiae a prima gentis origine. Paris, 1575.

Boke of Duke Huon of Burdeux, The, done into English by Lord Berners, edited by S. L. Lee for Early English Text Society, Nos. 40, 41, 43 & 50, Extra Series. London, 1882, 2 vols. in 3.

Bond, R. Warwick, Early Plays from the Italian, edited by R. W. Bond. Oxford, 1911.

Book of Homage to Shakespeare, A, edited by Israel Gollancz. Oxford, 1916.

Boswell-Stone, W. G., Shakspere's Holinshed; the Chronicle and the Historical Plays Compared. London, 1896.

Bourke, Ulick J., The Bull "Ineffabilis," translated and edited by U. J. Bourke. Dublin, 1868.

Bourne, Henry, Antiquitates Vulgares or the Antiquities of the Common People. Newcastle, 1725.

Bovet, Richard, Pandaemonium, or the Devil's Cloyster. Fairy Tales . . . ed. by W. C. Hazlitt. London, 1875.

Brand, John, Observations on the Popular Antiquities of Great Britain, revised by Sir Henry Ellis. London, 1849, 3 vols.

——— Popular Antiquities of Great Britain, edited by W. Carew Hazlitt. London, 1870, 3 vols.

Brathwaite, Richard, A Strappado for the Diuell, with introduction by J. W. Ebsworth. Boston, Lincolnshire, 1878.

Bray, Anna Eliza (Kempe) Stothard, A Description of the Part of Devonshire Bordering on the Tamar and the Tavy. London, 1836, 3 vols.

Breton, Nicholas, The Passionate Shepherd, edited by Frederic Ouvry. London, 1877.

BROOKE, C. F. TUCKER, The Shakespeare Apocrypha, edited by C. F. Tucker Brooke. Oxford, 1908.

——— Shakespeare of Stratford. New Haven, 1926.

BROTANEK, RUDOLF, Die englischen Maskenspiele. Wiener Beiträge zur englischen Philologie, Vol. XV, Wien and Leipzig, 1902.

BROWN, ARTHUR C. L., A Study in the Origins of Arthurian Romance; 1. Iwain. Studies and Notes in Philology and Literature, Vol. VIII. Boston, 1903.

BROWNE, SIR THOMAS, Works, Including Life and Correspondence, edited by Simon Wilkin. London, 1836, 4 vols.

BROWNE, WILLIAM, The Whole Works of William Browne, edited by W. C. Hazlitt. London, 1869, 2 vols.

BUCHAN, PETER, Gleanings of Scarce Old Ballads, with explanatory notes. Aberdeen, 1891.

Buggbears, The. Early Plays from the Italian, edited by R. W. Bond. Oxford, 1911.

BULLEN, A. H., A Collection of Old English Plays, edited by A. H. Bullen. London, 1882, 4 vols.

BULLOKAR, JOHN, The English Expositor Improv'd, revised by R. Browne. London, 1719.

BURR, GEORGE L., Literature of Witchcraft. Papers of the American Historical Association, Vol. IV, No. 3, New York, 1890.

——— Narratives of the Witchcraft Cases, 1648–1706, edited by G. L. Burr. New York, 1914.

——— The Witch-Persecutions, edited by G. L. Burr. Translations and Reprints from the Original Sources of European History, Vol. III, No. 4, Series of 1896. Philadelphia, 1897.

BURTON, ROBERT, The Anatomy of Melancholy, edited by A. R. Shilleto. London, 1896, 3 vols.

BUTLER, SAMUEL, Hudibras, edited by H. G. Bohn. London, 1859.

BYRD, WILLIAM, Psalmes, Sonets and Songs of Sadness and Pietie. Lyrics from the Songbooks of the Elizabethan Age, edited by A. H. Bullen. London, 1891.

CALVIN, JOHN, The Institutions of Christian Religion, translated by Thomas Norton. London, 1611.

Cambridge History of English Literature, edited by A. W. Ward and A. R. Waller. New York, 1907–1917, 14 vols.

CAMDEN, WILLIAM, Britain; or, A Chorographicall Description of England, Scotland and Ireland, translated by Philemon Holland. London, 1610.

——— Remains concerning Britain. London, 1870.

Campbell, John Francis, Popular Tales of the West Highlands. London, 1890, 4 vols.

Campbell, John Gregorson, Superstitions of the Highlands. Glasgow, 1902.

Campion, Thomas, Campion's Works, edited by Percival Vivian. Oxford, 1909.

Caradoc of Lhancarvan, The History of Wales written originally in British, Englished by Dr. Powell, edited by T. Evans. London, 1774.

Carew, Richard, Survey of Cornwall, with notes by Thomas Tonkin published from original mss. by Francis Lord de Dunstanville. London, 1811.

Cartwright, William, The Ordinary. Dodsley, Select Collection of Old Plays, Vol. X. London, 1780.

Casaubon, Merick, Of Credulity and Incredulity; in things Divine and Spiritual. London, 1670.

Castelain, Maurice, Ben Jonson: l'homme et l'œuvre. Paris, 1907.

Catholicon Anglicum, edited by Sidney J. H. Herrtage for Early English Text Society, No. 75. London, 1881.

Caxton, William, The Golden Legend or Lives of the Saints, Englished by William Caxton, edited by F. S. Ellis. London, 1900, 7 vols.

——— Six Bookes of Metamorphoseos in whyche ben conteyned The Fables of Ovyde translated out of Frensshe into Englysshe by William Caxton. London, 1819.

Chalmers, Alexander, The Works of the English Poets from Chaucer to Cowper, edited by Alexander Chalmers. London, 1810, 21 vols.

Chambers, E. K., The Elizabethan Stage. Oxford, 1923, 4 vols.

——— The Mediaeval Stage. Oxford, 1903, 2 vols.

——— The Fairy World, Appendix A. A Midsummer Night's Dream, Warwick edition. London [1911].

——— Shakespeare, a Survey. Oxford, 1926.

Chambers, Robert, Popular Rhymes of Scotland. London and Edinburgh, 1870.

Chantepie de la Saussaye, Pierre Daniel, The Religion of the Teutons, translated from Dutch by B. J. Vos. Boston and London, 1902.

Chapman, George, The Comedies and Tragedies; Pearson edition. London, 1873, 3 vols.

CHAPMAN, G., JONSON, B., MARSTON, J., Eastward Hoe. Students' Facsimile Edition, 1914.

CHAUCER, GEOFFREY, Complete Works, edited by W. W. Skeat. Oxford, 1894, 6 vols.; Oxford, 1897, Supplement.

CHETTLE, HENRY, Kind-Heart's Dream, edited by Edward F. Rimbault. Percy Society Publns. No. 5. London, 1841.

CHILD, FRANCIS JAMES, The English and Scottish Popular Ballads, edited by F. J. Child. Boston and New York, 1882, 1884, 1898, 5 vols., 10 parts.

CHURCHYARD, THOMAS, Bibliographical Miscellanies, Being a Selection of Curious Pieces, in Verse and Prose, by Philip Bliss. Oxford, 1813.

——— A discourse of the Queenes Majesties Entertainment in Suffolk and Norfolk, 1578. Nichols, The Progresses and Public Processions of Queen Elizabeth. London, 1823, 3 vols.

——— The First Parte of Churchyardes Chippes, containing Twelve severall Labours. London, 1575.

——— Frondes Caducae, reprinted by Alexander Boxwell. Auchinleck Press, 1816.

——— A Handfull of gladsome Verses given to the Queen's Majesty at Woodstock this Progress, 1578. E. K. Chambers, Warwick ed. of *A Midsummer Night's Dream,* App. A., The Fairy World.

——— The Life of Cardinal Wolsey by George Cavendish . . . to which is added Thomas Churchyard's *Tragedy of Wolsey,* with introduction by Henry Morley. London, 1887.

——— The Mirror of Man, and manners of Men. London, 1594.

——— A pleasant Discourse of Court and Wars. London, 1596.

——— A sad and solemne Funerall, of the right Honorable sir Francis Knowles. London, 1596.

——— The Worthines of Wales. London, 1776.

CLOBERY, CHRISTOPHER, Divine Glimpses of a Maiden Muse. London, 1659.

CLODD, EDWARD, Tom Tit Tot, an essay on savage philosophy in folk-tale. London, 1898.

Cobler of Canterburie, The, or An Invective against Tarltons Newes out of Purgatorie. Tarlton's Jests and News out of Purgatory, edited by J. O. Halliwell for the Shakespeare Society. London, 1844.

COCKAYNE, OSWALD, Leechdoms, Wortcunning, and Star-craft of Early England, edited by Oswald Cockayne. London, 1864, 3 vols.

Maske von Cole-Orton, Die. R. Brotanek, Die englischen Maskenspiele. Wiener Beiträge zur englischen Philologie, Vol. XV, Wien and Leipzig, 1902.

Collier, John Payne, A Bibliographical and Critical Account of the Rarest Books in the English Language, edited by J. P. Collier. New York, 1866, 4 vols.

——— Illustrations of Early English Popular Literature. London, 1863–1864, 2 vols.

——— New Facts Regarding the Life of Shakespeare. In a letter to Thomas Amyot. London, 1835.

Collins, William, The Poetical Works of Collins. The Poetical Works of Collins, Gray, and Beattie. London, 1839.

Common Prayer, The Book of the, and Administration of the Sacramentes, and other Rites and Ceremonies of the Churche after the use of the Churche of England. London, 1549.

Complaynt of Scotland, The, edited by J. Leyden, reëdited by J. A. H. Murray for Early English Text Society. London, 1872–1873.

Constable, Henry, Diana, or The Excellent Conceitful, Sonnets of H. C. An English Garner, New York, 1904, 2 vols.

Cooper, Thomas, An Admonition to the People of England, 1589, edited by Edward Arber. Birmingham, 1883.

Coote, Henry Charles, The Neo-Latin Fay. Folk Lore Record, Vol. II. London, 1879.

Corbet, Richard, The Poems of Bishop Corbet. The Works of the English Poets, edited by Alexander Chalmers, Vol. 5. London, 1810, 21 vols.

The Cornhill Magazine. London, 1881, Vol. XLIII.

Coryate, Thomas, Crudities, reprinted from edition of 1611. London, 1776, 3 vols.

Cotgrave, Randle, A Dictionarie of the French and English Tongues, compiled by Randle Cotgrave. London, 1611.

Cowley, Abraham, The Complete Works in Verse and Prose, edited by A. B. Grosart. Edinburgh, 1881, 2 vols.

Creighton, Mandell, The Age of Elizabeth. New York, 1898.

Crofts, J. E. V., A Life of Bishop Corbett, 1582–1635. Essays and Studies by members of The English Association, Vol. X. Oxford, 1924.

Croker, T. Crofton, Fairy Legends and Traditions of the South of Ireland, collected by T. C. Croker. London, 1834.

Crow, M. F., Elizabethan Sonnet-Cycles. London, 1896–1898, 4 vols.

CUMMING, J. G., The Isle of Man, Its History, Physical, Ecclesiastical, Civil and Legendary. London, 1848.

CUNNINGHAM, ALLAN, Traditional Tales of the English and Scottish Peasantry. London, 1874.

CUNNINGHAM, PETER, Extracts from the Accounts of the Revels at Court in the Reigns of Queen Elizabeth and King James I, edited by Peter Cunningham for The Shakespeare Society. London, 1842.

CUSHMAN, LYSANDER WILLIAM, The Devil and the Vice in the English Dramatic Literature before Shakespeare. Studien zur englischen Philologie, No. 6. Halle, 1900.

DALYELL, JOHN GRAHAM, The Darker Superstitions of Scotland. Edinburgh, 1834.

DANIEL, SAMUEL, The Complete Works in Verse and Prose, edited by A. B. Grosart. London, 1885–1896, 5 vols.

DAVIES, SIR JOHN, The Works in Verse and Prose, edited by A. B. Grosart. Blackburn, Lancashire, 1869–1876, 3 vols.

DAVIES, THOMAS, Dramatic Miscellanies: consisting of Critical Observations on Several Plays of Shakespeare. London, 1785, 3 vols.

DAVISON, FRANCIS, The Poetical Rhapsody: to which are added, Several other Pieces, with notes by Nicholas Harris Nicolas. London, 1826, 2 vols.

DAY, JOHN, The Works of John Day, edited by A. H. Bullen. Chiswick Press, Chancery Lane, London, 1881.

DEE, JOHN, The Private Diary of Dr. John Dee, and The Catalogue of his Library of Manuscripts, edited by J. O. Halliwell for the Camden Society, Vol. 19. London, 1842.

——— A true and Faithful Relation of What passed for many yeers between Dr. John Dee and Some Spirits . . . edited by Merick Casaubon. London, 1659.

DEKKER, THOMAS, Dramatic Works, Pearson reprints. London, 1873, 4 vols.

——— Non-dramatic Works, edited by Alexander B. Grosart. London, 1884–1886, 5 vols.

DELATTRE, FLORIS, English Fairy Poetry from the Origins to the Seventeenth Century. London, 1912.

DELONEY, THOMAS, Strange Histories of Songes and Sonets. London, 1607.

——— Works, edited by Francis Oscar Mann. Oxford, 1912.

DENHAM, MICHAEL A., The Denham Tracts, edited by James Hardy for the Folk-Lore Society, Nos. 29 & 35. London, 1880, 2 vols.

Discourse concerning Devils and Spirits, A. Reginald Scot, The Discoverie of Witchcraft, App. II, Nicholson rpt. London, 1886.

DITCHFIELD, P. H., The England of Shakespeare. London, 1917.

Documents Illustrating Elizabethan Poetry, by Sir Philip Sidney, George Puttenham and William Webbe, edited by Laurie Magnus. London, 1906.

DODSLEY, ROBERT, A Select Collection of Old Plays, edited by Robert Dodsley. London, 1780, 12 vols.

——— A Select Collection of Old English Plays, edited by Robert Dodsley, reëdited by W. C. Hazlitt. London, 1874–1876, 15 vols.

DOUCE, FRANCIS, An Essay on the Giants in Guildhall. The Gentleman's Magazine, Vol. 86, pt. 2. London, 1816.

——— Illustrations of Shakespeare, and of Ancient Manners. London, 1807, 2 vols.

DOUGLAS, GAWIN, The Aeneid of Virgil, translated into Scottish verse by Gawin Douglas, Bannatyne Club Publns. Edinburgh, 1839, 2 vols.

——— The Palice of Honour, Bannatyne Club Publns. Edinburgh, 1827.

DOYLE, ARTHUR CONAN, The Coming of the Fairies. New York, 1922.

DRAKE, NATHAN, Shakspeare and His Times. Paris, 1838, 2 vols. in 1.

DRAYTON, MICHAEL, Minor Poems, edited by Cyril Brett. Oxford, 1907.

——— The Muses Elizium, Spenser Soc. Publns. N. S. No. 5. Manchester, 1892.

——— Poemes Lyrick and Pastorall, Spenser Soc. Publns. N. S. No. 4. Manchester, 1891.

——— Poems, Spenser Soc. Publns. Nos. 45–46. Manchester, 1888, 2 vols.

——— The Poly-Olbion, Spenser Soc. Publns. N. S. Nos. 1–3. Manchester, 1889–1890.

DRUMMOND, WILLIAM, Notes of Ben Jonson's Conversations with William Drummond of Hawthornden, January, 1619, edited by D. Laing for the Shakespeare Society. London, 1842.

——— The Poems of William Drummond of Hawthornden, Maitland Club Publns. Edinburgh, 1832.

DRYDEN, JOHN, The Wife of Bath, Her Tale. The Poetical Works of John Dryden, Vol. IV. London, 1843–1844, 5 vols.

DuCange, C. D., Glossarium ad Scriptores Mediae & Infimae Latinitatis. London, 1688, 2 vols.

Dugdale, William, The Antiquities of Warwickshire. London, 1656.

——— Life, Diary and Correspondence, edited by William Hamper. London, 1827.

——— Monasticon Anglicanum, collected and published in Latin by William Dugdale. London, 1693, 3 vols.

Dunbar, William, Poems, edited by John Small for the Scottish Text Society. Edinburgh and London, 1893, 3 vols.

Earle, J., Microcosmography. London, 1732.

Early South-English Legendary, The, edited by Carl Horstmann for Early English Text Society, Vol. 87. London, 1887.

Eden, Richard, The First Three English books on America, edited by Edward Arber. Birmingham, 1885.

Edwards, T., The Canons of Criticism. London, 1765.

Ellacombe, Henry N., The Plant-Lore and Garden-Craft of Shakespeare. London, 1884.

Ellis, G., Specimens of Early English Metrical Romances, revised by J. O. Halliwell. London, 1848.

Ellison, Lee Monroe, The Early Romantic Drama at the English Court. Chicago, 1917.

Elton, Oliver, Michael Drayton, a Critical Study. London, 1905.

Elworthy, F. T., The Evil Eye. London, 1895.

Elyot, Thomas, Bibliotheca Eliotae, corrected by Thomas Cooper. London, 1559.

——— The Boke named The Gouernour, edited by Henry Herbert Stephen Croft. London, 1883, 2 vols.

Elze, Karl, Zum sommernachtstraum. Jahrbuch der deutschen Shakespeare-Gesellschaft, Vol. III. Berlin, 1868.

Encyclopaedia of Religion and Ethics, edited by James Hastings, Vol. 5. New York, 1908–1922, 12 vols. & Index.

England's Helicon, edited by A. H. Bullen. London, 1887.

Englands Parnassus, compiled by Robert Allot, 1600, edited by Charles Crawford. Oxford, 1913.

English Traditional Lore: Fairy Beliefs, etc. The Gentleman's Magazine Library, edited by G. L. Gomme, Vol. 4. London, 1885. 29 vols. in 30.

Erasmus, The Apophthegmes of Erasmus, translated by Nicholas Udall. Boston, Lincolnshire, 1877.

EVANS, H. A., English Masques, with introduction by H. A. Evans. London, 1897.

Examination of John Walsh, The, London, 1566. M. A. Murray, The Witch-Cult in Western Europe. Oxford, 1921.

Examination of Joan Willimott, The. A Collection of Rare and Curious Tracts relating to Witchcraft. London, 1838.

FAIRFAX, EDWARD, A Discourse of Witchcraft, As it was acted in the Family of Mr. Edward Fairfax . . . in the year 1621. Miscellanies of Philobiblon Soc., Vol. V. London, 1858–1859.

——— Godfrey of Bulloigne or the Recovery of Jerusalem, by Torquato Tasso. Done into English Heroical Verse by Edward Fairfax. London, 1687.

FAIRHOLT, F. W., The Civic Garland, Percy Society Publns., No. 61. London, 1845.

——— Lord Mayors' Pageants, Percy Soc. Publns., Nos. 38 & 43. London, 1843–1844, 2 vols.

FAREWELL, JAMES (?), The Irish Hudibras. London, 1689.

FARMER, JOHN S., Early English Dramatists, edited by J. S. Farmer. London, 1905–1908, 4 vols.
Six Anonymous Plays — First Series
Six Anonymous Plays — Second Series
Anonymous Plays — Third Series
Five Anonymous Plays — Fourth Series

FARMER, RICHARD, An Essay on the Learning of Shakespeare. Cambridge, 1767.

FEUILLERAT, A., Documents Relating to the Office of the Revels in the Time of Queen Elizabeth. Materialien zur Kunde des älteren englischen Dramas, Vol. 21. Louvain, 1908.

FIELD, NATHANIEL, A Woman is a Weathercock. Dodsley, Old English Plays, Hazlitt ed., Vol. XI. London, 1874–1876, 15 vols.

FILMER, ROBERT, An Advertisement to the Jury-Men of England, touching Witches. London, 1679.

FINETT, SIR JOHN, Finetti Philoxenis. London, 1656.

FLEAY, F. G., A Chronicle History of the Life and Works of Shakspere. London, 1886.

FLETCHER, JOHN, *See* Beaumont and Fletcher.

FLETCHER, J. B., Huon of Burdeux and the Fairie Queene. Journal of Germanic Philology, Vol. II. Bloomington, Ind., 1898–1899.

FLORIO, JOHN, A Worlde of Wordes. London, 1598.

Folk Lore Record, The. London, 1878–1883, 5 vols. in 6.

Folk Lore Journal, The. London, 1883–1889, 7 vols.

Folk-Lore. London, 1890– (*In progress*).

FORBY, ROBERT, The Vocabulary of East Anglia. London, 1830, 2 vols.

FORD, JOHN, Works, edited by William Gifford, revised by Alexander Dyce. London, 1869, 3 vols.

FOWLER, W. WARDE, Aeneas at the Site of Rome. Oxford, 1918.

FROISSART, SIR JOHN, Chronicles of England, France, Spain, Portugal, Scotland, Brittany, Flanders, and the adjoining Countries, translated by Lord Berners; rptd. from Pynson's ed. of 1523 & 1525. London, 1812, 2 vols.

FULLER, THOMAS, The Holy State and the Profane State. Cambridge, 1642.

Gammer Gvrtons Nedle by Mr. S. Mr. of Art, edited by H. F. B. Brett-Smith; The Percy Reprints. Boston and New York, 1920.

GASCOIGNE, GEORGE, Complete Works, edited by J. W. Cunliffe. Cambridge, 1907–1910, 2 vols.

GAY, JOHN, Poetical Works, edited by John Underhill. London, 1893, 2 vols.

GEOFFREY OF MONMOUTH, Historia Regum Britanniae, translated by Sebastian Evans. London and New York, 1911.

GERVASE OF TILBURY, Otia Imperialia. Einer Auswahl neu herausgegeben von Felix Liebrecht. Hannover, 1856.

GERVINUS, G. G. Shakespeare Commentaries, translated by F. E. Bunnett. New York, 1875.

GIFFARD, GEORGE, A Dialogue concerning Witches and Witchcrafts, Percy Society Publns., Vol. 8. London, 1843.

GIRALDUS CAMBRENSIS, Historical Works, edited by Thomas Wright. London, 1887.

——— Itinerarium Cambriae, cum annotationibus Davidis Poweli. London, 1806.

GLANVIL, JOSEPH, A Blow at Modern Sadducism in some Philosophical Considerations About Witchcraft. London, 1668.

——— Palpable Evidence of Spirits and Witchcraft. London, 1668.

——— A philosophical Endeavor in the Defence of the Being of Witches and Apparitions. London, 1668.

——— Saducismus Triumphatus. London, 1681.

Glossographia Anglicana Nova. London, 1707.

GOLDING, ARTHUR, The .xv. Bookes of P. Ouidius Naso, entytuled Metamorphosis, translated . . . into English meeter by Arthur Golding; edited by W. H. D. Rouse. London, 1904.

GOMME, G. L., The Handbook of Folklore, Folk-Lore Society Publns., No. 20. London, 1890.

GOODMAN, GODFREY, The Court of King James the First, edited by J. S. Brewer. London, 1839, 2 vols.

GOOGE, BARNABE, Eglogs, Epytaphes, and Sonets 1563, edited by Edward Arber. London, 1871.

——— The Popish Kingdome or reigne of Antichrist, written in Latin Verse by Thomas Naogeorgus, Englyshed by Barnabe Googe; rpt. edited by Robert Charles Hope. London, 1880.

——— The Zodiake of life, written by Marcellus Palingenius Stellatus; translated by Barnabie Googe. London, 1588.

GÖRBING, FRIEDRICH, Die Elfen in den englischen und schottischen Balladen. Halle, 1899.

GOSSE, EDMUND, Seventeenth Century Studies. London, 1883.

GOWER, GRANVILLE LEVESON, A Glossary of Surrey Words. London, 1893.

GOWER, JOHN, The English Works of John Gower, edited by G. C. Macaulay for the Early English Text Society, Nos. 81–82. London, 1900–1901, 2 vols.

GREENE, ROBERT, James the Fourth. The Minor Elizabethan Drama, edited by A. H. Thorndike. London, 1910, 2 vols.

——— Life and Complete Works, edited by A. B. Grosart. London, 1881–1886, 15 vols.

GREENLAW, EDWIN, Spenser's Fairy Mythology. Studies in Philology, Vol. 15. Chapel Hill, N. C., 1918.

GREG, W. W., Pastoral Poetry and Pastoral Drama. London, 1906.

GREGOR, WALTER, Notes on the Folk-Lore of the Northeast of Scotland, Folk-Lore Society Publns., Vol. 7. London, 1881.

GRESHAM, JAMES, The Picture of Incest, edited by A. B. Grosart. Manchester, 1876.

GREVILLE, FULKE, LORD BROOKE, Works in Verse and Prose, edited by A. B. Grosart. London, 1870, 4 vols.

GREY, ZACHARY, Critical, Historical, and Explanatory Notes on Shakespeare. London, 1754, 2 vols.

Grim, The Collier of Croydon. Dodsley, Old Plays, Vol. XI. London, 1780, 12 vols.

GRIMM, JACOB, Teutonic Mythology, translated by James S. Stallybrass. London, 1880–1888, 4 vols.

GROSE, FRANCIS, Antiquities of England and Wales. London, 1783–1797, 8 vols.

——— A Glossary of Provincial and Local Words used in England, with supplement by Samuel Pegge. London, 1839.

GUILPIN, EDWARD, Skialetheia, or a Shadowe of Truth (1598). Occasional Issues of Unique or Very Rare Books, edited by A. B. Grosart, Vol. VI. Manchester, 1878, 17 vols.

HALL, JOSEPH, Complete Poems, edited by A. B. Grosart. Manchester, 1879.

——— Works, edited by Philip Wynter. Oxford, 1862, 10 vols.

HALLIWELL, JAMES ORCHARD, A Catalogue of Chapbooks, Garlands & Popular Histories. London, 1849.

——— A Dictionary of Archaic and Provincial Words, Obsolete Phrases, Proverbs, and Ancient Customs, from the Fourteenth Century. London, 1847, 2 vols.

——— Illustrations of the Fairy Mythology of *A Midsummer Night's Dream,* edited by J. O. Halliwell for the Shakespeare Society. London, 1845.

——— An Introduction to Shakespeare's *Midsummer Night's Dream.* London, 1841.

——— The Literature of the Sixteenth and Seventeenth Centuries Illustrated by Reprints of Very Rare Tracts, edited by J. O. Halliwell. London, 1851.

——— Memoranda on the *Midsummer Night's Dream.* Brighton, 1879.

——— The Poetry of Witchcraft. London, 1853.

HARDWICK, CHARLES, Traditions, Superstitions, and Folk Lore. London, 1872.

HARINGTON, SIR JOHN, Nugae Antiquae, edited by Thomas Park. London, 1804, 2 vols.

HARMAN, THOMAS, A Caueat or Warening for Commen Cursetors vulgarely called Vagabones. *Bound with:* John Awdeley, The Fraternitye of Vacabondes, Early English Text Society. London, 1869.

HARPER, CARRIE ANNA, The Sources of The British Chronicle History in Spenser's *Faerie Queene.* Philadelphia, 1910.

Harper's Dictionary of Classical Literature and Antiquities, edited by Harry Thurston Peck. New York, 1897.

HARRIES, FREDERICK J., Shakespeare and the Welsh. London, 1919.

HARRISON, W., Harrison's Description of England in Shakspere's Youth, edited by F. J. Furnivall. London, 1877–1908, 4 parts.

HARSNET, SAMUEL, A Declaration of egregious Popish Impostures. London, 1603.

HART, JOHN S., An Essay on the Life and Writings of Edmund Spenser, with a special exposition of *The Fairy Queen.* New York & London, 1847.

HARTLAND, EDWIN SIDNEY, The Science of Fairy Tales. London, 1891.

HARVEY, GABRIEL, Works, edited by A. B. Grosart. London, 1884, 3 vols.

HAWES, STEPHEN, The Conversyon of Swerers: A joyfull Medytacyon to all Englonde of the Coronacyon of Kynge Henry the Eyght, edited by David Laing for the Abbotsford Club. Edinburgh, 1865.

——— The Pastime of Pleasure, edited by William Edward Mead for Early English Text Society, No. 173. London, 1928 (for 1927).

HAWKINS, CHARLES H., Noctes Shaksperianae, edited by C. H. Hawkins. London, 1887.

HAZLITT, W. CAREW, Catalogue of Early English Miscellanies formerly in the Harleian Library, Camden Society Publns., Vol. 87. London, 1862.

——— English Proverbs and Proverbial Phrases. London, 1907.

——— Fairy Tales, Legends and Romances illustrating Shakespeare, edited by W. C. Hazlitt. London, 1875.

——— Inedited Poetical Miscellanies 1584–1700. London, 1870.

——— Remains of the Early Popular Poetry of England, collected and edited by W. C. Hazlitt. London, 1864–1866, 4 vols.

——— Tales and Legends of National Origin or Widely Current in England from Early Times, edited by W. C. Hazlitt. London, 1892.

Heliconia, edited by T. Park. London, 1815, 3 vols.

HENDERSON, THOMAS F., Scottish Vernacular Literature. London, 1898.

HENDERSON, WILLIAM, Notes on the Folk Lore of the Northern Counties of England and the Borders, Folk Lore Society Publns., Vol. II. London, 1879.

HENRYSON, ROBERT, Poems and Fables, edited by D. Laing. Edinburgh, 1865.

——— Robene and Makyne and The Testament of Cresseid, edited by George Chalmers for the Bannatyne Club. Edinburgh, 1824.

HENSE, CARL CONRAD, Shakespeare Untersuchungen und Studien. Halle a S., 1884.

HENSLOWE, Henslowe's Diary, edited by W. W. Greg. London, 1904–1908, 2 vols.

——— Henslowe Papers, Being Documents Supplementary to Henslowe's Diary, edited by W. W. Greg. London, 1907.

HERFORD, CHARLES HAROLD, Studies in the Literary Relations of England and Germany in the Sixteenth Century. Cambridge, 1886.

HERFORD, C. H., and PERCY SIMPSON, Ben Jonson, edited by Herford and Simpson. Oxford, 1925–1927, 3 vols.

HERON, ROBERT, Observations made in a Journey through the Western Counties of Scotland in the autumn of 1792. Perth, 1793, 2 vols.

HERRICK, ROBERT, Poetical Works, edited by F. W. Moorman. Oxford, 1915.

HEYLYN, PETER, Cosmographie in four Books contayning the Chorographie & Historie of the whole World . . . London, 1677, 4 books & app. in 1 vol.

——— Mikrokosmos. Oxford, 1631.

HEYWOOD, JOHN, Dramatic Writings, edited by John S. Farmer. London, 1905.

HEYWOOD, THOMAS, Dramatic Works, Pearson edition. London, 1874, 6 vols.

——— The Hierarchie of the blessed Angells. London, 1635.

HEYWOOD, THOMAS and RICHARD BROOME, The Late Lancashire Witches, 1634. The Poetry of Witchcraft, edited by J. O. Halliwell. London, 1853.

Highland Papers, edited by J. R. N. Macphail for Scottish History Society, Vol. III (Publns., 2d ser., Vol. XX). Edinburgh, 1920.

HOBBES, THOMAS, Leviathan, rpt. of 1651 edition, with an essay by W. G. Pogson Smith. Oxford, 1909.

HOLINSHED, RAPHAEL, Chronicles of England, Scotland, and Ireland. London, 1807–1808, 6 vols.

HONE, WILLIAM, The Year Book of Daily Recreation and Information. London, 1838.

Honorable Entertainment, The, given to the Queenes Majestie in Progresse, at Elvetham in Hampshire by the Earle of Hertford, 1591. London, 1591.

HOOKER, RICHARD, Of the Laws of Ecclesiastical Polity, edited by R. W. Church. Oxford, 1868.

HORMAN, WILLIAM, Vulgaria, 1519. Cf. Catholicon Anglicum, note p. 113.

HOWELL, JAMES, Epistolae Ho-Elianae. London, 1645.

HOWELLS, W., Cambrian Superstitions. Tipton, 1831.

HULL, ELEANOR, Folklore of the British Isles. London, 1928.

HULOET, RICHARD, Huloets Dictionarie, Newelye corrected, amended, set in order and enlarged by John Higgins. London, 1572.

HUNDT, R., Shakspeares Sturm und Sommernachtstraum. Dramburg, 1878.

HUNT, M. L., Thomas Dekker, Columbia Studies in English. New York, 1911.

HUNTER, JOSEPH, New Illustrations of the Life, Studies, and Writings of Shakespeare. London, 1845, 2 vols.

Huon de Bordeaux, Chanson de Geste; publiee . . . par MM. F. Guessard et C. Grandmaison. Paris, 1860.

HUTCHINSON, FRANCIS, An Historical Essay concerning Witchcraft. London, 1720.

JACK, ADOLPHUS A., A Commentary on the Poetry of Chaucer and Spenser. Glasgow, 1920.

Jacob and Esau, The Historie of. Six Anonymous Plays, Second Series, edited by J. S. Farmer. London, 1906.

JAMES VI OF SCOTLAND, The Workes of the Most High and Mightie Prince, James. London, 1616.

JAMIESON, ROBERT, Popular Ballads and Songs, edited by Robert Jamieson. Edinburgh, 1806.

JEAFFRESON, JOHN CORDY, Middlesex County Records, edited by J. C. Jeaffreson for the Middlesex County Records Society. London, 1886–1892, 4 vols.

JOHNSON, SAMUEL, A Dictionary of the English Language, by Robert Gordon Latham, founded on that of Dr. Samuel Johnson; edited by H. J. Todd. London, 1866, 2 vols.

——— A Journey to the Western Islands of Scotland. London, 1775.

——— The Plays of William Shakespeare, with notes by Samuel Johnson and George Steevens. London, 1778, 10 vols.

——— Johnson on Shakespeare. Essays and Notes edited by Walter Raleigh. London, 1908.

JONSON, BEN, The Devil is an Ass, edited by William Savage Johnson; Yale Studies in English, No. 29. New York, 1905.

——— Masques and Entertainments, edited by Henry Morley. London, 1890.

——— Ben Jonson's Sad Shepherd with Waldron's Continuation, edited by W. W. Greg. Materialien zur Kunde des älteren englischen Dramas, Elfter Band. Louvain, 1905.

——— Works, edited by William Gifford. London, 1846.

JORDAN, J. C., Robert Greene, Columbia Studies in English. New York, 1915.

KEIGHTLEY, THOMAS, The Fairy Mythology. London, 1833, 2 vols.

KEITH, ALEXANDER, Scottish Ballads: Their Evidence of Authorship and Origin. Essays and Studies by members of The English Association, Vol. XII. Oxford, 1926.

KER, W. P., The Craven Angels. The Modern Language Review, Vol. VI. Cambridge, 1911.

KERMODE, P. M. C., Manx Crosses. London, 1907.

KING, WILLIAM, Miscellanies in Prose and Verse. London, 1704.

KIRK, ROBERT, Secret Commonwealth, edited by Andrew Lang. London, 1893.

KITTREDGE, GEORGE L., The Friar's Lantern and Friar Rush. Publns. of the Modern Language Association of America, Vol. XV, New Series, Vol. VIII. Baltimore, 1900.

——— Witchcraft in Old and New England. Cambridge, Mass., 1929.

KOEPPEL, EMIL, Quellen-Studien zu den Dramen: George Chapman's, Philip Massinger's, und John Ford's Quellen und Forschungen . . . Vol. 82. Strassburg, 1897.

——— Quellen-Studien zu den Dramen: Ben Jonson's, John Marston's, und Beaumont's und Fletcher's Münchener Beiträge . . . Vol. XI. Erlangen, 1895.

KYD, THOMAS, Works, edited by F. S. Boas. Oxford, 1901.

KYTELER, LADY ALICE, Contemporary narrative of the proceedings against Dame Alice Kyteler, prosecuted for sorcery in 1324, edited by Thomas Wright for the Camden Society, Vol. 24. London, 1843.

LAING, DAVID, Select Remains of the Ancient and Popular Poetry of Scotland, edited by William and David Laing, reëdited by John Small. Edinburgh, 1885.

LAING, JEANIE M., Notes on Superstition and Folk Lore, with introduction by D. H. Edwards. Edinburgh, 1885.

LAMBARDE, WILLIAM, Dictionarium Angliae Topographicum & Historicum; an Alphabetical Description of the Chief Places in England and Wales. London, 1730.

Lancelot du Lac, 1553 ed. Cf. E. K. Chambers, The Fairy World, App. A to A Midsummer Night's Dream.

LANEHAM, ROBERT, Robert Laneham's Letter: Describing a Part of the Entertainment unto Queen Elizabeth at the Castle of Kenilworth in 1575, edited by F. J. Furnivall. New York and London, 1907.

LANGLAND, WILLIAM, The Vision of William concerning Piers the Plowman, edited by W. W. Skeat. Oxford, 1886, 2 vols.

LAVATER, LUDWIG, Of Ghostes and Spirites walking by nyght, . . . translated by R. H. London, 1572.

LAW, ROBERT, Law's Memorials, edited by Charles Sharpe. Edinburgh, 1819.

LAYAMON, Laȝamons Brut, or Chronicle of Britain, edited by Sir Frederic Madden. London, 1847, 3 vols.

LEA, HENRY CHARLES, A History of the Inquisition of Spain. New York, 1907, 4 vols.

LEE, SIR SIDNEY, A Life of William Shakespeare. New York, 1924.

——— Elizabethan Sonnets, edited by Sidney Lee. Westminster, 1904, 2 vols.

LEGGE, F., Witchcraft in Scotland. The Scottish Review, Vol. 18. Paisley and London, 1891.

LELAND, JOHN, The Itinerary of John Leland, edited by Lucy Toulmin Smith. London, 1906–1910, 5 vols.

LELOYER, PIERRE, Discovrs, et Histoires des Spectres, Visions et Apparitions . . . Paris, 1605.

LEVINS, PETER, Manipulus Vocabulorum, edited by Henry B. Wheatley for Early English Text Society. London, 1867.

LEYDEN, JOHN, Poetical Works, with memoir by Thomas Brown. London and Edinburgh, 1875.

——— Scenes of Infancy, 2d edition. Edinburgh, 1811.

LILLY, WILLIAM, William Lilly's History of His Life and Times from the year 1602 to 1681; rpt. Hunt and Clarke, London, 1826. Autobiography, Vol. II, pub. by Hunt and Clarke.

——— A Rare Collection of Tracts. London, 1660.

LLEWELLYN, MARTIN, Men-miracles; with other poemes. London, 1646.

LODGE, THOMAS, Complete Works, Hunterian Club edition. Glasgow, 1883, 4 vols.

LONG, EDGAR, Drayton's Eighth Nymphal. Studies in Philology, Vol. 13. Chapel Hill, N. C., 1916.

LOOMIS, ROGER SHERMAN, Celtic Myth and Arthurian Romance. New York, 1927.

LUCE, MORTON, Shakespeare, the Man and His Work. London, 1913.

LUPTON, Thousand Notable Things. Cf. John Brand, Popular Antiquities of Great Britain, Vol. I, p. 207. London, 1870.

Lust's Dominion. Dodsley, Old English Plays, Hazlitt edition, Vol. 14. London, 1874–1876, 15 vols.

LYDGATE, JOHN, Lydgate's Fall of Princes, edited by Henry Bergen for Early English Text Society. London, 1924–1927, 4 vols.

LYLY, JOHN, Complete Works, edited by R. W. Bond. Oxford, 1902, 3 vols.

LYNDESAY, DAVID, Poems, with introduction by John Nichol for Early English Text Society. London, 1865–1871, 2 vols.

Lyrics from the Song-Books of the Elizabethan Age, edited by A. H. Bullen. London, 1891.

MACARTHUR, JOHN R., The Influence of Huon of Burdeux upon the *Fairie Queene*. The Journal of Germanic Philology, Vol. 4. Bloomington, Ind., 1902.

MACCULLOCH, J. A., Fairy. Hastings' Encyclopaedia of Religion and Ethics, Vol. V. New York, 1908–1922, 12 vols.

——— The Mingling of Fairy and Witch Beliefs in Sixteenth and Seventeenth Century Scotland, Folk-Lore Society Publns. London, 1921.

MACGREGOR, ALEXANDER, Highland Superstitions. Stirling and London, 1901.

MACHYN, HENRY, The Diary of Henry Machyn, edited by John G. Nichols for the Camden Society, No. 42. London, 1848.

MACKAY, CHARLES, Memoirs of Extraordinary Popular Delusions and the Madness of Crowds. London, 1852, 2 vols.

MACRITCHIE, DAVID, The Testimony of Tradition. London, 1889.

Maitland Club, Miscellany of the. Edinburgh, 1833–1847, 4 vols.

MAJOR, JOHN, A History of Greater Britain, translated and edited by A. Constable for the Scottish History Society. Edinburgh, 1892.

MAP, WALTER, De Nugis Curialium, edited by Montague Rhodes James. Oxford, 1914.

——— De Nugis Curialium (Courtiers' Trifles), Englished by Frederick Tupper and Marbury Bladen Ogle. New York, 1924.

MARLOWE, CHRISTOPHER, Works, edited by C. F. Tucker Brooke. Oxford, 1910.

MARSTON, JOHN, Works, edited by A. H. Bullen. London, 1887, 3 vols.

MARTIN, MARTIN, Description of the Western Islands of Scotland. J. Pinkerton, General Collection of Voyages and Travels, Vol. 3. London, 1808–1814, 17 vols.

MASEFIELD, JOHN, Shakespeare and Spiritual Life. Oxford, 1924.

MASSINGER, PHILIP, Dramatick Works, edited by Mason & Colman. London, 1779, 4 vols.

Materialien zur Kunde des älteren englischen Dramas, edited by W. Bang, Vols. 9, 11, 21. Louvain, 1902–1914, 43 vols.

MAURY, L. F. A., Croyances et légendes du moyen âge. Paris, 1896.

——— Les Fees du moyen âge. Paris, 1843.

Maydes Metamorphosis, The. A Collection of Old English Plays, edited by A. H. Bullen, Vol. I. London, 1882, 4 vols.

MAYNE, JASPER, The City Match, a Comedy. Dodsley, Old English Plays, Hazlitt ed., Vol. 13. London, 1874–1876, 15 vols.

Melusine, compiled by Jean D'Arras; edited by A. K. Donald for Early English Text Society. London, 1895.

MELVILLE, SIR JAMES, Memoirs of His Own Life, edited by T. Thomson for The Bannatyne Club. Edinburgh, 1827.

Merry Devill of Edmonton, The. Students' Facsimile Edition, 1911.

Merry pranks of Robin Goodfellow, The. Illustrations of the Fairy Mythology of *A Midsummer Night's Dream* edited by J. O. Halliwell. London, 1845.

MIDDLETON, CHRISTOPHER, The Famous Historie of Chinon of England, edited by William Edward Mead for Early English Text Society. London, 1925.

MIDDLETON, THOMAS, Works, edited by A. H. Bullen. London, 1885. 8 vols.

Midnight's Watch, The, or Robin Goodfellow his serious observation. Illustrations of the Fairy Mythology of *A Midsummer Night's Dream,* edited by J. O. Halliwell. London, 1845.

MILLER, FRANK JUSTUS, Ovid Metamorphoses, translated by Frank Justus Miller, Books I–VIII. London, 1916, 2 vols.

MILTON, JOHN, Complete Poetical Works, Cambridge edition. Boston and New York, 1899.

MINSHEU, JOHN, The Guide into the tongues. London, 1617.

Mirror for Magistrates, A, edited by Joseph Haslewood. London, 1815, 3 vols.

Misogonus. Early Plays from the Italian, edited by R. W. Bond. Oxford, 1911.

Montemayor, Jorge de, Diana, translated by Bartholomew Yong. London, 1598.

Montgomerie, Alexander, Poems, edited by George Stevenson. Edinburgh and London, 1910.

Moore, Arthur William, Folk-Lore of the Isle of Man, collected by Arthur William Moore. London, 1891.

Moorman, F. W., The Pre-Shakespearean Ghost, *and* Shakespeare's Ghosts. Modern Language Review, Vol. I. London, 1906.

——— William Browne His Britannia's Pastorals and the Pastoral Poetry of the Elizabethan Age. Quellen und Forschungen zur Sprach und Culturgeschichte der germanischen Völker, Vol. 81. Strassburg, 1897.

More, Henry, A Collection of Several Philosophical Writings. London, 1712.

More, Sir Thomas, The Utopia of Sir Thomas More, in Latin from the edition of March, 1518, and in English from the first edition of Ralph Robynson's translation; edited by J. H. Lupton. Oxford, 1895.

Morgan, J., Phoenix Britannicus, Vol. I. London, 1732.

Morley, George, Shakespeare's Greenwood. London, 1900.

Moryson, Fynes, The Itinerary of Fynes Moryson, published by James MacLehose & Sons. Glasgow, 1907–1908, 4 vols.

Munday, Anthony (?), Fidele and Fortunio the Two Italian Gentlemen; Malone Society Reprints. London, 1909.

Munday, Anthony, John a Kent and John a Cumber, edited by J. P. Collier for the Shakespeare Society. London, 1851.

——— The Downfall of Robert Earl of Huntington. Collier, Five Old Plays. London, 1828–1829.

Munday, Anthony, and Henry Chettle, The Death of Robert Earl of Huntington. Collier, Five Old Plays. London, 1828–1829.

Murray, M. A., Organisations of Witches in Great Britain. Folk-Lore, Vol. 28. London, 1917.

——— The Witch-Cult in Western Europe. Oxford, 1921.

Mushacke, Wilhelm, Beiträge zur Geschichte des Elfenreiches in Sage und Dichtung. Crefeld, 1891.

Napier, Arthur S., Old English Glosses, edited by A. S. Napier. Oxford, 1900.

NAPIER, JAMES, Old Ballad Folk-Lore. The Folk Lore Record, Vol. II. London, 1879.

Narcissus a Twelfe Night Merriment, edited by Margaret L. Lee. London, 1893.

NARES, ROBERT, A Glossary, edited by J. O. Halliwell and T. Wright. London, 1882, 2 vols.

NASHE, THOMAS, Works, edited by R. B. McKerrow. London, 1904–1910, 5 vols.

NEILSON, WILLIAM ALLAN, and A. H. THORNDIKE, The Facts about Shakespeare. New York, 1913.

New English Dictionary on Historical Principles, A, edited by James A. H. Murray. Oxford, 1888–1928, 10 vols.

NEWCASTLE, LADY, Poems and Fancies. London, 1653.

NICHOLS, JOHN, The Progresses and Public Processions of Queen Elizabeth, edited by John Nichols. Edinburgh and Perth, 1823, 3 vols.

——— The Progresses, Processions, and Magnificent Festivities, of King James the First, edited by John Nichols. London, 1828, 4 vols.

NICHOLS, JOHN GOUGH, London Pageants. London, 1837.

NICOLAS, SIR HARRIS, Memoirs of the Life and Times of Sir Christopher Hatton, K. G. London, 1847.

NORTHALL, G. F., English Folk-Rhymes, collected by G. F. Northall. London, 1892.

Notes and Queries, 2d ser., Vol. 7, edited by W. J. Thoms. London, Jan. & June, 1859.

NOTESTEIN, WALLACE, A History of Witchcraft in England from 1558 to 1718. Washington, 1911.

NUTT, ALFRED, The Fairy Mythology of English Literature: Its Origin and Nature. Folk-Lore, Vol. 8. London, 1897.

——— Studies on the Legend of the Holy Grail. Folk-Lore Journal, No. 23. London, 1888.

O'CURRY, EUGENE, Lectures on the Manuscript Material of Ancient Irish History. Dublin, 1878.

O'GRADY, STANDISH H., Silva Gadelica, edited by S. H. O'Grady. London, 1892, 2 vols.

OLAUS MAGNUS, A Compendious History of the Goths, Swedes, & Vandals, and other Northern Nations. London, 1658.

——— De Gentibus Septentrionalibus Historia. Ambergae, 1599.

——— Gentivm Septentrionaliv̄ Historiae Breviarium. Lvgd. Batavorvm, 1652.

Old English Miscellany, An, edited by Richard Morris for the Early English Text Society. London, 1872.

OLIPHANT, E. H. C., The Plays of Beaumont and Fletcher. New Haven, Conn., 1927.

OSGOOD, CHARLES G., A Concordance to the Poems of Edmund Spenser, compiled and edited by C. G. Osgood. Philadelphia 1915.

OVID, P. Ovidii Nasonis Metamorphoseon, edited by Fridericus Polle. Leipzig, 1912.

OWEN, ANEURIN, Ancient Laws and Institutes of Wales, edited by A. Owen. London, 1841.

PADELFORD, FREDERICK MORGAN, Early Sixteenth Century Lyrics, edited by F. M. Padelford. Boston and London, 1907.

PALSGRAVE, JEAN, Lesclarcissement de La Langue Francayse. Paris, 1852.

Paradise of Dainty Deuices, The, edited by Sir Egerton Brydges. London, 1810.

PARKES, W., Curtaine Drawer of the World, edited by A. B. Grosart. Manchester, 1876.

Passionate Pilgrim, The, edited by Sidney Lee. Oxford, 1905.

PASTON, The Paston Letters, edited by J. Gairdner. Westminster, 1900–1901, 4 vols.

PATON, LUCY ALLEN, Studies in the Fairy Mythology of Arthurian Romance. Boston, 1903.

PECOCK, REGINALD, The Repressor of Over Much Blaming of the Clergy, edited by Churchill Babington. London, 1860, 2 vols.

PEELE, GEORGE, The Battle of Alcazar; Malone Society Reprints. Chiswick Press, London, 1907.

——— The Old Wives' Tale; Malone Society Reprints. London, 1909.

PEELE, GEORGE and ROBERT GREENE, Dramatic Works, edited by A. Dyce. London, 1879.

PENNANT, THOMAS, A Tour in Scotland and a Voyage to the Hebrides. J. Pinkerton, General Collection of Voyages and Travels, Vol. 3. London, 1808–1814, 17 vols.

PEPYS, SAMUEL, The Diary of Samuel Pepys, edited by H. B. Wheatley. London and New York, 1893–1898, 9 vols.

Pepysian Garland, A: Black-Letter Broadside Ballads of the years 1595–1639, edited by H. E. Rollins. Cambridge, 1922.

Percy, Thomas, Bishop Percy's Folio Manuscript Ballads and Romances, edited by J. W. Hales and F. J. Furnivall. London, 1867, 3 vols.

——— Reliques of Ancient English Poetry, collected by Thomas Percy, edited by George Gilfillan. Edinburgh and London, 1858, 3 vols.

Percy, William, The Faery Pastorall or Forrest of Elues dedicated to the Roxburghe Club. London, 1824.

Perrault, Charles, Popular Tales, edited by Andrew Lang. Oxford, 1888.

Phaër, Thomas, The whole .xii. Bookes of the Aeneidos of Virgill, conuerted into English meeter by Thomas Phaër, newly set forth by Thomas Twyne. London, 1573.

Phillips, Edward, The New World of Words, compiled by Edward Phillips. London, 1706.

Philotus, rpt. of Charteris edition for the Bannatyne Club. Edinburgh, 1835.

Phipson, Emma, The Animal-Lore of Shakespeare's Time. London, 1883.

Phoenix Nest, The, rpt. of 1593 edition. London, 1926.

Pinkerton, John, General Collection of Voyages and Travels. London, 1808–1814, 17 vols.

——— Scotish Poems, collected by J. Pinkerton. London, 1792, 3 vols.

Pitcairn, Robert, Criminal Trials in Scotland, edited by R. Pitcairn. Edinburgh, 1833, 3 vols. in 2.

Pleasant Treatise of Witches, A. London, 1673.

Plummer, Charles, Elizabethan Oxford; Reprints of Rare Tracts, Oxford Historical Society, Vol. 8. Oxford, 1887.

Poole, Josua, The English Parnassus. London, 1677.

Popular Mythology of the Middle Ages. The Quarterly Review, Vol. 22. London, 1820.

Potts, Thomas, The Wonderful Discoverie of Witches in the countie of Lancaster, rpt. for Chetham Society. Manchester, 1845.

Powell, Frederick York, The First Nine Books of the Danish History of Saxo Grammaticus, translated by Oliver Elton, edited by F. Y. Powell. London, 1894.

Pranks of Puck, The. Illustrations of the Fairy Mythology of *A Midsummer Night's Dream,* edited by J. O. Halliwell. London, 1845.

Proctor, Thomas, A Gorgious Gallery of Gallant Inventions. *Rpt.* Heliconia, Vol. I. London, 1814.

Proescholdt, Ludwig, The Sources of Shakespeare's *Midsummer Night's Dream.* Halle, 1878.

Promptorium Parvulorum, edited by Albertus Way for the Camden Society. London, 1843–1865, 2 vols.

Promptorium Parvulorum, edited by A. L. Mayhew for the Early English Text Society. London, 1908.

Prothero, G. W., Select Statutes and Other Constitutional Documents Illustrative of the Reigns of Elizabeth and James I, edited by G. W. Prothero. Oxford, 1906.

Pvritaine, The, Or The Widdow of Watling-streete. Students' Facsimile Edition, 1911.

Puttenham, Richard, The Arte of English Poesie; Arber's English Reprints. Birmingham, 1869.

Quarterly Review, The. London, 1820, Vol. 22; London, 1873–1874, Vols. 134–137.

Queenes Majesties Entertainment at Woodstocke, The, edited by J. W. Cunliffe. Publns. of Mod. Lang. Assn. of America. Baltimore, 1911, Vol. 26.

Quiller-Couch, Sir Arthur, Notes on Shakespeare's Workmanship. New York, 1917.

Ramsay, Allan, The Ever Green; a Collection of Scots Poems, rpt. of 1724 edition. Glasgow, 1875, 2 vols.

——— The Gentle Shepherd. London, 1763.

Randolph, Thomas, Poetical and Dramatic Works, edited by W. C. Hazlitt. London, 1875, 2 vols.

Ravenscroft, Thomas, Selections from the Works of Thomas Ravenscroft, Roxburghe Club Publns. London, 1822.

Ray, John, A Collection of English Words not generally used, edited by W. W. Skeat for the English Dialect Society. London, 1874.

Reeves, W. P., Shakespeare's Queen Mab. Modern Language Notes, Vol. 17. Baltimore, 1902.

Reliquiae Antiquae, edited by T. Wright and J. O. Halliwell. London, 1845, 2 vols.

Reyher, Paul, Les Masques Anglais. Paris, 1909.

Rhys, John, Celtic Folklore, Welsh and Manx. Oxford, 1901, 2 vols.

——— Lectures on the Origin and Growth of Religion as Illustrated by Celtic Heathendom. London, 1888.

——— Studies in the Arthurian Legend. Oxford, 1891.

RITSON, JOSEPH, Fairy Tales, collected by Joseph Ritson. London, 1831.

ROBERT OF GLOUCESTER, Robert of Gloucester's Chronicle, edited by Thomas Hearne. Oxford, 1724, 2 vols.

ROBERTS, PETER, The Cambrian Popular Antiquities. London, 1815.

Robin Goodfellow; his mad prankes, and merry Jests. J. O. Halliwell, Illustrations of the Fairy Mythology of *A Midsummer Night's Dream*. London, 1845.

ROLLINS, HYDER E., Old English Ballads, edited by H. E. Rollins. Cambridge, 1920.

Romance of King Orfeo, The. W. C. Hazlitt, Fairy Tales. London, 1875.

Romance of William of Palerne, The, reëdited by W. W. Skeat for the Early English Text Society. London, 1867.

ROOT, R. K., Classical Mythology in Shakespeare; Yale Studies in English, No. 19. New Haven, 1903.

ROTHSCHILD, J. A. DE, Shakespeare and His Day. London, 1906.

Round about our Coal Fire; or, Christmas Entertainments. Rpt. of 1740 edition. London, 1883.

ROWLANDS, SAMUEL, Complete Works, edited by Edmund Gosse for the Hunterian Club. Glasgow, 1880, 3 vols.

Roxburghe Ballads, The, printed for the Ballad Society. London, 1874–1899, 9 vols.

Rvsh, The Historie of Frier, rpt. of 1st ed., London, 1620. London, 1810.

St. Gregory or Gregorius auf dem Steine. Herrig, Archiv für das Studium der neueren Sprachen und Literaturen, Vol. 57. Braunschweig, 1877.

SANDS, J., Curious Superstitions in Tiree. The Celtic Magazine, Vol. 8. Inverness, 1883.

SANDYS, GEORGE, Ovid's Metamorphosis, Englished by George Sandys. London, 1640.

SAVAGE, F. G., The Flora and Folk Lore of Shakespeare. London, 1923.

SCHELLING, FELIX E., Shakespeare and "Demi-Science." Philadelphia, 1927.

SCHOFIELD, W. H., The Lay of Guingamor. Harvard Studies and Notes in Philology and Literature, Vol. 5. Boston, 1896.

——— The Lays of Graelent and Lanval, rpt. from Publns. of the Modern Language Assn. of America, Vol. 15, No. 2. Baltimore, 1900.

SCHÜCKLING, LEVIN L., The Fairy Scene in *The Merry Wives* in Folio & Quarto. Modern Language Review, Vol. 19. Cambridge, England, 1924.

SCOT, REGINALD, The Discoverie of Witchcraft, edited by Brinsley Nicholson. London, 1886.

——— Scot's Discovery of Witchcraft. London, 1651.

SCOTT, SIR WALTER, Letters on Demonology and Witchcraft. New York, 1830.

——— Minstrelsy of the Scottish Border. Edinburgh and London, 1803, 3 vols.

Scottish History Society, Miscellany of the, edited by George F. Warner. Edinburgh, 1893–1926, 4 vols.

SEAGER, H. W., Natural History in Shakespeare's Time. London, 1896.

Secret History of the Court of James the First, The. Edinburgh, 1811, 2 vols.

SELDEN, JOHN, The Historie of Tithes. London, 1618.

——— Titles of Honor. London, 1672.

SEMPILL, ROBERT, The Sempill ballates . . . To which are added Poems by Sir James Semple of Beltrees. Edinburgh, 1872.

Severall notorious and lewd Cousonages of John West and Alice West, The. *Rpt.* W. C. Hazlitt, Fairy Tales. London, 1875.

SHADWELL, THOMAS, The Lancashire Witches and Tegue o Divelly the Irish Priest. The Poetry of Witchcraft, edited by J. O. Halliwell. London, 1853.

SHAKESPEARE, WILLIAM, A New Variorum Edition of Shakespeare, edited by Horace Howard Furness. Philadelphia, 1871–1928, 20 vols.

——— The Plays of William Shakespeare, with notes by Samuel Johnson. London, 1765, 8 vols.

——— The Plays of William Shakespeare, with notes by Samuel Johnson and George Steevens. London, 1778, 10 vols.

——— The Plays and Poems of William Shakspeare, edited by Edmond Malone. London, 1821, 21 vols.

——— The Plays of William Shakespeare, printed from Mr. Steevens's last edition, edited by J. Nichols. London, 1797, 8 vols.

——— The Works of Shakespeare, edited by Mr. Theobald. London, 1772, 12 vols.

——— The Works of William Shakespeare, edited by Richard Grant White. Boston, 1865, 12 vols.

——— The First Sketch of Shakespeare's Merry Wives of Windsor, edited by J. O. Halliwell for The Shakespeare Society. London, 1842.

——— Shakespere's Merry Wives of Windsor, Facsimile of First Quarto, 1602. London, 1881.

——— A Midsommer Nights Dreame, Variant edition. Facsimile rpt. of First Folio, 1623, edited by Henry Johnson. Boston and New York, 1888.

——— A Midsummer-Night's Dream, Warwick ed., edited by E. K. Chambers. London, 1911.

Shakespeare's England, edited by Sir Walter Raleigh, Sir Sidney Lee, and C. T. Onions. Oxford, 1917, 2 vols.

Sharpe, Charles Kirkpatrick, A Historical Account of the Belief in Witchcraft in Scotland. London, 1884.

Sheavyn, Phoebe A. B., The Literary Profession in the Elizabethan Age. Manchester, 1909.

Shirley, James, Dramatic Works and Poems, with notes by William Gifford, edited by A. Dyce. London, 1833, 6 vols.

Sidgwick, Frank, The Sources and Analogues of *A Midsummer-Night's Dream*. London, 1908.

Sidney, Sir Philip, Complete Works, edited by Albert Feuillerat. Cambridge, 1912–1926, 4 vols.

——— Sir P. S. His Astrophel & Stella. Lee, Elizabethan Sonnets, Vol. I. Westminster, 1904, 2 vols.

Sikes, Wirt, British Goblins. London, 1880.

Sinclair, Sir John, The Statistical Account of Scotland. Edinburgh, 1791–1799, 21 vols.

Sinclar, George, Satan's Invisible World Discovered. Edinburgh, 1685.

Singer, Charles, Early English Magic and Medicine, from Proceedings of the British Academy. Oxford, 1920.

Skelton, John, Poetical Works, edited by A. Dyce. London, 1843, 2 vols.

Skinner, Stephano, Etymologicon Linguae Anglicanae, edited by Thomas Henshaw. London, 1671.

Spalding, Thomas Alfred, Elizabethan Demonology. London, 1880.

Spalding Club, Miscellany of the, Vol. I. Aberdeen, 1841.

SPENCER, JOHN, Things New and Old, collected by John Spencer with preface by Thomas Fuller. London, 1658.

SPENSER, EDMUND, Complete Poetical Works, Cambridge edition, edited by Neil Dodge. Boston and New York, 1908.

STANYHURST, RICHARD, Translation of the first Four Books of the Aeneis of P. Virgilius Maro, edited by Edward Arber. London, 1880.

STOLL, ELMER EDGAR, Shakespeare Studies. New York, 1927.

STOW, JOHN, The Annales, or Generall Chronicle of England, begun by John Stow, continued by Edmond Howes. London, 1615.

——— A Survey of London, edited by C. L. Kingsford. Oxford, 1908, 2 vols.

STRUTT, JOSEPH, Horda Angel-Cynnan. London, 1775–1776, 3 vols.

——— Sports and Pastimes of the People of England. London, 1810.

STUBBES, PHILIP, The Anatomie of Abuses, rptd. from 3d edition of 1585, under superintendence of William B. D. D. Turnbull. London and Edinburgh, 1836.

SUCKLING, SIR JOHN, The Poems, Plays and Other Remains, edited by W. C. Hazlitt. London, 1892, 2 vols.

SURREY, HENRY, EARLE OF, Certain Bokes of Virgiles Aenaeis, turned into English meter by Henry, Earle of Surrey; Roxburghe Club Publns. London, 1814.

SYMONDS, JOHN, Ben Jonson. New York, 1886.

SYNGE, JOHN MILLINGTON, The Aran Islands. Boston, 1911.

Tarlton's Jests, and News Out Of Purgatory, edited by J. O. Halliwell for the Shakespeare Society. London, 1844.

TAYLOR, JOHN, Works of John Taylor the Water-Poet, comprised in The Folio Edition of 1630, Spenser Society Publns. Manchester, 1869, 3 vols. in 1.

——— Works of John Taylor the Water Poet, not included in the folio volume of 1630, Spenser Society Publns. Manchester, 1870–1878, 5 vols.

——— A Short Relation of a Journey through Wales . . . in 1652, edited by J. O. Halliwell. London, 1859.

Tell-Trothes New-Yeares Gift, edited by F. J. Furnivall for the New Shakspere Society, Ser. VI, No. 2. London, 1876.

THISELTON-DYER, T. F., British Popular Customs, Present and Past. London, 1876.

——— Folk Lore of Shakespeare. London, 1883.

THOMAS OF ERCELDOUNE, The Romance and Prophecies of Thomas of Erceldoune, edited by James A. H. Murray for Early English Text Society. London, 1875.

THOMS, WILLIAM J., Early English Prose Romances, edited by W. J. Thoms. London and New York [1907].

——— Three Notelets on Shakespeare. London, 1865.

THORNDIKE, ASHLEY H., The Influence of Beaumont and Fletcher on Shakspere. Worcester, 1901.

——— The Minor Elizabethan Drama, edited by A. H. Thorndike. London and New York, 1910, 2 vols.

THORNDIKE, ASHLEY H., and W. A. NEILSON, The Facts about Shakespeare. New York, 1913.

THORPE, BENJAMIN, The Homilies of the Anglo-Saxon Church . . . in the original Anglo-Saxon, with English version by Benj. Thorpe for the Aelfric Society. London, 1844–1846, 2 vols.

Famous History of Tom Thumb, The. Percy Society Publns., Vol. 23. London, 1858.

TICKELL, THOMAS, Works. The Works of Celebrated Authors, Vol. 2. London, 1750, 2 vols.

TIDDY, R. J. E., The Mummers' Play. Oxford, 1923.

Tottel's Miscellany, Arber's English reprints. London, 1870.

Towneley Plays, The, reëdited by George England with notes by A. W. Pollard for Early English Text Society. London, 1897.

TURBERVILLE, GEORGE, Epitaphes, Epigrams, Songs and Sonets, edited by J. P. Collier. London, 1870.

TUSSER, THOMAS, Five Hundred Points of Good Husbandry, edited by William Mavor. London, 1812.

TYNDALE, WILLIAM, An Answer to Sir Thomas More's Dialogue, The Supper of the Lord after the true meaning of John VI and I Cor. XI; edited by Henry Walter for the Parker Society. Cambridge, 1850.

——— Doctrinal Treatises, edited by Henry Walter for the Parker Society. Cambridge, 1848.

——— Expositions and Notes on Sundry Portions of The Holy Scriptures, edited by Henry Walter for the Parker Society. Cambridge, 1849.

Typographical Antiquities, edited by Joseph Ames, William Herbert and T. F. Dibdin. London, 1810–1819, 4 vols.

TYRWHITT, THOMAS, The Poetical Works of Geoffrey Chaucer, edited by Thomas Tyrwhitt. London, 1866.

UDALL, NICHOLAS (?), Ralph Roister Doister. Thorndike, Minor Elizabethan Drama, Vol. 2. London, 1910.

Valiant Welshman, The, 1615. Students' Facsimile Edition, 1913.

VOLLHARDT, WILLIAM, Die Beziehungen des Sommernachtstraums zum italienischen Schäferdrama. Leipzig, 1899.

WALDRON, GEORGE, A Description of the Isle of Man, edited by William Harrison for the Manx Society. Douglas, 1865.

WALTER, JAMES, Shakespeare's True Life. London, 1890.

WALTHER, MARIE, Malory's Einfluss auf Spenser's *Faerie Queene*. Eisleben, 1900.

WARD, ADOLPHUS WILLIAM, A History of English Dramatic Literature to the Death of Queen Anne. London and New York, 1899, 3 vols.

WARNER, WILLIAM, Albion's England. Works of the English Poets, edited by A. Chalmers, Vol. 4. London, 1810.

WARTON, THOMAS, The History of English Poetry, from the Close of the Eleventh to the Commencement of the Eighteenth Century. London, 1824, 4 vols.

——— Observations on *The Fairy Queen* of Spenser. London, 1807, 2 vols. in 1.

WEBER, HENRY, Metrical Romances of the Thirteenth, Fourteenth, and Fifteenth Centuries, edited by Henry Weber. Edinburgh, 1810, 3 vols.

WEBSTER, JOHN (1580?–1625?), Works, edited by A. Dyce. London, 1859.

WEBSTER, JOHN (1610–1682), The Displaying of Supposed Witchcraft. London, 1676.

WENTZ, W. Y. EVANS, The Fairy-Faith in Celtic Countries. London, New York, Toronto and Melbourne, 1911.

WHEATLEY, HENRY B., Chronological Notices of the Dictionaries of the English Language. Transactions of the Philological Society, 1865. London and Berlin, 1865.

——— The Folklore of Shakespeare. Folk-Lore, Vol. 27. London, 1916.

WHETSTONE, GEORGE, Promos and Cassandra. Students' Facsimile Edition, 1910.

WILEY, EDWIN, A Study of the Supernatural in Three Plays of Shakespeare. Berkeley, 1913.

WILLIAM OF NEWBURGH, Historia Rerum Anglicarum, edited by Richard Howlett. London, 1884–1885, 2 vols.

WILLIS, NATHANIEL, Mount Tabor, or Private Exercises of a Penitent Sinner. Cf. Brand, Observations on the Popular Antiquities of Great Britain, edited by Sir Henry Ellis, Vol. II, p. 485. London, 1849, 3 vols.

Wily Beguiled, 1606. The Malone Society Reprints, 1912.

WIMBERLY, LOWRY CHARLES, Folklore in the English & Scottish Ballads. Chicago, 1928.

WINWOOD, SIR RALPH, Memorials of Affairs of State in the Reigns of Queen Elizabeth and King James I, edited by Edmund Sawyer. London, 1725, 3 vols.

Wisdome of Doctor Dodypoll, The. Students' Facsimile Edition, 1912.

Witchcraft, A Collection of Rare and Curious Tracts Relating to. Rptd. verbatim from original editions. London, 1838.

WITHER, GEORGE, Fair Virtue, The Mistress of Philarete. London, 1818.

——— Juvenilia, printed for the Spenser Society. Manchester, 1871.

WITHINGTON, ROBERT, English Pageantry. Cambridge, Mass., 1918–1920, 2 vols.

WOOD-MARTIN, W. G., Traces of the Elder Faiths of Ireland. London, New York, Bombay, 1902, 2 vols.

WORTH, R. N., Devon Topography (15 pamphlets, no title page, place or date of publn.).

——— A History of Devonshire. London, 1886.

WRIGHT, THOMAS, Anglo-Saxon and Old English Vocabularies, edited by Richard P. Wülcker. London, 1884, 2 vols.

——— Essays on Subjects Connected with the Literature, Popular Superstitions, and History of England in the Middle Ages. London, 1846, 2 vols.

YEATS, W. B., The Celtic Twilight. London, 1893.

ZUPITZA, JULIUS, Aelfrics Grammatik und Glossar, edited by J. Zupitza. Sammlung englischer Denkmäler in kritischen Ausgaben, Erster Band. Berlin, 1880.

TEXTS IN WHICH REFERENCES TO THE FAIRIES OCCUR

The numbers following each entry refer to pages in this book.

Addison, Joseph, The Spectator, Nos. 12, 110, 117, 419: 33.
Aldhelm, Aenigmata: 227.
Aubrey, John, Miscellanies upon Various Subjects: 98, 141.
——— Natural History of Wiltshire: 107, 215.
——— Remains of Gentilisme and Judaisme.
Austin, Henry, The Scourge of Venus or The Wanton Lady: 250.

Bacon, Francis, Apophthegms: 237.
Bale, John, Three Laws: 15, 19.
Barnes, Barnabe, Parthenophil and Parthenope.
Bartholomew Iscanus, Paenetential: 186.
Beaumont, Francis and John Fletcher, The Fair Maid of the Inn.
——— The Faithful Shepherdess: 40, 100, 101, 122, 133, 136, 158.
——— The Honest Man's Fortune: 129.
——— The Knight of the Burning Pestle: 235.
——— The Little French Lawyer: 136.
——— The Lover's Progress.
——— Monsieur Thomas: 38, 73, 84, 90.
——— The Night-Walker, or The Little Thief: 74, 90, 231, 235.
——— The Pilgrim: 73, 74, 92, 94, 105, 135, 168.
——— The Scornful Lady: 92.
——— Wit at Several Weapons: 136.
Beaumont, John, An Historical, Physiological and Theological Treatise of Spirits, Apparitions, Witchcrafts, and other Magical Practices: 33, 44, 139, 170.
Boswell-Stone, W. G., Shakspere's Holinshed: 62, 91, 139.
Bourne, Henry, Antiquitates Vulgares: 33, 54, 63, 87, 112, 126, 217.
Bovet, Richard, Pandaemonium: 66, 68, 69, 90, 107, 108, 124.
Brand, John, Popular Antiquities of Great Britain.
Browne, Sir Thomas, Pseudodoxia Epidemica: 18, 138.
Browne, William, Britannia's Pastorals: 24, 72, 105, 109, 114, 119, 136, 142, 200, 208, 209, 210.
——— An Elegie on the Countesse Dowager of Pembroke: 62.

——— Fido: an Epistle to Fidelia: 20.
——— The Shepheards Pipe: 129, 142, 208.
Buggbears, The: 20, 40, 61, 82, 83, 222, 224, 228, 229.
BURTON, ROBERT, The Anatomy of Melancholy: 17, 19, 25, 26, 27, 43, 45, 57, 58, 63, 72, 79, 92, 120, 130, 137, 139, 146, 200, 231, 240, 248, 253.
BUTLER, SAMUEL, Hudibras: 18, 152, 230, 235.
BYRD, WILLIAM, Psalms, Sonnets and Songs of Sadness and Pietie: 87.

CALVIN, JOHN, The Institutions of Christian Religion: 152.
CAMDEN, WILLIAM, Britannia: 33, 37, 84, 137, 139, 166.
——— Remains concerning Britain.
CAMPION, THOMAS, A Book of Ayres: 120, 134.
CARTWRIGHT, WILLIAM, The Ordinary: 38.
Catholicon Anglicum: 53.
CAXTON, WILLIAM, Six Bookes of Metamorphoseos in whyche ben conteyned The Fables of Ovyde. Translated out of Frensshe into Englysshe by William Caxton: 62.
CHAMBERS, ROBERT, Popular Rhymes of Scotland: 123.
CHAPMAN, GEORGE, An Humerous Dayes Myrth: 62, 143.
——— Eastward Hoe: 147.
CHAUCER, GEOFFREY, Sir Thopas.
——— The Marchantes Tale: 100, 103, 185.
——— The Milleres Tale: 37.
——— The Squieres Tale.
——— The Tale of the Man of Laws.
——— The Tale of the Wyf of Bathe: 28, 103.
——— The Wife of Bath's Prologue.
CHILD, FRANCIS JAMES, The English and Scottish Popular Ballads: 149.
CHURCHYARD, THOMAS, A Discourse of the Queenes Majesties Entertainment in Suffolk and Norfolk: 16, 35, 51, 59, 70, 75, 80, 82, 89, 90, 100, 103, 125, 126.
——— A Handful of Gladsome Verses: 130, 230, 235, 241.
CLOBURY, CHRISTOPHER, Divine Glimpses of a Maiden Muse: 135, 235, 248.
Cobler of Canterburie, The, or An Invective against Tarltons Newes out of Purgatorie: 247.
COCKAYNE, OSWALD, Ed., Leechdoms, Wortcunning, and Starcraft of Early England: 137.

COLLINS, WILLIAM, An Ode on the Popular Superstitions of the Highlands of Scotland: 115.
Common Conditions: 16, 20.
Complaynt of Scotland, The.
CONSTABLE, HENRY, Sonnet to Chloris: 20.
CORBET, RICHARD, The Faery's Farewell: 29, 63, 81, 93, 128, 133.
——— Iter Boreale: 100, 230, 245, 253.
COTGRAVE, RANDLE, A Dictionarie of the French and English Tongues: 233.
COWLEY, ABRAHAM, Complete Works in Verse and Prose.
CUNNINGHAM, ALLAN, Traditional Tales of the English and Scottish Peasantry.
CUNNINGHAM, PETER, Extracts from the Accounts of the Revels at Court in the Reigns of Queen Elizabeth and King James I: 83, 89.

DALYELL, JOHN GRAHAM, The Darker Superstitions of Scotland: 140, 174.
DEKKER, THOMAS, Old Fortunatus: 83, 124.
——— The Belman of London: 122.
——— Lanthorne and Candle-light.
——— Newes from Hell: 110.
——— The Ravens Almanacke.
——— The seven deadly Sinnes of London: 155, 252.
——— The Whore of Babylon: 200.
Discourse concerning Devils and Spirits, A: 41, 46, 58, 70, 80, 87, 97, 99, 105, 112, 117, 136, 154, 157.
DOUGLAS, GAWIN, The Aeneid of Virgil, translated into Scottish Verse.
The Aucht Buke: 15, 49, 79.
The Proloug of the Saxt Buke: 233.
——— The Palice of Honour: 19.
DOYLE, ARTHUR CONAN, The Coming of the Fairies: 66.
DRAYTON, MICHAEL, Englands Heroicall Epistles: 202.
——— Idea, the Shepheard's Garland: 202.
——— Mortimeriados (The Barons' Wars).
——— The Muses Elizium: 20, 206.
——— Nimphidia: 24, 92, 130, 160, 202, 203, 204, 205, 206, 207, 230, 235, 241, 249, 253, 255.
——— Poly-Olbion: 202.
——— The Quest of Cynthia.

DRYDEN, JOHN, The Wife of Bath, Her Tale.
DUNBAR, WILLIAM, The Golden Targe: 15, 87.

Early South-English Legendary, The: 41, 190.
EDEN, RYCHARDE, Decades: 49, 52, 59.
ELYOT, SIR THOMAS, Bibliotheca Eliotae: 25, 53, 59, 70, 83, 151.
Examination of John Walsh: 83, 84, 169.
Examination of Joan Willimott: 69, 168.

FAIRFAX, EDWARD, A Discourse of Witchcraft: 32, 60, 61, 153, 232.
——— Translation of Godfrey of Bulloigne: 109, 199.
FAREWELL, JAMES (?), Irish Hudibras: 116, 152.
FIELD, NATHANIEL, A Woman is a Weathercock: 129.
FLETCHER, JOHN, *See* Beaumont and Fletcher.
FLORIO, JOHN, A Worlde of Wordes: 53, 59, 70, 83, 151, 233.
FORBY, ROBERT, The Vocabulary of East Anglia: 237.
FORD, JOHN, The Sun's Darling: 92.
FROISSART, SIR JOHN, Chronicles of England, France, Spain, Portugal, Scotland, Brittany, Flanders and the adjoining Countries: 15, 52.
FULLER, THOMAS, The Holy State and the Profane State.

Gammer Gurtons Nedle: 16, 137, 229, 251.
GAY, JOHN, Fables: The Mother, the Nurse and the Fairy: 157.
GERVASE OF TILBURY, Otia Imperialia: 189, 190, 226.
GIFFARD, GEORGE, A Dialogue concerning Witches and Witchcrafts: 37, 166, 235, 259.
GIRALDUS CAMBRENSIS, Itinerarium Cambriae cum annotationibus Davidis Poweli: 189, 190.
——— The Itinerary through Wales and the Description of Wales, translated by Sir Richard Colt.
GLANVIL, JOSEPH, A Blow at Modern Sadducism in some Philosophical Considerations About Witchcraft.
——— Saducismus Triumphatus: 144, 170.
Godly Queen Hester: 19.
GOLDING, ARTHUR, Translation of The xv. Bookes of P. Ouidius Naso, entytuled Metamorphosis: 15, 21, 50, 59, 79, 105, 164, 181, 185, 229.
GOOGE, BARNABE, Translation of The Popish Kingdom of Naogeorgus: 16, 224.
——— Translation of The Zodiake of Life: 92.
GREENE, ROBERT, Groats worth of Wit, bought with a Million of Repentance: 78.

——— James the Fourth: 134, 180, 188.

GREVILLE, FULKE, Caelica.

——— Letter to the Marquess Buckingham.

Grim, the Collier of Croydon: 222, 239, 240, 243, 245, 247, 249, 251, 256, 257, 258, 262.

GUILPIN, EDWARD, Skialetheia.

HALL, JOSEPH, Complete Poems.

——— Carmen Funebre Caroli Horni: 20, 40.

——— The Invisible World: 32.

HALLIWELL, JAMES O., Illustrations of the Fairy Mythology of *A Midsummer Night's Dream:* 224.

HARINGTON, SIR JOHN, Orlando Furioso in English Heroical Verse.

HARMAN, THOMAS, A Caveat or Warening for Commen Cursetors vulgarely called Vagabones: 237, 251.

HARSNET, SAMUEL, A Declaration of egregious Popish Impostures: 18, 40, 60, 62, 146, 200, 247, 248.

HARVEY, GABRIEL, Letters between Spenser and Harvey.

——— Pierces Supererogation: 223.

HAZLITT, W. CAREW, Fairy Tales, Legends and Romances illustrating Shakespeare: 107.

HENSLOWE, Henslowe Papers, Being Documents Supplementary to Henslowe's Diary: 88, 95.

HERON, ROBERT, Observations made in a Journey through the Western Counties of Scotland in the Autumn of 1792: 118, 246.

HERRICK, ROBERT, Hesperides: 24, 119, 131, 162, 202, 208, 210, 211, 248.

HEYLYN, PETER, Cosmographie: 47, 48, 215.

HEYWOOD, THOMAS, The Brazen Age.

——— The Hierarchie of the blessed Angells: 25, 57, 58, 70, 86, 114, 144, 230, 232, 254.

——— If you Know not Me, You Know Nobody: 135.

HEYWOOD, THOMAS and RICHARD BROOME, The Late Lancashire Witches: 116, 122, 235, 260, 261.

Highland Papers: 101, 175.

Historie of Jacob and Esau, The: 16, 19, 74, 79, 195.

HOBBES, THOMAS, Leviathan: 18, 21, 45, 57, 63, 116, 153, 156.

HOLINSHED, RAPHAEL, Chronicles of England, Scotland and Ireland: 71, 168.

Honorable Entertainment, The, gieven to the Queenes Majestie in

Progresse, at Elvetham in Hampshire, by the Right Honorable, the Earle of Hertford, 1591: 35, 77, 95, 104, 180, 186.
HORMAN, WILLIAM, Vulgaria: 53, 151.
HULOET, RICHARD, Huloets Dictionarie, corrected by John Higgins: 52, 60.
Huon of Burdeux, The Boke of Duke (Berners translation): 15, 36, 44, 56, 80, 81, 95, 96, 118, 127, 139, 180, 187, 188, 197, 222.

JAMES VI OF SCOTLAND, Daemonologie: 25, 52, 57, 63, 79, 97, 112, 138, 167, 200, 222, 234, 241, 258.
JOHNSON, SAMUEL, A Dictionary of the English Language: 19.
——— A Journey to the Western Islands of Scotland.
——— The Plays of William Shakespeare, with notes by Johnson and Steevens: 1, 14, 17, 65.
John Bon and Mast Parson: 16.
JONSON, BEN, The Alchemist: 20, 30, 78, 89, 94, 121, 126, 132, 133, 142.
——— The Devil is an Ass: 168, 235, 243, 244, 247, 250, 256, 257, 258, 259.
——— Eastward Hoe: 147.
——— Epicoene, or The Silent Woman: 143.
——— Every Man Out of His Humor.
——— The Gipsies Metamorphosed: 74, 88, 92.
——— Love Restored: 231, 239, 240, 241, 242, 245, 249.
——— The New Inn.
——— Oberon, the Fairy Prince: 24, 35, 60, 77, 89, 100, 104, 109.
——— The Sad Shepherd: 158, 168, 200, 212, 230, 232, 243, 251, 259, 260.
——— The Satyr: 35, 77, 95, 104, 117, 121, 129, 130, 136, 139, 143, 152, 212, 243, 255.
——— A Tale of a Tub.
——— Underwoods: 155.

KING, WILLIAM, Miscellanies in Prose and Verse: 214.
King Darius: 16.
King and a poore Northerne Man, The.
KIRK, ROBERT, Secret Commonwealth: 12, 29, 34, 35, 45, 46, 58, 60, 70, 91, 105, 106, 107, 108, 112, 113, 114, 115, 116, 126, 136, 141, 154, 162, 234.

LAING, DAVID, Select Remains of the Ancient and Popular Poetry of Scotland.

Lancelot du Lac: 28.

LANGLAND, WILLIAM, The Vision of William concerning Piers the Plowman: 228.

LAVATER, LUDWIG, De spectris lemuribus et magnis atque insolitis fragonibus . . . *translated as* Of Ghostes and Spirites walking by nyght: . . . 58, 83.

LAW, ROBERT, Memorials.

LAYAMON, Brut: 191.

LELOYER, PIERRE, Discovrs, et Histoires des Spectres, Visions et Apparitions des Esprits, Anges, Demons, et Ames, se Monstrans visibles auz hommes: 32.

LEVINS, PETER, Manipulus Vocabulorum: 51, 71.

LEYDEN, JOHN, Scenes of Infancy: 124.

LILLY, WILLIAM, History of His Life and Times from the Year 1602 to 1681: 81, 140, 169.

LLEWELLYN, MARTIN, Men-miracles; with other poemes: 131.

LODGE, THOMAS, Phillis Honoured with Pastoral Sonnets: 101.

——— Wit's Misery.

LUPTON, Thousand Notable Things: 137.

Lust's Dominion: 31, 125.

LYDGATE, JOHN, Fall of Princes.

LYLY, JOHN, Endimion: 31, 62, 71, 79, 121, 122, 125, 181.

——— Euphues: 72.

——— Gallathea: 20, 80, 92, 100.

LYNDESAY, SIR DAVID, Ane Satyre of the thrie Estaits: 55, 56, 110.

——— The Testament and Complaynt of our Soverane Lordis Papyngo.

Maitland Club, Miscellany of the: 174, 175.

MAJOR, JOHN, Exposition in Matthew: 15, 233, 238.

MAP, WALTER, De Nugis Curialium (James ed.): 190.

——— Courtiers' Trifles *translation of* De Nugis Curialium by Tupper and Ogle.

MARLOWE, CHRISTOPHER, The Tragedie of Dido Queene of Carthage (with Thomas Nashe): 17, 160.

Marriage of Wit and Science: 20.

MARSTON, JOHN, The Scourge of Villanie.

——— Eastward Hoe: 147.

MARTIN, MARTIN, Description of the Western Islands of Scotland: 161, 162, 247.

Maske von Cole-Orton, Die: 84, 85, 141, 230, 247, 255.

MASSINGER, PHILIP, The Fatal Dowry: 129, 142.
Maydes Metamorphosis, The: 52, 96, 120, 133, 198.
MAYNE, JASPER, The City Match.
Medulla Grāmatice: 20, 51, 71, 79.
Merry Devill of Edmonton, The: 38.
Merry pranks of Robin Goodfellow, The: 235.
MIDDLETON, CHRISTOPHER, The Famous Historie of Chinon of England: 21, 42, 92, 103, 109, 121, 197.
MIDDLETON, THOMAS, Anything for a Quiet Life: 157.
——— The Changeling: 157.
——— The Spanish Gipsy: 81.
——— The Witch: 121, 260, 261.
Midnight's Watch, The, or Robin Goodfellow his serious observation: . . . 241, 254.
MILTON, JOHN, At a Vacation Exercise in the College.
——— Comus: 40, 85, 136.
——— L'Allegro: 117, 235, 238, 241, 243, 245.
——— On the Morning of Christ's Nativity.
——— Paradise Lost: 213.
MINSHEU, JOHN, The Guide into the Tongues: 54, 70.
Mirror for Magistrates, A: 15, 17, 40, 57, 165.
Misogonus: 16, 20, 151, 160, 236, 241.
MONTGOMERIE, ALEXANDER, The Flyting of Montgomerie and Polwart: 20, 87, 97, 101, 102, 104.
MORE, HENRY, An Antidote against Atheism: 18, 25, 215.
MUNDAY, ANTHONY (?), Fidele and Fortunio, the Two Italian Gentlemen: 230.

NASHE, THOMAS, Pierce Penilesse, His Supplication to the Divell: 43, 58, 92.
——— Preface to Menaphon.
——— Strange Newes, of the Intercepting Certaine Letters; Foure Letters Confuted: 152.
——— Summers Last Will and Testament.
——— The Terrors of the Night: 52, 57, 103, 130, 135, 225, 253.
New Custom.
New Year's Gift addressed to the Queen, 1600: 81.
NEWCASTLE, LADY, Poems and Fancies: 152, 160, 213.
NICHOLS, JOHN, The Progresses and Public Processions of Queen Elizabeth: 35, 51, 59, 70, 75, 77, 80, 82, 89, 90, 95, 100, 103, 125, 126, 143, 180, 186.

NORTON, THOMAS, Letter to Sir Christopher Hatton: 223.
——— Translation of Calvin's The Institutions of Christian Religion: 152.

OLAUS MAGNUS, Gentivm Septentrionaliv Historiae Breviarium De Gentibus Septentrionalibus Historia, *translated as* A Compendious History of the Goths, Swedes, & Vandals: . . . 44, 64, 93.

PALSGRAVE, JEAN, Lesclarcissement de La Langue Francayse: 20, 79.
PASTON, The Paston Letters: 223.
PEELE, GEORGE, The Battle of Alcazar: 17, 40, 110.
PENNANT, THOMAS, A Tour in Scotland and a Voyage to the Hebrides: 137.
PEPYS, SAMUEL, Diary: 157.
Pepysian Garland, A (in Black-letter Broadside Ballads of the years 1595–1639): 233, 254.
PERCY, THOMAS, Reliques of Ancient English Poetry: 7.
PERCY, WILLIAM, The Faery Pastorall, or Forrest of Elves: 199.
PHAËR, THOMAS, Translation of the Aeneidos of Virgill: 15, 50, 79, 104.
PHILLIPS, EDWARD, The Fairies Fegaries: 132.
Philotus: 39, 110.
PITCAIRN, ROBERT, Criminal Trials in Scotland: 58, 62, 69, 78, 81, 88, 91, 93, 97, 104, 107, 108, 115, 118, 127, 128, 137, 138, 140, 149, 170, 171, 172, 173, 174, 175.
PITT, MOSES, An Account of Anne Jefferies in a Letter to Dr. Edward Fowler: 44, 69, 80, 87, 113, 157, 169.
Pleasant historie of Tom a Lincolne, The: 152.
Pleasant Treatise of Witches, A: 97, 156, 161, 216.
POOLE, JOSUA, The English Parnassus: 87, 116.
Pranks of Puck, The: 128, 152, 242, 255.
Promptorium Parvulorum: 52, 137.
Puritaine, The, or The Widdow of Watling-streete.
PUTTENHAM, RICHARD, The Arte of English Poesie: 17, 152, 155.

Queen Elizabeth at Quarrendon, Speeches to: 143.
Queen at Hengrave Hall and Chippenham, The, 1578: 143.
Queenes Majesties Progress at Woodstocke, The: 16, 35, 77, 85, 89, 97, 104, 134, 143, 185, 195.

RAMSAY, ALLAN, The Gentle Shepherd: 154.

RANDOLPH, THOMAS, Amyntas: 212.

RAVENSCROFT, THOMAS, A Brief Discourse of the true (but neglected) use of Charact'ring the Degrees . . .
  The Fayries Daunce: 123.
  The Urchins Daunce.

Richard Coer de Lion: 227.

ROBERT OF GLOUCESTER, Chronicle: 47, 191.

Robin Goodfellow; his mad prankes, and merry Jests: . . . 69, 87, 90, 93, 107, 118, 119, 123, 131, 132, 215, 232, 235, 238, 241, 242, 244, 245, 248, 250, 252, 255.

Romance of King Orfeo, The: 104, 214.

Round about our Coal Fire or Christmas Entertainments: 120, 127.

ROWLANDS, SAMUEL, More Knaues Yet? The Knaues of Spades and Diamonds: 17, 60, 231, 246, 248, 254.

St. Gregory or Gregorius auf dem Steine: 227.

SANDS, J., Curious Superstitions in Tiree: 153.

SCOT, REGINALD, Discovery of Witchcraft (1651 ed.): 17, 31, 41, 60, 61, 62, 63, 72, 79, 84, 102, 116, 153, 166, 181, 221, 222, 224, 228, 242, 244, 245, 246, 248, 253, 258.

SCOTT, SIR WALTER, Letters on Demonology and Witchcraft.
——— Minstrelsy of the Scottish Border: 2, 3, 23, 149, 219.

Scottish History Society, Miscellany of the.

SELDEN, JOHN, The Historie of Tithes: 224.

Severall notorious and lewd Cousonages of John West and Alice West, The: . . . 29, 89, 128, 142, 145.

SHADWELL, THOMAS, The Lancashire Witches and Tegue o Divelly, the Irish Priest: 260.

SHAKESPEARE, WILLIAM, Antony and Cleopatra: 178.
——— Comedy of Errors: 6, 37, 110, 120, 133, 177, 178.
——— Coriolanus.
——— Cymbeline: 37, 74, 80, 81, 90, 103, 112, 143, 178.
——— Hamlet: 102, 177.
——— Henry IV: 159, 177.
——— King Lear: 178.
——— Macbeth: 6, 84, 168, 178.
——— Merry Wives of Windsor: 4, 9, 20, 30, 75, 76, 77, 78, 82, 85, 86, 89, 93, 100, 117, 121, 125, 127, 129, 130, 134, 177, 178, 196, 218, 230, 240, 255.
——— Merry Wives of Windsor: the First Quarto, 1602: 75, 76, 77, 78, 255.

——— A Midsummer Night's Dream: 1, 2, 3, 4, 9, 10, 11, 12, 14, 18, 20, 23, 24, 45, 78, 88, 92, 93, 99, 101, 103, 125, 134, 136, 137, 143, 158, 176, 178, 179, 180, 181, 182, 183, 184, 185, 186, 187, 188, 191, 192, 193, 194, 195, 197, 198, 199, 200, 201, 202, 203, 204, 205, 206, 207, 208, 209, 211, 213, 215, 219, 220, 221, 225, 229, 230, 234, 235, 236, 240, 245, 249, 251, 253, 254, 255, 259, 260.

——— Pericles: 6, 73, 81, 90, 178.

——— Richard II: 6.

——— Richard III: 137.

——— Romeo and Juliet: 4, 9, 12, 23, 78, 131, 179, 194, 195, 199, 203, 209.

——— The Tempest: 4, 12, 93, 100, 113, 123, 136, 138, 178, 179, 196.

——— Venus and Adonis: 178.

——— Winter's Tale: 128, 146, 159, 160, 178.

SHIRLEY, JAMES, Love Tricks, 92.

——— Grateful Servant: 120.

——— Witty Fair One: 92.

Silva Gadelica: 115.

SINCLAR, GEORGE, Satan's Invisible World Discovered, 174.

SINCLAIR, SIR JOHN, The Statistical Account of Scotland: 107, 115.

Sinners Beware: 227.

SKINNER, STEPHEN, Etymologicon Linguae Anglicanae: 48, 156.

Spalding Club, Miscellany of the: 91, 97, 101, 112, 138, 174, 175.

SPENSER, EDMUND, Epithalamion: 229, 230.

——— The Faerie Queene: 14, 23, 25, 35, 152, 158, 159, 181.

——— Prosopopoia: or Mother Hubberds Tale.

——— The Shepheardes Calender: 24, 31, 34, 48, 63.

——— The Teares of the Muses.

——— Virgils Gnat.

STANYHURST, RICHARD, Translation of The First Four Books of the Aeneis of P. Virgilius Maro: 16, 19, 45, 79, 228, 229.

STEWARD, SIR SIMON, King Oberon's Apparel: 211, 212.

STRUTT, JOSEPH, Horda Angel-Cynnan: 33.

SYNGE, JOHN M., The Aran Islands: 43.

Tarltons Newes out of Purgatorie: 116, 222, 225, 230, 240, 243.

Tell-Trothes New-Yeares Gift: 225.

Thersites.

THOMAS, OF ERCELDOUNE, Romance and Phophecies: 149.

TICKELL, THOMAS, Kensington Garden: 214.
Towneley Plays, The.
Shepherds' Play, II: 150.
TUSSER, THOMAS, Five Hundred Points of Good Husbandry.
TYNDALE, WILLIAM, The Exposition of the First Epistle of St. John: 224, 237, 245.
——— The Obedience of a Christian Man: 224, 237, 245.

UDALL, NICHOLAS (?), Ralph Roister Doister: 15.

Valiant Welshman, The: 31, 78, 136.

WALDRON, GEORGE, A Description of the Isle of Man: 87, 93, 99, 119, 154, 155, 156.
WARNER, WILLIAM, Albion's England: 37, 109, 152.
——— Albions England (1612 quarto): 240, 242, 244, 246, 254.
WEBSTER, JOHN, The Displaying of supposed Witchcraft: 25, 32, 47, 70, 108, 138, 170, 216.
WEBSTER, JOHN, The Devil's Law-Case: 156.
WHETSTONE, GEORGE, The Historie of Promos and Cassandra: 20.
WILLIS, NATHANIEL, Mount Tabor, or, Private Exercise of a Penitent Sinner: 160.
Wily Beguiled: 232, 241, 243, 252, 256, 257.
Wisdome of Doctor Dodypoll, The: 94, 109, 118, 141, 197.

INDEX

Abductions, 124, 136, 148–50; of children, 7, 10, 99, 149n, 150–62; of nurses, 154; of witches, 163–75
Age of fairies, 46
Angels, fallen, 41
Anne of Denmark, fairy masques in honor of, 35, 36, 77
Appearance, of fairies, 65–91; of changelings, 155; of Robin Goodfellow, 237, 240, 254. *See also* Clothing: Size and figure
Ariel, 1
Avalon, 27

Bath water, set out for fairies, 118
Beauty of fairies, 72, 80–82
Berg-elfen, 2
Bestowing good fortune, 36, 37, 117, 132, 141–47
Bewitchment, 27, 28n, 150. *See also* Witches
Black fairies, 85
Bountiful fairies, 36, 37, 117, 132, 141–47
Bread, 112; as a charm, 161; and cream, 237, 246
Broom of Robin Goodfellow, 245
Brownie, 15, 233, 246n
Bugbears, fairies included among, 39

Cake making of fairies, 112
Cattle, fairy, 114
Changelings, 7, 10, 29, 99, 149n, 148–62, 183
Characteristics and personality, 5, 9n, 10, 91–110, 181. *See also* Evil fairies: Good fairies: Nature of fairies
Charms and spells, 30, 34, 37–39, 84, 161
Child—abstracting propensities, 7, 10, 29, 99, 148–62, 183
Children, altered by fairies, 151
Christmas, 102
Church of Rome, 62, 176
Churchyard, Thomas, royal entertainments of, 16, 51, 70, 75, 126
Classic mythology, identification of fairies with beings of, 15, 48–55, 61, 70, 104
Cleanliness, passion for, 129
Clothing, 66, 86–91, 187, 209, 237, 242–44
Cobham, Elianor, 165
Colors, of fairies, 40, 83–86; of fairy costumes, 86–88
Commonwealth of fairies, 103, 104, 180, 197
Corn, 113
Costumes of stage fairies, 86
Country of fairies. *See* Fairyland
Cream, 116; and bread, 237, 246

Dairy operations, 116
Dancing, 91–96
Days of fairy activity, 101
Definitions, of fairy, 1n, 14, 44, 52–54, 70; of elf, 19, 52, 53, 71; of changed children: of changeling, 151; of witch, 164n; of puck, 227; of hobgoblin, 229; of Robin Goodfellow, 233n
Dependent race, fairies never a, 120
Devils, fairies as, 25, 34, 36, 39, 55–61, 199; Robin Goodfellow as, 219, 224, 231, 240, 243, 247, 256–58
Diana, 181
Dictionaries, treatment of fairies and elves, 1n, 14, 19, 44, 51, 52–

54, 70, 71, 151; of Robin Goodfellow, 233n
Diminutive fairies. *See* Size and figure
Dirt and disorder, dislike of, 130
Diseases, caused and cured, 137
Domestic devils, 58, 60
Domestic interests of fairies, 111–47; of Robin Goodfellow, 238, 245
Domestic tyrants, 120, 136. *See also* Evil fairies
Dress, 66, 86–91, 187, 209, 237, 242–44
Drever, Jonet, 174
Dryads, 52, 53, 61, 70
Dunlop, Bessie, 69, 78, 91, 127, 140, 171
Dwelling place, 27, 47, 99, 105–10, 238; mortal invasion of, 122–24

Earthly life, 111–47
Ecclesiastiques, 45
Elizabeth, Queen, entertainments in honor of, 16, 35, 77, 90, 126, 186; presentation of gifts to, 143
Elves, 2, 8, 24n, 190; distinction between fairies and, 19–22, 50, 52; meaning of term, 19, 51, 52, 53, 71; origin of name, 48
Enchantments, 27, 28n, 150
Evil beings of classical mythology, 52–54
Evil fairies, 25, 33–40, 55–64, 136, 199. *See also* Punishments
Evil spirits, term repudiated by fairies, 43

Fairies, as real and actual beings, 27, 28–33, 65, 68, 232; Elizabethan and modern, compared, 65; disappearance of belief in, 176, 201
Fairies and elves, distinction between, 19–22, 50, 52
Fairy, meaning of term, 1n, 14, 44, 52, 54, 70, 151
Fairy creed, pre-Christian, 8
Fairy rings, 92, 99, 122
Fairyland, location of, 27, 47, 99, 105–10, 238; mortal invasion of, 122–24
Fallen angels, 41
Familiar beings, 65, 70, 221
Fata, definition, 53n
Fauns, 49, 51, 52, 70, 71
Feasting, 112, 118
Finnish fairy mythology, 2
Fire as a charm, 162n
Flour, 113
Flowers, fairies' association with, 185, 196, 199, 200, 207, 208
Folk fairies, 24–26; literary conceptions compared with, 1–11, 63; decline of belief in, 176, 193, 201
Folk hero, Robin Goodfellow as, 222–24, 225, 230, 236–53
Food, 46, 112–18, 209, 237, 246; fairies' dependence upon mortals for, 111
Foreknowledge, 139
Forests, habitation in, 99, 238
Fowlis, Lady Katherene Roiss, 175
Future, power to foretell, 139

Garrett, 40
Generosity, 36, 37, 117, 132, 141–47
Ghosts, 41, 44
Gibelins. *See* Guelfes and Gibelins
Gifts, 36, 37, 117, 132, 141–47
Goblin, 225; origin of name, 48
God, effect of name, 34n, 37
Goddesses, similarity between fairies and, 71
Good qualities of fairies, 10, 35, 40, 181, 193, 215; of Robin Goodfellow, 222. *See also* Generosity
Gothic fairy mythology, 2, 3, 5

Government of fairies, 103, 104, 180, 197
Gowdie, Issobell, 78, 88, 98, 108, 117, 175
Grant, the, 226n
Greek fairy lore. *See* Classic mythology
Guelfes and Gibelins, as origin of elfes and goblins, 48

Hair, unkempt, 131
Haldane, Issobell, 174
Hamadryads, 15, 51, 52, 53, 61, 70
"Hemton hamten," 244
Hillocks and hills, habitation in, 99, 106, 109
Hobgoblin, 16, 52; Robin Goodfellow as, 219, 226, 231, 253; meaning of term, 229
Horses, use of, 97–99
Hour, fairies', 102
Human affairs, fairies' interest in, 111–47

Incredible fairies, 192, 196, 202–11, 254, 255
Infernal spirits, 25, 33–40, 43, 55–64, 136, 199
Iron as a charm, 161

James I, fairy masques in honor of, 35, 36, 77
Jefferies, Anne, 43, 69, 80, 87, 113, 157, 169
Jesus, name invoked against fairies, 34n
Jewels, gifts of, 143
Joking, practical, 135, 223, 238, 251

Kingdom of fairies, 103, 104, 180, 197

Ladies of the fairies, 53, 71
Lamiae, 52–54, 71
Larva, 53
Latin fairy lore. *See* Classic mythology
Laughter of Robin Goodfellow, 237, 250
Law, recognition of witches by, 29, 34, 58, 164, 167, 168, 169
Laws and prohibitions, 120, 122–33
Lewingstoun, Christian, 140, 175
Licentiousness, dislike of, 133
Life on earth, 111–47
Lilly, William, 140, 169
Literary conceptions, of fairy mythology compared with folk fairies, 1–11, 63; of Robin Goodfellow, 219–21, 225, 230, 251, 253–62
Literary fairies of Shakespeare, 23n, 176–96; influence upon other writers, 197–218
Locomotion, means of, 91–99
Lovers, mortal, 8n, 27, 53, 148; Robin Goodfellow's interest in, 249

Mab, 23n, 117, 194, 196n, 203
McIlmichall, Donald dow, 174
Malignant fairies. *See* Wicked fairies
Man, Andro, 91, 101, 138, 173
Masks, 82
Masques in honor of royalty, 18, 35, 51, 70, 75, 77, 89, 90, 126, 143, 144n, 186
Matchmaking of Robin Goodfellow, 249
Middle nature of fairies, 41, 46
Milk, 116; custom of pouring upon stone, 246n
Modern fairies, photographs, 65
Monarchs, 104, 180
Money, gifts of, 141, 144
Moore, Thomas, and wife, 145
Morisone, Jonet, 175
Mortal, Robin Goodfellow as, 232

Mortals, fairies as, 27, 28–33, 65, 68, 176, 201; fairies as souls of departed, 41, 44; dependence upon, 111, 120; abduction of, 124, 136, 148–50, 154, 163–75. *See also* Changelings
Music, 93–96
Mythology. *See* Classic mythology

Naiad, 53, 59
Names, of fairy queens, 104; of Shakespearean fairies, 186
Nature of fairies, 23–41, 46, 48–64. *See also* Characteristics
Night, fairy activity during, 102
Night wanderers led astray, 135, 238, 252
Nymphs, 15, 49–53, 61, 70, 71

Oberon, 36, 80, 81, 139, 180, 181, 205, 209
Occupations, of fairies, 3, 27, 34, 186, 196; of Robin Goodfellow, 231, 238, 245, 248–49, 251–53
Origins, of Elizabethan fairies, 2, 3, 5, 7, 41–64; of Robin Goodfellow, 223–35

Page, Anne, 75, 76, 86
Peirsoun, Alesoun, 69, 128, 138, 148, 172
Personality and characteristics, 5, 9n, 10, 91–110, 181. *See also* Evil fairies: Good fairies: Nature of fairies
Pictures, of modern fairies, 65; of Robin Goodfellow, 238
Pinchings, 120, 133, 239
Poetic myths, 9n
Portuni, the, 226n
Pouke. *See* Puck
Practical joking, 135, 223, 238, 251
Precious stones, gifts of, 143
Privacy, laws insuring, 122–29
Prohibitions imposed upon mortals, 120, 122–33
Puck, 16; meaning of term, 219, 227, 252; Robin Goodfellow conceived as, 219, 220, 226, 252, 253
Puckerels, 16, 228
Puck-hairy, 243, 259
Pug, 256n, 257, 259
Punishments, 120, 122–37, 239

Queen of the Fairies, 104, 181, 184, 194, 195n, 199; names, 104. *See also* Mab

Religion, effect upon fairies, 29n, 31, 34n, 102
Reoch, Elspeth, 175
Rewarding virtue, 132, 249
Ridiculous fairies, 192, 196, 202–11, 254, 255
Riding horseback, 96–99
Rings, fairy, 92, 99, 122
Robin Goodfellow, 4, 16, 52, 116, 185, 219–62; as conceived by Shakespeare and his successors, 219–21, 225, 230, 251, 253–62; as devil, 219, 224, 231, 240, 243, 247, 256–58; as folk hero, 222–24, 225, 230, 236–53; fame and popularity, 222; as a British spirit, 222, 224; origin and race, 223–35; names, 223, 225, 235, 236; as practical joker, 223, 238, 251; employments of, 231, 238, 245, 248–49, 251–53; association with witches, 232, 258–60; as a mortal, 232; a Brownie in Scotland, 233; appearance and figure, 237, 240, 254; clothing, 237, 242–44; desire for bread and cream, 237, 246; broom and threshing flail of, 245; matchmaking instincts, 249
Roman Catholic Church, 62, 176

Royal masques and entertainments, 16, 35, 51, 70, 75, 77, 89, 90, 126, 143, 144n, 186
Royalty, presentation of gifts to, 143
Rulers, 104, 180; names of, 104
Rural beliefs. *See* Folk fairies

Satan. *See* Devils
Satyrs, 51, 52, 70, 71
Scandinavian fairy mythology, 5
Scotland, conception of fairies in, 3, 5, 15, 16, 45, 46, 57, 58; belief in brownies, 233, 246n. *See also* Witches
Seasons of activity, 101
Second sight, 140
Shakespeare, fairies of, 23n, 176–96; compared with folk fairies, 1–11; influence upon other writers, 197–218, 230, 253, 255–62; conception of Robin Goodfellow, 219–21, 225, 230, 251, 253–55
Sickness caused and cured, 137
Sinclair, Isobel, 140n, 174
Singing, 94
Sixpence pieces in shoes, 141
Size and figure, of fairies, 2, 6, 7, 8, 66–80, 187–91, 194, 197n, 198, 201, 203, 209, 213, 215, 217; of Robin Goodfellow, 237, 240, 254
Skebister, Bessie, 140n
Strix, definition, 53, 54
Sublunary devils, 58, 60
Summertime, 101

Terrestrial devils, 26, 58, 231, 240
Teutonic fairy tradition, 8, 9
Titania, 181
Travellers led astray, 135, 238, 252
Treasure, association of fairies with, 144
Tyrrye, Joan, 69

Unchastity, punishment for, 133
Underground fairyland, 105

Virtue, rewarding, 132, 249
Visors, 82, 86

Walsh, John, 83, 169
Water, association of fairies with, 100
Watery devils, 26, 58, 59, 72
Wearing apparel, 66, 86–91, 187, 209, 237, 242–44
Weir, Jean, 174
West, Alice and John, 29, 128, 145
Wicked beings of classical mythology, 52–54
Wicked fairies, 25, 33–40, 55–64, 136, 199. *See also* Punishments
Willimott, Joan, 69, 168
Winter, inactivity during, 101
Witches and witchcraft, 16, 36, 46, 163–75; legal recognition of, 29, 34, 58, 164, 167, 168, 169; association of Robin Goodfellow, with, 232, 258–60. *See also names of witches*
Wood spirits of classic literature, 51